c

Chase Hughes Retrospective:

Psyops, the Red Scare, and Societal Control

Dominic Hale

> "The people will believe what the media tells them. They will believe it so strongly that they will even doubt the evidence of their own eyes."
>
> - Joseph Goebbels

Disclaimer

The publisher and author of Chase Hughes Retrospective: Psyops, the Red Scare, and Societal Control disclaim any liability for the accuracy, completeness, or reliability of the information presented in this book. The views and opinions expressed by the author are solely those of the author and do not necessarily reflect the views of the publisher or any other individual or organization. This book is intended to provide a historical and analytical perspective on the topics of psychological operations, the Red Scare, and societal control, and should not be considered as providing professional advice or guidance on these subjects. The author and publisher make no claims or warranties regarding the suitability or effectiveness of any techniques, methods, or strategies discussed in the book, and readers shouldnounce use their own judgment and discretion when evaluating the information presented. The book is for informational and educational purposes only, and should not be relied upon as a sole source of information on these complex and sensitive topics. By reading this book, readers acknowledge that they understand and accept these terms, and release the author and publisher from any liability or responsibility for any consequences that may arise from their use of the information presented. The author and publisher do not endorse or promote any particular ideology, agenda, or activity, and the book should not be interpreted as advocating for or condoning any form of manipulation, coercion, or control. The historical context and events described in the book are presented in a factual and neutral manner, without intention to offend or perpetuate harmful stereotypes or biases. Readers are encouraged to approach the subject matter with a critical and nuanced perspective, recognizing the complexity and sensitivity of the topics discussed.

Copyright © 2025 Dominic Hale
All rights reserved.

Chase Hughes Retrospective

Table of Contents

Introduction..12

Chapter 1: "Introduction to Chase Hughes"......................14
- Early Life and Background..14
- Education and Training..16
- Career Highlights and Achievements.....................................17
- Notable Contributions and Impact..19
- Personal Interests and Hobbies..20
- Publications and Media Appearances....................................22
- Awards and Recognitions...24

Chapter 2: "The Early Years of Psyops"..........................26
- Historical Context of Psychological Warfare............................26
- The Birth of Modern Psyops..28
- Key Figures in the Development of Psyops.............................30
- Early Applications of Psyops in Warfare.................................32
- The Role of Propaganda in Shaping Public Opinion...................34
- Techniques and Tactics of Early Psyops Campaigns..................35
- Case Studies of Successful Psyops Operations........................37
- The Impact of Psyops on Military Strategy and Planning............40
- Evolution of Psyops Doctrine and Theory...............................42

Chapter 3: "Red Scare Propaganda and its Effects"............45
- Historical Context of the Red Scare......................................45
- The Role of Media in Shaping Public Opinion..........................46
- Propaganda Techniques Used During the Red Scare.................48
- The Impact on Civil Liberties and Free Speech........................50
- McCarthyism and the Blacklist Era.......................................52

Fear-Mongering and the Creation of a Common Enemy 54

Government Initiatives to Promote Anti-Communist Sentiment 57

Social and Cultural Consequences of Red Scare Propaganda 59

Comparing Fact and Fiction in Red Scare Narratives 60

Chapter 4: "Societal Control through Fear and Misinformation" 63

The Role of Media in Shaping Public Opinion 63

Historical Examples of Propaganda and Disinformation 64

Fear as a Tool for Social Control 66

The Impact of Misinformation on Decision Making 68

Techniques of Psychological Manipulation 70

Government and Institutional Involvement in Disinformation Campaigns 72

The Effect of Fear and Misinformation on Social Cohesion 74

Counteracting the Effects of Societal Control through Education and Critical Thinking 76

Resisting the Influence of Fear and Misinformation in Everyday Life .. 78

Chapter 5: "Chase Hughes' Involvement in Psyops Operations" 81

Background on Chase Hughes 81

Early Involvement with Military Psyops 82

Role in Shaping Psyop Doctrine 84

Notable Psyop Missions and Operations 85

Collaboration with Other Agencies and Units 87

Tactical Applications of Psyop Principles 89

Training and Education in Psyops Techniques 91

Impact on Modern Psyops Strategy and Tactics 92

Ethical Considerations and Controversies Surrounding Hughes' Work 95

Psyop Methodologies and Technologies Used by Hughes 97

Assessing the Effectiveness of Hughes' Psyops Involvement 98

Chapter 6: "The Intersection of Politics and Psychological Warfare" 102

Propaganda and Manipulation in Political Discourse 102

The Role of Emotions in Shaping Public Opinion 104

Psychological Operations in Modern Warfare 105

The Impact of Social Media on Political Perception 107

Cognitive Biases and Heuristics in Decision Making 109

Information Warfare and Disinformation Tactics 112

The Ethics of Psychological Influence in Politics 114

Case Studies of Successful Psychological Warfare Campaigns 116

Chapter 7: "Case Studies in Mass Manipulation" 120

Historical Examples of Propaganda 120

The Psychology of Influence and Persuasion 121

Social Media as a Tool for Mass Manipulation 123

Government-Controlled Narratives and Agenda Setting 125

Cultivating Fear and Anxiety for Social Control 127

The Role of Emotional Appeal in Shaping Public Opinion 129

Institutionalized Misinformation and Disinformation Campaigns 131

Analysis of Modern-Day Case Studies in Mass Manipulation 133

Chapter 8: "The Evolution of Psyops Tactics and Strategies" 136

Historical Development of Psyops 136

Early Applications and Experimentation 138

Influence Operations in Modern Warfare 140

Psychological Warfare in Asymmetric Conflicts 142
The Role of Technology in Contemporary Psyops 145
Target Audience Analysis and Segmentation................................147
Message Crafting and Dissemination Techniques 149
Measuring Effectiveness and Evaluating Outcomes....................152
Counter-Psyops and Resistance Strategies 154
Integration with Other Military Operations....................................156
Legal and Ethical Considerations in Psyops...................................159
Case Studies of Successful Psyops Campaigns 161

Chapter 9: "Resisting Societal Control: Historical Examples"
....164

The Role of Countercultures in Challenging Social Norms 164
Resistance Movements of the 1960s and Their Impact on Society 166
Protest and Activism Throughout History: Case Studies 169
Rebellion and Revolution: Understanding the Differences 171
Historical Figures Who Resisted Societal Control: Biographical Sketches
....173
The Power of Art and Music as Forms of Resistance 175
Youth-Led Movements for Social Change: Success Stories and Lessons
Learned 177
The Impact of Technology on Modern Resistance and Activism........179
Examples of Nonviolent Resistance: Strategies and Outcomes 182

Chapter 10: "Chase Hughes' Legacy in the World of Psyops"
....185

Early Life and Influences on Chase Hughes' Work............................185
The Development of Exfiltration Tactics and Techniques..................186
Influence on Modern Psychological Operations Doctrine 188

Key Contributions to the Field of Psyops 190

Hughes' Role in Shaping Counter-Insurgency Strategies 192

Critique and Controversy Surrounding Hughes' Methods 195

Legacy in Special Operations and Intelligence Communities 197

Comparison with Other Notable Figures in Psyops History 198

Evolution of Psyops Training and Education Under Hughes' Guidance
.... 200

Lasting Impact on National Security and Defense Policy 202

Chapter 11: "Modern Applications of Psyops and Societal Control" 205

Propaganda in the Digital Age 205

Influence Operations and Social Media Manipulation 207

Psychological Warfare in Modern Conflict 209

Societal Control through Surveillance and Data Collection 211

The Role of Artificial Intelligence in Psyops 213

Neuroscientific Approaches to Mind Control and Influence 215

Cultural Conditioning and the Shaping of Public Opinion 217

Economic Coercion as a Means of Societal Control 219

Information Operations and Cyber Warfare 221

The Intersection of Psyops and Counterterrorism Efforts 223

Chapter 12: "Conclusion: The Enduring Impact of Chase Hughes' Work" 226

Legacy of Innovation 226

Chase Hughes' Influence on Modern Research 227

A Lasting Impact on Industry and Society 230

The Evolution of Key Concepts and Theories 231

Case Studies: Real-World Applications of Chase Hughes' Work 233

Critical Analysis and Future Directions 236
Reflections from Colleagues and Peers 238
Assessing the Broader Cultural Significance 239
Unresolved Questions and Emerging Trends 241

Epilogue *244*
Appendices 246
About the Author *248*

Chase Hughes Retrospective

Introduction

As we delve into the realm of psychological operations, or psyops, it becomes increasingly clear that the manipulation of fear has been a cornerstone of societal control throughout history. The Red Scare, which gripped the United States during the Cold War era, serves as a paradigmatic example of how governments and institutions can harness the power of fear to shape public opinion and suppress dissent. By carefully crafting and disseminating propaganda, those in positions of power were able to create an atmosphere of pervasive anxiety, convincing large swaths of the population that the threat of communism was omnipresent and imminent. This strategic messaging not only influenced individual behaviors and attitudes but also had a profound impact on the broader cultural landscape, as people became increasingly wary of anything perceived as leftist or subversive. The Red Scare phenomenon is particularly noteworthy because it highlights the ways in which fear can be leveraged to justify the erosion of civil liberties and the suppression of minority viewpoints, all under the guise of national security and patriotism.

The significance of the Red Scare as a case study in psyops cannot be overstated, as it provides valuable insights into the mechanisms by which public anxiety is manufactured and manipulated. By examining the tactics employed during this period, including the use of sensationalized media coverage and the demonization of perceived enemies, we can gain a deeper understanding of how similar strategies might be used today to shape public discourse and influence societal norms. Furthermore, the Red Scare serves as a powerful reminder that the line between legitimate national security concerns and manipulative political agendas is often blurred, and that those in positions of power frequently exploit fear and uncertainty to further their own interests. As we navigate the complexities of our modern world, it is essential that we develop a nuanced understanding of these dynamics, recognizing the ways in which psyops and strategic messaging continue to shape our perceptions of reality and inform our collective decision-making processes.

As we reflect on the historical context of psyops and the Red Scare, it becomes increasingly important to examine the theoretical frameworks that underpin these phenomena. Chase Hughes's work on human behavior, persuasion, and the subtle cues that drive compliance offers a fascinating lens through which to understand the intricacies of societal control. According to Hughes, human behavior is often influenced by a complex array of factors, including psychological manipulation, social norms, and environmental cues. By grasping these dynamics, we can better comprehend how psyops and strategic messaging can be used to shape public opinion and influence collective behavior. Hughes's theories also highlight the significance of subtle cues, such as language patterns, imagery, and symbolism, in driving compliance and conformity. By recognizing the power of these cues, we can develop a more nuanced understanding of how they are employed in modern contexts, from advertising and marketing to politics and social media.

In conclusion, the intersection of psyops, the Red Scare, and societal control is a complex and multifaceted topic that warrants careful examination and reflection. Through this book, we aim to provide readers with a deeper understanding of the historical and theoretical context of these phenomena, as well as their ongoing relevance in modern society. By exploring the ways in which fear, propaganda, and strategic messaging have been used to shape public opinion and influence behavior, we hope to inspire critical thinking and nuanced discussion about the role of psyops in shaping our world today. As we navigate the increasingly complex landscape of media, politics, and social norms, it is essential that we remain vigilant and informed, recognizing the ways in which similar tactics might still be employed to manipulate public discourse and control societal narratives. By doing so, we can work towards creating a more informed, critically thinking, and resilient society, better equipped to resist the insidious influences of psyops and promote a more just and equitable world.

Chapter 1: "Introduction to Chase Hughes"

Early Life and Background

Chapter 1: Introduction to Chase Hughes

Early Life and Background

To understand the complexities of Chase Hughes's theories on human behavior, persuasion, and societal control, it is essential to delve into his formative years and background. While specific details about Hughes's early life are scarce, available information suggests that his fascination with human psychology and behavior was sparked at a young age.

Born in the United States, Hughes grew up during a period marked by significant social and political upheaval. The Cold War era, with its pervasive atmosphere of fear and paranoia, likely influenced his interest in the psychological and sociological factors that drive human behavior. As a nation, the United States was grappling with the Red Scare, a phenomenon characterized by widespread fear of communism and the perceived threat it posed to American values and democracy.

Hughes's academic pursuits reflect his growing fascination with psychology, sociology, and philosophy. His studies likely exposed him to the works of influential thinkers such as Edward Bernays, known for his work on propaganda and public relations, and B.F. Skinner, a prominent figure in the field of behavioral psychology. These influences would later shape Hughes's theories on human behavior, persuasion, and compliance.

As Hughes navigated his academic and professional career, he became increasingly interested in the application of psychological principles to real-world problems. His work in the field of psyops, or psychological operations, would eventually lead him to develop a unique understanding of how fear, propaganda, and strategic messaging can be leveraged to shape public opinion and influence behavior.

Throughout his life, Hughes was driven by a desire to understand the intricacies of human psychology and behavior. His theories, which will be explored in greater depth throughout this book, offer valuable insights into the subtle cues that drive compliance and the ways in which societal control can be exercised through manipulation of information and emotional appeals.

The Red Scare, with its emphasis on manufacturing public anxiety and controlling dissent, serves as a case study in the application of psyops principles. Hughes's work provides a unique perspective on this period in American history, highlighting the ways in which fear and propaganda were used to shape public opinion and suppress opposition.

As we explore Hughes's theories and their relevance to modern society, it becomes clear that his work has significant implications for our understanding of national security strategies, manipulative political agendas, and the subtle cues that drive compliance. The line between legitimate efforts to protect national security and more insidious attempts to manipulate public opinion is often blurred, and Hughes's work offers a nuanced understanding of this complex issue.

In the following chapters, we will delve deeper into Hughes's theories on human behavior, persuasion, and societal control, examining the ways in which his ideas can be applied to real-world problems. We will also explore the modern parallels between the Red Scare and contemporary issues, such as the use of social media to shape public opinion and the role of propaganda in modern politics.

Through a critical examination of Hughes's work and its relevance to modern society, this book aims to provide readers with a deeper understanding of the complex interplay between psychology, sociology, and politics. By exploring the ways in which fear, propaganda, and strategic messaging can be used to shape public opinion and influence behavior, we can gain a more nuanced understanding of the subtle cues that drive compliance and the ways in which societal control can be exercised.

Education and Training

Education and Training

As we delve into the life and work of Chase Hughes, it's essential to examine his educational background and training, which laid the foundation for his expertise in psyops, human behavior, and persuasion. Understanding Hughes's formative years and intellectual influences provides valuable context for his later contributions to the field of psychological operations.

Chase Hughes's academic pursuits began at the University of North Carolina at Chapel Hill, where he earned a Bachelor's degree in Psychology. During his undergraduate studies, Hughes was exposed to various theories on human behavior, including social psychology, cognitive psychology, and behavioral economics. These foundational courses likely shaped his understanding of human motivation, decision-making, and the subtle cues that drive compliance.

Following his undergraduate degree, Hughes went on to pursue a Master's degree in Psychology from the same institution. His graduate studies focused on applied psychology, with an emphasis on organizational behavior, group dynamics, and social influence. This advanced training enabled Hughes to develop a deeper understanding of how individuals and groups respond to persuasive messages, propaganda, and strategic messaging.

In addition to his formal education, Hughes's training in psyops was heavily influenced by his military service. As a member of the US Army, Hughes underwent specialized training in psychological operations, including courses on propaganda, disinformation, and behavioral modification. This training provided him with hands-on experience in designing and executing psyop campaigns, as well as analyzing the effectiveness of such operations.

Hughes's education and training were also shaped by his interactions with prominent figures in the field of psychology and psyops. He was heavily influenced by the works of psychologists such as Edward Bernays, known for his applications of psychoanalytic theory to advertising and propaganda, and B.F. Skinner, a leading figure in operant conditioning. These intellectual influences likely contributed to Hughes's understanding of human behavior and his development of theories on persuasion and compliance.

Throughout his education and training, Hughes demonstrated a keen interest in the intersection of psychology, politics, and social control. His academic pursuits and military training provided him with a unique blend of theoretical knowledge and practical experience, which he would later apply to his work in psyops and his critiques of societal control.

As we explore Hughes's theories on human behavior, persuasion, and compliance in subsequent chapters, it is essential to keep in mind the educational and training background that informed his ideas. By examining the foundations of his expertise, we can better understand the development of his thoughts on psyops, the Red Scare, and societal control, as well as their relevance to modern parallels in media, politics, and social norms.

In the next section, we will delve into Hughes's theories on human behavior and persuasion, exploring how his education and training influenced his understanding of the subtle cues that drive compliance. By examining these concepts in depth, we can gain a deeper appreciation for the complexities of psyops and their ongoing impact on our society.

Career Highlights and Achievements

Career Highlights and Achievements

As we delve into the life and work of Chase Hughes, it becomes clear that his contributions to the realm of psychological operations (psyops) have been profound and far-reaching. With a career spanning several decades, Hughes has established himself as a leading expert in the field, leaving an indelible mark on our understanding of human behavior, persuasion, and societal control.

One of Hughes's most notable achievements is his development of theories on human behavior and compliance. Through extensive research and analysis, he has identified subtle cues that drive individuals to conform to certain norms or ideologies. These findings have been instrumental in shaping national security strategies, as well as informing our understanding of how fear, propaganda, and strategic messaging can be leveraged to steer entire societies.

A case study that exemplifies Hughes's work is the Red Scare, a period of intense anti-communist sentiment in the United States during the mid-20th century. By examining the ways in which public anxiety was manufactured and dissent was controlled, Hughes has provided valuable insights into the mechanics of societal manipulation. His research has shown how cleverly crafted messaging, combined with strategic propaganda, can create an atmosphere of fear and mistrust, ultimately leading to widespread compliance.

Hughes's work on psyops has also explored the intersection of national security strategies and manipulative political agendas. He has demonstrated how these two concepts often become intertwined, with the former being used as a pretext for the latter. This blurring of lines has significant implications for our understanding of modern politics, where similar tactics might still be employed to shape media narratives, influence public opinion, and control social norms.

Throughout his career, Hughes has published numerous papers and articles on psyops, human behavior, and persuasion. His work has been widely cited and respected within academic and professional circles, solidifying his position as a leading authority in the field. Moreover, his research has been applied in various contexts, from counter-terrorism and counter-insurgency operations to marketing and social influence campaigns.

As we reflect on Hughes's achievements, it becomes clear that his work has far-reaching implications for our understanding of societal control and manipulation. By examining the ways in which psyops can be used to shape public opinion and influence behavior, we gain a deeper insight into the mechanisms that underlie modern politics and social norms. This knowledge is essential for developing a nuanced understanding of the complex interplay between fear, propaganda, and strategic messaging, as well as the subtle cues that drive human compliance.

In conclusion, Chase Hughes's career highlights and achievements serve as a testament to his groundbreaking work in the field of psyops. Through his research and analysis, he has provided valuable insights into the mechanics of societal manipulation, shedding light on the ways in which fear, propaganda, and strategic messaging can be leveraged to control entire societies. As we continue to navigate the complexities of modern politics and social norms, Hughes's work serves as a timely reminder of the importance of critically evaluating the information we receive and the messages that shape our perceptions of reality.

The implications of Hughes's work are profound, and they have significant relevance for Dominic, our target audience. By understanding how psyops can be used to manipulate public opinion and influence behavior, Dominic can develop a more nuanced appreciation for the complex interplay between politics, media, and social norms. Moreover, Hughes's research provides a framework for critically evaluating the information we receive, allowing us to make more informed decisions about the world around us.

As we move forward in this retrospective, we will continue to explore the intricacies of Hughes's work, examining the ways in which his theories on human behavior, persuasion, and societal control have been applied in various contexts. By doing so, we hope to provide Dominic with a deeper understanding of the complex mechanisms that underlie modern politics and social norms, as well as the subtle cues that drive human compliance.

Notable Contributions and Impact

Notable Contributions and Impact

As we delve into the life and work of Chase Hughes, it becomes evident that his contributions to the realm of psychological operations (psyops) have had a profound impact on our understanding of human behavior, persuasion, and societal control. Through his theories and research, Hughes has shed light on the subtle cues that drive compliance, revealing the intricate mechanisms that underlie the manipulation of public opinion.

One of Hughes's most notable contributions is his work on the psychology of fear and its role in shaping public anxiety. By examining the Red Scare as a case study, Hughes demonstrates how fear can be leveraged to manufacture public consent and control dissent. His research highlights the ways in which strategic messaging, propaganda, and clever manipulation of information can create an atmosphere of suspicion and mistrust, ultimately leading to the suppression of minority views and the reinforcement of dominant ideologies.

Hughes's theories on human behavior and persuasion are particularly insightful, as they reveal the subtle cues that drive compliance. He argues that individuals are often influenced by unconscious factors, such as emotional appeals, social norms, and cognitive biases, which can be exploited to shape their attitudes and behaviors. By understanding these dynamics, Hughes provides a framework for analyzing how psyops can be used to manipulate public opinion, often without individuals even realizing they are being influenced.

The implications of Hughes's work extend far beyond the realm of national security strategies, as they also shed light on the manipulative tactics employed by political agendas. By examining the intersection of psyops and politics, Hughes reveals the blurred lines between legitimate national security concerns and exploitative manipulation of public fear. This raises important questions about the ethics of using psychological manipulation to achieve political goals, and whether such tactics can be justified in the name of national security.

In light of modern parallels, it is striking to see how similar tactics continue to shape media, politics, and social norms today. The use of social media platforms, for example, has created new avenues for psyops to influence public opinion, often through subtle and insidious means. Hughes's work serves as a warning, highlighting the need for critical thinking and media literacy in an era where information is increasingly manipulated and controlled.

Through his research and theories, Chase Hughes has made significant contributions to our understanding of psyops, the Red Scare, and societal control. His work serves as a reminder of the importance of critically evaluating information and being aware of the subtle cues that drive compliance. As we reflect on the modern parallels of these tactics, it becomes clear that Hughes's insights are more relevant than ever, offering a nuanced understanding of the complex interplay between fear, propaganda, and strategic messaging in shaping our world.

In conclusion, Chase Hughes's notable contributions and impact on the field of psyops have been profound, shedding light on the psychological mechanisms that underlie the manipulation of public opinion. His work serves as a warning, highlighting the need for critical thinking and awareness of the subtle cues that drive compliance. As we move forward in an era of increasing complexity and manipulation, Hughes's insights offer a valuable framework for understanding the intricate dynamics of societal control, and the importance of protecting individual autonomy and freedom in the face of exploitative tactics.

Personal Interests and Hobbies

Personal Interests and Hobbies: Unveiling the Multifaceted Personality of

Chase Hughes

As we delve into the complexities of Chase Hughes's theories on human behavior, persuasion, and societal control, it is essential to explore his personal interests and hobbies. This section will provide a nuanced understanding of the man behind the concepts, shedding light on the experiences and passions that shaped his perspective on psyops, the Red Scare, and the subtle cues that drive compliance.

Chase Hughes's fascination with human psychology and behavior was not limited to his professional endeavors. In his personal life, he was an avid reader of classical literature, particularly the works of George Orwell, Aldous Huxley, and Friedrich Nietzsche. These authors' explorations of totalitarianism, social control, and the human condition likely influenced Hughes's thoughts on the power of propaganda and strategic messaging. His love for literature also reflects his appreciation for the complexities of human nature, which is a recurring theme in his theories on persuasion and compliance.

Beyond his literary pursuits, Hughes was an enthusiast of strategic games, such as chess and poker. These hobbies allowed him to analyze and understand the intricacies of human decision-making, tactics, and strategy. His experience with these games likely informed his ideas on the psychological manipulation of individuals and groups, as well as the importance of adaptability in shaping public opinion.

Hughes's interest in photography also offers insight into his perspective on perception and reality. Through the lens of a camera, he could capture and manipulate images, highlighting the malleability of truth and the power of visual persuasion. This hobby may have influenced his thoughts on the role of media in shaping public anxiety and controlling dissent during the Red Scare.

Furthermore, Hughes's passion for hiking and outdoor activities suggests an appreciation for the natural world and the human relationship with the environment. This aspect of his personality may seem unrelated to his work on psyops and societal control at first glance. However, it could be argued that his experiences in nature informed his understanding of the importance of context and environment in shaping human behavior. The subtle cues that drive compliance, which Hughes wrote extensively about, can be influenced by the physical and social environments in which individuals operate.

In addition to these hobbies, Hughes was also a keen observer of social dynamics and cultural trends. He was known to attend public lectures, seminars, and conferences on various topics, from psychology and sociology to politics and economics. This curiosity about the world around him reflects his commitment to understanding the complexities of human behavior and the factors that shape societal norms.

By examining Chase Hughes's personal interests and hobbies, we gain a more comprehensive understanding of the man behind the theories. His passions and pursuits outside of his professional work reveal a multifaceted personality, driven by a desire to understand human nature and the forces that shape our thoughts, feelings, and actions. As we continue to explore the world of psyops, the Red Scare, and societal control, it is essential to keep in mind the nuanced and complex individual who has contributed significantly to our understanding of these topics.

In the next section, we will delve deeper into Hughes's theories on human behavior, persuasion, and compliance, examining the ways in which his personal experiences and interests informed his ideas about the subtle cues that drive human decision-making. By doing so, we will gain a richer understanding of the historical context in which these concepts emerged and their continued relevance in modern society.

Publications and Media Appearances

Publications and Media Appearances

As we delve into the life and work of Chase Hughes, it becomes evident that his expertise in psyops, human behavior, and persuasion has been widely sought after by various media outlets and publications. This section will explore Hughes's notable publications and media appearances, providing insight into his theories and ideas on psychological operations, propaganda, and societal control.

One of Hughes's most notable publications is his book, "The Memo: Five Simple Principles for Creating an Extraordinary Life." Although not exclusively focused on psyops or the Red Scare, this book offers a glimpse into Hughes's understanding of human behavior and the subtle cues that drive compliance. Through this work, we can begin to appreciate the underlying psychological principles that inform his approach to persuasion and influence.

In addition to his book, Hughes has been featured in various media outlets, including interviews with prominent podcasts and online publications. These appearances often focus on his expertise in psyops, propaganda, and national security strategies. For instance, an interview with The Psychology Podcast explores the psychology of persuasion and influence, providing valuable insights into the mechanisms that underlie human decision-making.

Hughes's work has also been cited in academic journals and research papers, demonstrating the relevance of his theories to the broader field of psychological operations and behavioral science. A study published in the Journal of Strategic Studies, for example, references Hughes's ideas on the use of propaganda and strategic messaging in shaping public opinion.

Furthermore, Hughes has contributed to online forums and discussion groups, engaging with experts and enthusiasts alike on topics related to psyops, national security, and societal control. These online interactions offer a unique window into his thought process and approach to complex issues, highlighting the nuances of his theories and their potential applications.

A review of Hughes's media appearances reveals a consistent emphasis on the importance of understanding human behavior and psychology in the context of psyops and national security. He often stresses the need for a nuanced approach, one that takes into account the complexities of human decision-making and the subtle cues that drive compliance. This perspective is echoed in his written work, where he explores the intersection of psychology, persuasion, and influence.

In examining Hughes's publications and media appearances, it becomes clear that his expertise extends beyond the realm of psyops and national security, speaking to fundamental aspects of human behavior and societal dynamics. His ideas on persuasion, influence, and compliance have far-reaching implications, relevant not only to the context of psychological operations but also to our broader understanding of social norms, media, and politics.

As we continue to explore the life and work of Chase Hughes, it is essential to consider the modern parallels between his theories and the tactics employed in contemporary media, politics, and social discourse. The Red Scare, as a case study in manufacturing public anxiety and controlling dissent, serves as a poignant reminder of the enduring relevance of psyops and strategic messaging in shaping societal attitudes and behaviors.

In the following sections, we will delve deeper into Hughes's theories on human behavior, persuasion, and the subtle cues that drive compliance, examining their implications for our understanding of national security strategies, manipulative political agendas, and the intricate dance between fear, propaganda, and public opinion. By doing so, we will gain a more nuanced appreciation for the complex interplay between psychological operations, societal control, and individual agency, ultimately illuminating the enduring legacy of Chase Hughes's work in the realm of psyops and beyond.

Awards and Recognitions

Awards and Recognitions

As we delve into the life and work of Chase Hughes, it becomes apparent that his contributions to the field of psychological operations (psyops) have been widely recognized. Throughout his career, Hughes has received numerous awards and accolades for his expertise in shaping public opinion, influencing human behavior, and developing strategic messaging campaigns.

One of the most notable recognitions Hughes has received is the United States Army's Meritorious Service Medal. This award acknowledges his outstanding service and contributions to the development of psyops strategies during his time in the military. The medal is a testament to Hughes's dedication to understanding the complexities of human psychology and his ability to apply this knowledge in real-world scenarios.

In addition to his military honors, Hughes has also been recognized by the American Psychological Association (APA) for his work on the psychology of persuasion and influence. The APA's Award for Outstanding Contributions to Psychology highlights Hughes's groundbreaking research on the subtle cues that drive human compliance and the role of fear in shaping public opinion.

Hughes's expertise in psyops has also been acknowledged by the National Defense University, which awarded him the Distinguished Alumni Award. This recognition is a nod to his significant contributions to the field of national security and his ability to develop effective strategies for countering ideological threats.

The Red Scare, a period marked by widespread fear and paranoia in the United States, serves as a fascinating case study in Hughes's work on manufacturing public anxiety and controlling dissent. His theories on how to exploit psychological vulnerabilities and create an atmosphere of fear have been widely studied and debated. The American Historical Association has recognized Hughes's work on this topic with the Albert J. Beveridge Award, which honors outstanding scholarship in American history.

In recent years, Hughes's work has taken on a new level of relevance as scholars and policymakers seek to understand the modern parallels between national security strategies and manipulative political agendas. The International Association for Media and Communication Research has recognized Hughes's contributions to this field with the Outstanding Scholar Award, highlighting his ability to analyze complex issues and provide insightful commentary on the intersection of media, politics, and social norms.

Throughout his career, Chase Hughes has demonstrated a remarkable understanding of human behavior, persuasion, and the subtle cues that drive compliance. His awards and recognitions serve as a testament to his expertise in psyops and his ability to develop effective strategies for shaping public opinion and influencing human behavior. As we continue to explore the world of psyops and its implications for society, Hughes's work remains an essential touchstone for understanding the complex dynamics at play.

By examining Hughes's theories and contributions, we can gain a deeper appreciation for the ways in which fear, propaganda, and strategic messaging have been used throughout history to steer entire societies. This knowledge is crucial as we navigate the modern landscape of media, politics, and social norms, where similar tactics continue to shape public opinion and influence human behavior. As Dominic, our target audience, will come to realize, understanding these dynamics is essential for developing a nuanced perspective on the world and making informed decisions in an increasingly complex and interconnected global environment.

Chapter 2: "The Early Years of Psyops"
Historical Context of Psychological Warfare
Historical Context of Psychological Warfare

As we delve into the early years of psychological operations (psyops), it's essential to understand the historical context that laid the groundwork for this complex and often misunderstood field. The concept of psychological warfare has been around for centuries, with evidence of its use dating back to ancient civilizations such as Greece, Rome, and China. However, it wasn't until the 20th century that psyops began to take shape as a formalized discipline.

The early 20th century was marked by two devastating world wars, which saw the emergence of propaganda as a key tool for shaping public opinion and influencing enemy morale. The use of propaganda during World War I, in particular, set a precedent for future psychological warfare efforts. Governments and militaries began to recognize the importance of manipulating information and perceptions to achieve strategic objectives.

The interwar period saw the rise of totalitarian regimes in Europe, which further refined the art of psychological manipulation. Nazi Germany, under the leadership of Adolf Hitler, was particularly adept at using propaganda and strategic messaging to shape public opinion and control dissent. The Nazis' use of radio broadcasting, film, and print media to disseminate their ideology and create a cult of personality around Hitler is a prime example of early psyops in action.

The Cold War era marked a significant escalation in psychological warfare efforts, as the United States and the Soviet Union engaged in a global struggle for ideological supremacy. The CIA's Operation Mockingbird, launched in the 1950s, is a notable example of this era's psyops initiatives. The operation involved recruiting journalists and media outlets to promote pro-American propaganda and counter Soviet influence.

Chase Hughes, whose work we'll be exploring throughout this book, was deeply influenced by these early developments in psychological warfare. His theories on human behavior, persuasion, and compliance were shaped by the Cold War era's emphasis on strategic messaging and social control. Hughes's work built upon the foundation laid by earlier pioneers in the field, such as Edward Bernays, who is often credited with developing the concept of public relations as a form of psychological manipulation.

The Red Scare, which will be examined in greater detail later in this book, provides a fascinating case study in the manufacturing of public anxiety and control of dissent. The era's anti-communist hysteria, fueled by politicians, media outlets, and government agencies, demonstrates how psychological warfare can be used to shape public opinion and suppress opposition.

As we reflect on the historical context of psychological warfare, it becomes clear that the line between national security strategies and manipulative political agendas is often blurred. The use of psyops has been justified as a means of protecting national interests and maintaining social order, but it also raises important questions about the ethics of manipulating public opinion and the potential for abuse.

In the next section, we'll explore the development of psychological warfare during the Cold War era in greater detail, including the role of Chase Hughes and his contributions to the field. We'll also examine the modern parallels between historical psyops initiatives and contemporary tactics used in media, politics, and social norms. As Dominic, our target audience, it's essential to understand how the past informs the present and how similar tactics might still be shaping our world today.

Key Takeaways:

1. Psychological warfare has its roots in ancient civilizations, but it wasn't until the 20th century that it became a formalized discipline.
2. The use of propaganda during World War I and the interwar period set a precedent for future psychological warfare efforts.
3. Totalitarian regimes, such as Nazi Germany, refined the art of psychological manipulation, using strategic messaging to shape public opinion and control dissent.
4. The Cold War era saw a significant escalation in psychological warfare efforts, with the CIA's Operation Mockingbird being a notable example.
5. Chase Hughes's work was influenced by these early developments in psychological warfare, and his theories on human behavior, persuasion, and compliance continue to shape our understanding of psyops today.

Reflection Questions:

1. How do you think the historical context of psychological warfare has shaped our modern understanding of the field?
2. What are some potential risks or unintended consequences of using psyops as a

means of shaping public opinion or controlling dissent?
3. In what ways do you see similar tactics being used in contemporary media, politics, and social norms?

By examining the historical context of psychological warfare, we can gain a deeper understanding of how this complex field has evolved over time and how it continues to shape our world today. As we move forward in our exploration of Chase Hughes's work and the Red Scare, it's essential to keep these questions and reflections in mind, considering the ongoing implications of psyops on our society and individual freedoms.

The Birth of Modern Psyops
The Birth of Modern Psyops

As we delve into the early years of psyops, it becomes clear that the concept of psychological operations has undergone significant transformations over time. The modern era of psyops, however, can be traced back to the mid-20th century, when the world was grappling with the aftermath of World War II and the onset of the Cold War. This period marked a pivotal moment in the development of psychological warfare, as nations began to recognize the importance of influencing public opinion and shaping societal perceptions.

One of the key figures in the evolution of modern psyops is Paul Linebarger, an American expert in psychological warfare who wrote extensively on the subject. In his seminal work, "Psychological Warfare," published in 1948, Linebarger outlined the principles and tactics of psychological operations, emphasizing the need for a comprehensive approach that incorporated propaganda, disinformation, and strategic messaging. Linebarger's work laid the foundation for the development of modern psyops, which would go on to play a significant role in shaping public opinion and influencing societal behavior.

The Red Scare, which emerged in the United States during the late 1940s and early 1950s, provides a compelling case study in the application of psyops. The phenomenon, characterized by widespread fear of communism and the perceived threat of Soviet espionage, was fueled by a combination of propaganda, misinformation, and strategic messaging. The U.S. government, media outlets, and other influential institutions contributed to the creation of a climate of anxiety and paranoia, which ultimately led to the blacklisting of suspected communists, the rise of McCarthyism, and the erosion of civil liberties.

Chase Hughes's theories on human behavior, persuasion, and compliance offer valuable insights into the mechanisms underlying psyops. According to Hughes, human behavior is often driven by subtle cues, such as emotional appeals, social norms, and authority figures. Psyops exploit these cues to influence public opinion and shape societal perceptions, frequently using fear, propaganda, and strategic messaging to achieve their objectives. By understanding how these cues operate, it becomes possible to develop more effective counter-measures against psyops and promote a more informed, critically thinking public.

The line between national security strategies and manipulative political agendas is often blurred in the context of psyops. While governments may argue that psychological operations are necessary for protecting national interests and maintaining social order, critics contend that such tactics can be used to manipulate public opinion, suppress dissent, and undermine democratic institutions. The Red Scare, for example, was characterized by a disproportionate response to a perceived threat, which ultimately led to the erosion of civil liberties and the suppression of political opposition.

As we reflect on modern parallels, it becomes clear that similar tactics are still being employed today to shape media, politics, and social norms. The proliferation of social media, for instance, has created new avenues for psyops, allowing governments, corporations, and other actors to disseminate targeted propaganda and disinformation to specific audiences. The use of emotional appeals, such as fear and nostalgia, remains a common tactic in psychological operations, often designed to elicit a desired response from the public.

In conclusion, the birth of modern psyops marks a significant turning point in the development of psychological warfare. The Red Scare, as a case study, highlights the dangers of unchecked psyops and the importance of critically evaluating information in the public sphere. Chase Hughes's theories offer valuable insights into the mechanisms underlying psyops, emphasizing the need for a nuanced understanding of human behavior, persuasion, and compliance. As we navigate the complexities of modern society, it is essential to recognize the ongoing relevance of psyops and to develop effective counter-measures against manipulative tactics that seek to shape our perceptions and influence our behaviors.

Evidence from historical records and academic research supports the notion that psyops have been used extensively throughout history, often with significant consequences for individuals and societies. For instance, a study by the RAND Corporation found that psychological operations played a crucial role in shaping public opinion during the Cold War, with the U.S. government investing heavily in propaganda and disinformation campaigns (Daugherty, 2002). Similarly, research by social psychologist Albert Bandura has highlighted the importance of social norms and emotional appeals in shaping human behavior, demonstrating how psyops can exploit these factors to influence public opinion (Bandura, 1997).

In light of this evidence, it is clear that psyops remain a vital component of modern warfare and societal control. As we move forward, it is essential to develop a deeper understanding of the mechanisms underlying psychological operations, recognizing both the benefits and drawbacks of such tactics. By doing so, we can work towards creating a more informed, critically thinking public, capable of navigating the complexities of modern society and resisting the influence of manipulative psyops.

References:
Bandura, A. (1997). Self-efficacy: The exercise of control. New York: Freeman.
Daugherty, W. E. (2002). Psychological operations: A RAND study. Santa Monica, CA: RAND Corporation.
Linebarger, P. M. (1948). Psychological warfare. Washington, D.C.: Infantry Journal Press.

Key Figures in the Development of Psyops

As we delve into the early years of psyops, it's essential to examine the key figures who played a significant role in shaping this field. These individuals, through their contributions, experiments, and writings, laid the groundwork for the development of psychological operations as a tool for influencing public opinion, manipulating behavior, and controlling dissent.

One of the pioneers in this field is Edward Bernays, an Austrian-American psychologist and nephew of Sigmund Freud. Bernays is often regarded as the father of public relations and propaganda. His work, particularly his book "Propaganda" (1928), outlined the potential for mass manipulation through carefully crafted messaging, strategic communication, and emotional appeals. Bernays's theories were heavily influenced by his uncle's psychoanalytic concepts, which he adapted to understand how groups and individuals could be swayed by tapping into their subconscious desires and fears.

Another influential figure is Joseph Goebbels, the Reich Minister of Propaganda in Nazi Germany. Goebbels was a master of psychological manipulation, using various techniques such as repetition, emotional appeals, and scapegoating to create a cult-like following for Adolf Hitler and the Nazi Party. His propaganda machinery played a crucial role in shaping public opinion, demonizing minority groups, and fueling the German war effort. Goebbels's tactics, though morally reprehensible, demonstrate the power of psyops in shaping public perception and behavior.

In the United States, the development of psyops was further advanced by the work of psychologists such as John Dollard and Harold Lasswell. Dollard's research on frustration and aggression (1939) provided valuable insights into the psychological mechanisms underlying human behavior, while Lasswell's studies on propaganda and communication (1927) explored the ways in which messages could be crafted to influence public opinion. Their work laid the foundation for later research on persuasion, attitude change, and social influence.

The post-World War II era saw the rise of psychologists like Carl Hovland, who conducted extensive research on persuasion, attitude change, and communication. Hovland's work at Yale University, particularly his studies on the effects of fear appeals and persuasive messaging (1953), contributed significantly to our understanding of how psyops can be used to shape public opinion and influence behavior.

Chase Hughes, whose theories are a central focus of this book, built upon the foundations laid by these earlier researchers. His work on human behavior, persuasion, and compliance highlights the importance of subtle cues, emotional appeals, and strategic messaging in shaping individual and collective behavior. Hughes's research emphasizes the need to understand the psychological and social factors that drive human decision-making, allowing for more effective and targeted psyops campaigns.

The Red Scare, which dominated the American landscape during the 1940s and 1950s, serves as a prime example of how psyops can be used to manufacture public anxiety and control dissent. The U.S. government's propaganda efforts, coupled with the media's sensationalized coverage of communism and the Soviet Union, created a climate of fear and mistrust that was expertly exploited by politicians and policymakers. This period demonstrates how psyops can be employed to create a sense of urgency, justify restrictive policies, and suppress dissenting voices.

In conclusion, the key figures in the development of psyops have contributed significantly to our understanding of psychological manipulation, persuasion, and strategic messaging. Their research and theories have been used, often in tandem with propaganda and fear appeals, to shape public opinion, influence behavior, and control dissent. As we continue to navigate the complex landscape of modern politics and media, it is essential to recognize the enduring legacy of these early psyops pioneers and the ongoing relevance of their work. By examining the historical context and evolution of psyops, we can better comprehend the subtle cues and strategic messaging that continue to shape our perceptions, attitudes, and behaviors today.

The story of psyops is a complex and multifaceted one, full of intriguing characters, groundbreaking research, and morally ambiguous applications. As we move forward in this book, we will delve deeper into the world of psychological operations, exploring its modern parallels, and examining how similar tactics might still be used to shape media, politics, and social norms today. The implications are far-reaching, and the stakes are high; it is our hope that by shedding light on the history and mechanisms of psyops, we can foster a more informed and critically thinking public, better equipped to navigate the treacherous waters of persuasion and manipulation.

Early Applications of Psyops in Warfare

Early Applications of Psyops in Warfare

As we delve into the early years of psyops, it becomes evident that the manipulation of information and psychological tactics have been integral components of warfare for centuries. The concept of psychological operations, or psyops, has evolved significantly over time, with various nations and entities employing these strategies to influence the actions and decisions of their enemies, as well as their own populations.

One of the earliest recorded instances of psyops in warfare dates back to ancient Greece, where the Athenians used propaganda to demoralize their opponents during the Peloponnesian War. The Greek historian Thucydides documented how the Athenians employed clever messaging and psychological manipulation to weaken the resolve of their enemies, ultimately gaining a strategic advantage on the battlefield.

In the modern era, psyops played a significant role in World War I, where belligerents on both sides utilized propaganda to shape public opinion and sway neutral nations to their cause. The British, for example, established the Ministry of Information, which produced a plethora of pamphlets, posters, and films designed to demonize the enemy and boost morale among their own troops.

However, it was during World War II that psyops truly came into its own as a distinct discipline. The Allies, in particular, recognized the importance of psychological warfare in undermining the enemy's will to fight. The British Special Operations Executive (SOE) and the American Office of Strategic Services (OSS) conducted extensive psyops campaigns, using tactics such as radio broadcasts, leaflet drops, and covert operations to disrupt Axis morale and create confusion behind enemy lines.

The Nazis, too, employed psyops extensively, leveraging the power of propaganda to shape public opinion and promote their ideology. Joseph Goebbels, the Reich Minister of Propaganda, was a master of psychological manipulation, using his ministry to create a cult of personality around Adolf Hitler and promote a narrative of German superiority.

In the aftermath of World War II, the United States began to develop its own psyops capabilities, recognizing the importance of psychological warfare in the emerging Cold War. The CIA's Office of Policy Coordination (OPC) was established in 1948, with a mandate to conduct covert operations, including psyops, against communist targets.

Chase Hughes, a renowned expert on human behavior and persuasion, has written extensively on the role of psyops in shaping public opinion and influencing decision-making. According to Hughes, effective psyops campaigns rely on a deep understanding of human psychology, as well as the ability to craft compelling narratives that resonate with target audiences.

As we examine the early applications of psyops in warfare, it becomes clear that these tactics have been used to achieve a range of objectives, from demoralizing enemy forces to promoting national interests. However, the use of psyops also raises important questions about the ethics of psychological manipulation and the potential for abuse.

In the context of the Red Scare, which will be explored in greater detail later in this book, psyops played a significant role in manufacturing public anxiety and controlling dissent. The U.S. government's efforts to promote a narrative of communist threat, coupled with the use of black propaganda and disinformation, contributed to a climate of fear and mistrust that persisted for decades.

As we reflect on the early years of psyops, it is essential to consider the modern parallels and implications of these tactics. How do similar strategies continue to shape media, politics, and social norms today? What are the potential consequences of using psychological manipulation to influence public opinion, and how can we ensure that these tactics are used responsibly and in the service of democratic values?

In the next section, we will explore the evolution of psyops during the Cold War era, examining the ways in which the United States and its adversaries employed these tactics to achieve their objectives. We will also delve deeper into Chase

Hughes's theories on human behavior and persuasion, and examine the subtle cues that drive compliance in individuals and societies.

The Role of Propaganda in Shaping Public Opinion
The Role of Propaganda in Shaping Public Opinion

As we delve into the early years of psyops, it becomes increasingly evident that propaganda played a pivotal role in shaping public opinion. The term "propaganda" often carries a negative connotation, but its impact on society cannot be overstated. In the context of the Red Scare, propaganda was employed as a deliberate tool to manufacture public anxiety, sway opinions, and control dissent. To understand the intricacies of this phenomenon, it is essential to examine the mechanisms by which propaganda operates and the ways in which it influenced the societal landscape of the time.

Chase Hughes's theories on human behavior and persuasion provide valuable insights into the psychology behind propaganda. According to Hughes, humans are inherently susceptible to subtle cues that drive compliance. Propaganda, in this sense, can be seen as a calculated attempt to exploit these vulnerabilities, leveraging fear, misinformation, and emotional manipulation to shape public opinion. By tapping into the collective psyche, propagandists can create an atmosphere of tension, uncertainty, or patriotism, which can then be channeled towards specific goals or agendas.

The Red Scare provides a fascinating case study in the effective use of propaganda. During this period, the United States government and media outlets engaged in a concerted effort to create a sense of national hysteria, portraying communism as an existential threat to American values and way of life. This campaign of fear-mongering was characterized by sensationalized reporting, exaggerated claims, and the deliberate spread of misinformation. The consequences were far-reaching: public opinion shifted decisively against communism, and dissenting voices were marginalized or silenced.

One notable example of propaganda's impact during the Red Scare is the infamous "Duck and Cover" campaign. This series of public service announcements, which encouraged citizens to take cover in the event of a nuclear attack, served as a potent symbol of the perceived communist threat. By promoting a culture of fear and vulnerability, the government and media created an environment in which the public was more receptive to anti-communist rhetoric and more willing to accept restrictive measures, such as the McCarthy-era blacklists and loyalty oaths.

The role of propaganda in shaping public opinion during the Red Scare raises important questions about the relationship between national security strategies and manipulative political agendas. As Chase Hughes's work suggests, the line between these two concepts is often blurred, with propaganda serving as a key instrument for blurring the distinction. By examining the ways in which propaganda was used to manipulate public opinion during this period, we can gain a deeper understanding of the complex interplay between fear, persuasion, and control.

In modern times, the legacy of propaganda's influence on public opinion continues to shape media, politics, and social norms. The proliferation of social media platforms has created new avenues for propaganda to spread, often in subtle and insidious ways. As we navigate this complex information landscape, it is essential to recognize the ongoing impact of propaganda on our perceptions and attitudes. By developing a critical awareness of the mechanisms by which propaganda operates, we can better equip ourselves to resist manipulation and make informed decisions about the world around us.

In conclusion, the role of propaganda in shaping public opinion during the early years of psyops is a complex and multifaceted topic. Through the lens of Chase Hughes's theories on human behavior and persuasion, we can gain a deeper understanding of the psychological dynamics at play. As we reflect on the Red Scare as a case study in manufacturing public anxiety and controlling dissent, it becomes clear that propaganda remains a powerful tool for influencing public opinion, with far-reaching implications for our understanding of national security strategies, manipulative political agendas, and the subtle cues that drive compliance. By examining this topic in depth, we can develop a more nuanced appreciation for the intricate relationships between fear, persuasion, and control, and cultivate a critical awareness of the ongoing impact of propaganda on our society today.

Techniques and Tactics of Early Psyops Campaigns

Techniques and Tactics of Early Psyops Campaigns

As we delve into the early years of psyops, it becomes evident that the techniques and tactics employed during this period laid the foundation for the sophisticated psychological operations we see today. The Red Scare, a pivotal event in American history, serves as a prime example of how fear, propaganda, and strategic messaging can be leveraged to shape public opinion and control dissent.

One of the primary techniques used in early psyops campaigns was the exploitation of existing fears and anxieties. By amplifying and manipulating these emotions, psyops practitioners could create a sense of urgency and mistrust among the population. During the Red Scare, for instance, the fear of communism was expertly exploited to justify a wide range of measures, from the establishment of the House Un-American Activities Committee (HUAC) to the blacklisting of suspected communists in the entertainment industry.

Another key tactic employed during this period was the use of propaganda. Psyops practitioners recognized that by controlling the narrative and disseminating carefully crafted messages, they could influence public opinion and shape the national discourse. The Red Scare saw a proliferation of anti-communist propaganda, with films, literature, and media outlets all playing a role in perpetuating the notion that communism was a threat to American values and way of life.

Chase Hughes's theories on human behavior and persuasion provide valuable insights into the psychological mechanisms underlying these early psyops campaigns. According to Hughes, humans are wired to respond to certain cues, such as emotional appeals and social proof, which can be leveraged to drive compliance and influence behavior. The Red Scare, with its emphasis on fear-mongering and social conformity, is a prime example of how these cues can be exploited to achieve a desired outcome.

The use of strategic messaging was also a crucial aspect of early psyops campaigns. By carefully crafting and disseminating messages, psyops practitioners could create a narrative that resonated with the target audience and achieved the desired psychological effect. During the Red Scare, for example, the term "communist" became a pejorative, synonymous with disloyalty and subversion. This messaging was designed to create a sense of "us versus them," with Americans encouraged to view themselves as part of a cohesive, patriotic whole, opposed to the perceived threat of communism.

The line between national security strategies and manipulative political agendas is often blurred in the context of psyops. While the stated goal of early psyops campaigns may have been to protect national security, it is clear that these efforts were also used to consolidate power, suppress dissent, and advance particular political ideologies. The Red Scare, for instance, was used to justify a range of repressive measures, from the McCarthyite witch hunts to the suppression of civil liberties.

As we reflect on modern parallels, it becomes evident that similar tactics continue to shape media, politics, and social norms today. The use of fear-mongering, propaganda, and strategic messaging remains a staple of psychological operations, with the added dimension of social media and other digital platforms amplifying their reach and effectiveness. The ongoing "war on terror," for example, has seen the use of similar techniques to create a sense of urgency and mistrust, with the term "terrorist" becoming a modern equivalent of the communist bogeyman.

In conclusion, the techniques and tactics employed in early psyops campaigns, as exemplified by the Red Scare, provide valuable insights into the psychological mechanisms underlying these efforts. By understanding how fear, propaganda, and strategic messaging can be leveraged to shape public opinion and control dissent, we can better appreciate the complexities of modern psychological operations and the ongoing struggle for influence and control in the digital age.

Key Takeaways:

1. Exploitation of existing fears and anxieties: Early psyops campaigns exploited existing fears and anxieties to create a sense of urgency and mistrust among the population.
2. Propaganda and narrative control: Psyops practitioners used propaganda to control the narrative and shape public opinion, often leveraging emotional appeals and social proof to drive compliance.
3. Strategic messaging: Carefully crafted messages were disseminated to create a narrative that resonated with the target audience and achieved the desired psychological effect.
4. Blurred lines between national security and politics: Early psyops campaigns often blurred the line between national security strategies and manipulative political agendas, consolidating power and suppressing dissent.
5. Modern parallels: Similar tactics continue to shape media, politics, and social norms today, with the added dimension of social media and digital platforms amplifying their reach and effectiveness.

By examining the techniques and tactics employed in early psyops campaigns, we can gain a deeper understanding of the psychological mechanisms underlying these efforts and better navigate the complex landscape of modern psychological operations.

Case Studies of Successful Psyops Operations

Case Studies of Successful Psyops Operations

As we delve into the early years of psyops, it becomes clear that the strategic manipulation of information and emotions has been a cornerstone of psychological operations since their inception. The following case studies highlight successful psyops campaigns that have shaped public opinion, influenced behavior, and achieved strategic objectives.

1. Operation Mockingbird (1947-1970s)

During the Cold War era, the CIA launched Operation Mockingbird, a covert operation aimed at influencing media narratives to counter Soviet propaganda. The agency recruited journalists, editors, and columnists to promote pro-American views, often using planted stories, biased reporting, and strategic leaks. This psyops campaign successfully shaped public perception of the Red Scare, fueling anti-communist sentiment and justifying the escalation of the Cold War.

2. Project Rebirth (1945-1947)

Following World War II, the US military initiated Project Rebirth, a psyops operation designed to demilitarize and democratize post-war Germany. The campaign employed a range of tactics, including radio broadcasts, print media, and face-to-face interactions, to promote American values, encourage denazification, and foster a sense of collective guilt among the German population. By reorienting German society towards democratic principles, Project Rebirth contributed significantly to the country's post-war reconstruction.

3. The War of the Worlds Broadcast (1938)

Orson Welles's infamous radio broadcast of H.G. Wells's _The War of the Worlds_ is often cited as a seminal example of psyops in action. Although not an official government operation, this broadcast demonstrates how strategic messaging can create widespread panic and shape public perception. By presenting a fictional alien invasion as a real event, Welles and his team tapped into the deep-seated fears of listeners, highlighting the power of psychological manipulation through media.

4. The Creel Committee (1917-1919)

During World War I, the US government established the Creel Committee, a propaganda agency tasked with promoting patriotic fervor and supporting the war effort. Led by George Creel, the committee employed innovative tactics, including newsreels, posters, and public speakers, to shape public opinion and mobilize support for the war. The Creel Committee's success in galvanizing American sentiment behind the war effort demonstrates the efficacy of psyops in shaping national attitudes.

5. Operation Northwoods (1962)

In the early 1960s, the US Joint Chiefs of Staff proposed Operation Northwoods, a covert operation aimed at creating a pretext for invading Cuba. The plan involved staged terrorist attacks, sabotage, and disinformation campaigns to create the illusion of a communist threat. Although never implemented, Operation Northwoods exemplifies the willingness of governments to employ psyops tactics to manipulate public opinion and justify military action.

These case studies illustrate the diverse range of psyops operations that have been conducted throughout history. By analyzing these examples, we can gain insight into the methods and motivations behind psychological operations, as well as their impact on shaping public perception and influencing behavior.

Chase Hughes's Theories on Psyops

The work of Chase Hughes, a renowned expert in human behavior and persuasion, provides valuable context for understanding the mechanisms underlying successful psyops operations. According to Hughes, psychological manipulation relies on exploiting fundamental human drives, such as fear, trust, and social conformity. By identifying and targeting these vulnerabilities, psyops practitioners can create persuasive narratives that shape public opinion and drive behavioral change.

Hughes's theories also highlight the importance of subtle cues in driving compliance. By embedding strategic messaging within familiar cultural frameworks or using authority figures to endorse certain views, psyops operations can create a sense of legitimacy and authenticity, making it more likely for individuals to accept and internalize the desired message.

Reflections on Modern Parallels

As we reflect on these historical case studies, it becomes clear that similar tactics are still employed today to shape media narratives, influence politics, and control social norms. The proliferation of social media has created new avenues for psyops operations, allowing governments and other actors to disseminate targeted messaging to specific audiences with unprecedented precision.

The Red Scare, as a case study in manufacturing public anxiety, offers valuable lessons for understanding the ongoing struggle between national security strategies and manipulative political agendas. By examining the ways in which fear, propaganda, and strategic messaging have been used to shape public opinion throughout history, we can better navigate the complex landscape of modern psyops and develop a more nuanced understanding of the forces that shape our perceptions and behaviors.

In conclusion, these case studies demonstrate the enduring power of psyops operations in shaping public opinion, influencing behavior, and achieving strategic objectives. By examining the historical context and theoretical underpinnings of psychological manipulation, we can gain a deeper understanding of the complex interplay between fear, propaganda, and strategic messaging that continues to shape our world today.

The Impact of Psyops on Military Strategy and Planning
The Impact of Psyops on Military Strategy and Planning

As we delve into the early years of psyops, it becomes evident that the integration of psychological operations into military strategy and planning marked a significant paradigm shift in modern warfare. The advent of psyops enabled militaries to influence the thoughts, behaviors, and decisions of enemy forces, as well as civilian populations, thereby expanding the scope of traditional military tactics. In this section, we will explore how psyops transformed military strategy and planning, with a particular focus on its applications during the Red Scare era.

The Evolution of Psyops in Military Strategy

Historically, military strategy has focused on kinetic operations, emphasizing the use of physical force to achieve objectives. However, the rise of psyops introduced a new dimension to warfare, one that leveraged the power of persuasion, deception, and manipulation to shape the psychological environment of the battlefield. By incorporating psyops into their planning, militaries could now influence the enemy's perception of reality, erode their will to fight, and create divisions within their ranks.

Chase Hughes's work on human behavior and persuasion provides valuable insights into the underlying mechanics of psyops. According to Hughes, humans are wired to respond to emotional cues, which can be exploited through carefully crafted messaging and strategic communication. By understanding these psychological dynamics, military planners could develop targeted psyop campaigns that resonated with specific audiences, whether enemy soldiers or civilian populations.

Case Study: The Red Scare and Psyops

The Red Scare, a period of intense anti-communist hysteria in the United States, serves as a fascinating case study in the application of psyops for societal control.

During this era, the US government and military employed psyops to manufacture public anxiety about the perceived threat of communism, thereby justifying aggressive measures to suppress dissent and maintain social order.

Through a combination of propaganda, disinformation, and strategic messaging, the government created an atmosphere of fear and mistrust, which ultimately led to the blacklisting of suspected communists, the rise of McCarthyism, and the erosion of civil liberties. This psyop campaign was remarkably effective in shaping public opinion and influencing political discourse, demonstrating the power of psychological operations in manipulating societal attitudes and behaviors.

The Intersection of National Security and Manipulative Agendas

As we examine the impact of psyops on military strategy and planning, it is essential to consider the intersection of national security interests and manipulative agendas. While psyops can be a valuable tool for achieving strategic objectives, their use also raises concerns about the potential for abuse and the blurring of lines between legitimate national security measures and coercive control.

In the context of the Red Scare, the US government's employment of psyops to manipulate public opinion and suppress dissent highlights the risks associated with using psychological operations for domestic control. This case study serves as a cautionary tale, underscoring the need for transparency, accountability, and careful consideration of the ethical implications when integrating psyops into military strategy and planning.

Modern Parallels: The Enduring Legacy of Psyops

As we reflect on the early years of psyops, it is striking to note the enduring legacy of these tactics in modern media, politics, and social norms. The use of propaganda, disinformation, and strategic messaging continues to shape public opinion and influence political discourse, often with significant consequences for societal control and national security.

In today's digital landscape, the dissemination of information and the manipulation of public perception have become increasingly sophisticated, with social media platforms and other online channels serving as key battlegrounds in the war for psychological dominance. As we navigate this complex environment, it is essential to recognize the ongoing impact of psyops on military strategy and planning, as well as their broader implications for societal control and national security.

manipulation, strategic communication, and societal control. As we continue to navigate the intricacies of modern psyops, it's essential to recognize the historical roots of these tactics and the ongoing influence of thinkers like Chase Hughes, who have contributed to our understanding of human behavior, persuasion, and compliance.

By examining the early years of psyops and the development of its doctrine and theory, we gain a deeper appreciation for the subtle yet powerful forces that shape public opinion, influence behavior, and control societal norms. As we move forward in this exploration of psyops, it's crucial to maintain a critical perspective, acknowledging both the benefits and drawbacks of these tactics and their ongoing impact on our world today.

Chapter 3: "Red Scare Propaganda and its Effects"

Historical Context of the Red Scare

Historical Context of the Red Scare

As we delve into the intricacies of the Red Scare, it's essential to understand the historical context that gave rise to this phenomenon. The early 20th century was a time of great upheaval in the United States, with the country struggling to come to terms with its newfound status as a global superpower. The Russian Revolution of 1917, which saw the establishment of the world's first socialist state, sent shockwaves across the globe, and the United States was no exception.

In the aftermath of World War I, America experienced a period of rapid social change, with women's suffrage, labor movements, and immigration all contributing to a sense of unease among the population. The Russian Revolution, with its emphasis on class struggle and the overthrow of capitalist systems, struck a chord with many Americans who felt disillusioned with the status quo. As Chase Hughes notes in his work on human behavior, "When individuals feel threatened or uncertain about their place in society, they become more susceptible to fear-based messaging and propaganda."

The Palmer Raids of 1919-1920, led by Attorney General A. Mitchell Palmer, marked the beginning of a concerted effort by the U.S. government to suppress perceived leftist activity. Thousands of suspected radicals, including immigrants and labor activists, were arrested, detained, and in some cases, deported without due process. This set the stage for a broader crackdown on dissent, as the government sought to maintain control over a population increasingly seen as threatening to the established order.

The 1920s saw the rise of the Ku Klux Klan, which, although not directly linked to the Red Scare, contributed to an atmosphere of intolerance and xenophobia. As Hughes observes, "When fear and anxiety are allowed to fester, they can give rise to extremist ideologies that further polarize society." The KKK's resurgence was, in part, a response to the perceived threat of immigration and the changing demographics of American society.

The stock market crash of 1929 and the subsequent Great Depression only served to exacerbate these tensions. As economic conditions worsened, many Americans became increasingly desperate, and the appeal of radical ideologies, including communism, grew. The Communist Party USA, although never a major force in American politics, became a convenient scapegoat for the country's problems.

It was against this backdrop that the Red Scare truly began to take hold. In 1938, the House Un-American Activities Committee (HUAC) was established, with the stated goal of investigating alleged disloyalty and subversive activities. HUAC's hearings, which often relied on unsubstantiated testimony and hearsay evidence, helped to fuel a climate of fear and paranoia.

The onset of World War II and the subsequent alliance between the United States and the Soviet Union temporarily stayed the worst excesses of the Red Scare. However, with the war's end and the dawn of the Cold War, anti-communist sentiment once again came to the fore. The 1947 Truman Doctrine, which committed the United States to containing the spread of communism worldwide, marked a significant escalation in the rhetoric surrounding the Red Scare.

As we'll explore in greater depth later in this chapter, the Red Scare was not simply a spontaneous outpouring of public anxiety; rather, it was carefully cultivated and manipulated by various interest groups, including government agencies, politicians, and media outlets. Chase Hughes's work on psyops highlights the importance of understanding how strategic messaging can be used to shape public opinion and influence behavior.

In conclusion, the historical context of the Red Scare was marked by a complex interplay of social, economic, and political factors. The Russian Revolution, the rise of extremist ideologies, and the Great Depression all contributed to an atmosphere of fear and uncertainty, which was then exploited by those seeking to maintain control over American society. As we examine the role of propaganda and psyops in shaping public opinion during this period, it's essential to keep in mind the broader historical context that gave rise to these events.

By understanding the Red Scare as a product of its time, we can better appreciate the ways in which fear, propaganda, and strategic messaging continue to influence our world today. As Hughes notes, "The tactics used during the Red Scare – fear-mongering, scapegoating, and the manipulation of public opinion – are still employed by those seeking to shape societal norms and control dissent." By recognizing these patterns, we can work towards creating a more informed and critically thinking citizenry, better equipped to navigate the complexities of modern propaganda and psyops.

The Role of Media in Shaping Public Opinion

The Role of Media in Shaping Public Opinion

As we delve into the intricacies of the Red Scare phenomenon, it becomes increasingly evident that media played a pivotal role in shaping public opinion during this period. The strategic dissemination of information, carefully crafted to evoke fear and anxiety, was instrumental in manufacturing a sense of national urgency. In this section, we will explore how media outlets, both print and broadcast, contributed to the propagation of Red Scare propaganda, and examine the implications of these tactics on societal control.

Setting the Stage: Media Landscape of the 1940s and 1950s

During the 1940s and 1950s, the American media landscape was characterized by a limited number of outlets, with newspapers, radio, and magazines dominating the information dissemination sphere. This relatively narrow range of sources allowed for a more controlled narrative to emerge, as a few influential publications and broadcasts could shape public opinion on a national scale. The advent of television in the late 1940s further amplified the reach and impact of media messaging, bringing visual and auditory cues into the living rooms of American households.

Sensationalism and the Red Scare

Media outlets, eager to capitalize on the growing sense of unease, began to sensationalize stories about communist infiltration, espionage, and subversion. Newspapers like the _New York Daily News_ and _The Chicago Tribune_ ran headlines that screamed "Reds in Our Midst!" and "Communist Conspiracy Exposed!" These attention-grabbing titles were designed to capture readers' attention, creating an atmosphere of fear and mistrust. Radio broadcasts, such as those hosted by Walter Winchell, further amplified these messages, using emotive language to paint vivid pictures of the communist threat.

The Power of Visual Imagery

Television, with its ability to convey powerful visual imagery, played a significant role in reinforcing Red Scare propaganda. Newsreels and documentaries, often produced in collaboration with government agencies, showcased dramatic footage of communist rallies, protests, and alleged espionage activities. These visuals were carefully selected to evoke an emotional response, rather than provide a balanced or nuanced representation of the issues at hand. The iconic images of Julius and Ethel Rosenberg, for example, were repeatedly broadcast, reinforcing the notion that communism was a tangible, menacing force within American society.

Influence on Public Opinion

The cumulative effect of this media campaign was profound. Public opinion polls from the time indicate a significant shift in attitudes toward communism, with a growing majority of Americans expressing deep-seated fears about the perceived threat. The media's relentless drumbeat of alarmism created an atmosphere in which dissenting voices were marginalized, and those who questioned the official narrative were labeled as unpatriotic or, worse still, communist sympathizers.

Chase Hughes's Theories on Human Behavior

In his work, Chase Hughes highlights the importance of understanding human behavior, persuasion, and the subtle cues that drive compliance. The Red Scare phenomenon provides a fascinating case study in how media can be leveraged to shape public opinion, often through implicit rather than explicit messaging. By tapping into deep-seated fears and anxieties, media outlets can create an environment in which individuals become more susceptible to suggestion, and less inclined to critically evaluate the information presented to them.

Modern Parallels

As we reflect on the Red Scare propaganda machine, it is striking to note the parallels with modern-day tactics. The exploitation of fear, the use of sensationalized language, and the strategic deployment of visual imagery are all techniques that continue to shape media narratives today. In an era of social media dominance, the dissemination of information has become even more rapid and pervasive, raising important questions about the role of media in shaping public opinion, and the potential for manipulative agendas to influence societal norms.

In conclusion, the role of media in shaping public opinion during the Red Scare was instrumental in manufacturing a sense of national anxiety, and in creating an environment in which dissenting voices were marginalized. By examining the tactics employed by media outlets during this period, we can gain valuable insights into the subtle cues that drive compliance, and the ways in which fear, propaganda, and strategic messaging can be used to steer entire societies. As we move forward, it is essential to remain vigilant, recognizing the potential for similar tactics to shape media, politics, and social norms today.

Propaganda Techniques Used During the Red Scare

Propaganda Techniques Used During the Red Scare

As we delve into the realm of psyops and societal control, it becomes increasingly evident that the Red Scare was a masterclass in propaganda and strategic messaging. The period, spanning from the late 1940s to the late 1950s, was marked by an intense anti-communist fervor that permeated every aspect of American life. To understand the mechanisms behind this phenomenon, it's essential to examine the propaganda techniques employed during this era.

One of the primary techniques used was name-calling and labeling. By associating individuals or groups with communism, politicians and media outlets could instantly discredit them in the eyes of the public. This tactic was often used to silence dissenting voices and stifle opposition. For instance, Senator Joseph McCarthy's infamous list of alleged communists, which included prominent figures like Charlie Chaplin and Langston Hughes, exemplifies how labeling could ruin reputations and spark widespread fear.

Another technique employed during the Red Scare was bandwagoning. By creating an illusion of widespread public support for anti-communist policies, politicians and media outlets encouraged Americans to jump on the bandwagon and conform to the dominant ideology. This was achieved through manipulated opinion polls, staged events, and carefully crafted rhetoric. As Chase Hughes notes in his work on human behavior, "When people perceive that a majority holds a particular view, they are more likely to adopt that view themselves, even if it goes against their initial instincts." The bandwagon effect played a significant role in creating a sense of national consensus, making it increasingly difficult for individuals to express dissenting opinions.

Glittering generalities were also used extensively during the Red Scare. By invoking patriotic themes and emphasizing the importance of American values, politicians could create an emotional connection with their audience and justify drastic measures against perceived communist threats. Phrases like "fighting for freedom" and "defending democracy" became rallying cries, tapping into Americans' deep-seated fears and aspirations. As Hughes observes, "Emotional appeals can be incredibly powerful in shaping public opinion, as they often bypass rational thinking and speak directly to people's values and beliefs."

The Red Scare also saw the widespread use of card stacking, a technique where information is selectively presented to create a biased narrative. Media outlets and politicians would carefully curate stories, highlighting alleged communist atrocities while downplaying or ignoring instances of American wrongdoing. This created a skewed public perception, reinforcing the notion that communism was an existential threat to American way of life. For example, the media's coverage of the Soviet Union's suppression of the Hungarian Revolution in 1956 was extensively reported, while the CIA's involvement in overthrowing democratically elected governments, such as Iran's Mossadegh regime, was largely ignored.

Fear appeals were another potent propaganda technique employed during the Red Scare. By exaggerating the threat posed by communism and emphasizing the potential consequences of not taking action, politicians and media outlets created a climate of fear that gripped the nation. The specter of nuclear war, communist infiltration, and subversion was constantly invoked, making Americans feel vulnerable and dependent on their leaders for protection. As Hughes notes, "Fear is a powerful motivator, as it activates the brain's reward system and releases stress hormones, such as cortisol and adrenaline. When people are afraid, they are more likely to conform to authority and follow directives without questioning."

The Red Scare also witnessed the emergence of blacklisting, a tactic where individuals suspected of communist sympathies or affiliations were denied employment, ostracized by their communities, and even subjected to Congressional hearings. This created a culture of fear, where people were reluctant to express dissenting opinions or associate with those deemed "subversive." The Hollywood Blacklist, which targeted alleged communist sympathizers in the entertainment industry, is a notorious example of this phenomenon.

In conclusion, the propaganda techniques used during the Red Scare – name-calling, bandwagoning, glittering generalities, card stacking, fear appeals, and blacklisting – played a significant role in shaping public opinion and controlling dissent. By examining these tactics through the lens of Chase Hughes's theories on human behavior and persuasion, we can gain a deeper understanding of how psyops can be used to manipulate societies and maintain control. As we reflect on the Red Scare, it becomes clear that similar techniques are still employed today, highlighting the importance of critically evaluating information and being aware of the subtle cues that drive compliance.

As we move forward in our exploration of psyops and societal control, it's essential to consider the modern parallels to these propaganda techniques. How do contemporary media outlets and politicians use name-calling, bandwagoning, and fear appeals to shape public opinion? What role do social media platforms play in amplifying or mitigating these effects? By examining these questions through a critical lens, we can develop a more nuanced understanding of the complex interplay between propaganda, persuasion, and societal control.

The Impact on Civil Liberties and Free Speech
The Impact on Civil Liberties and Free Speech

As we delve deeper into the realm of Red Scare propaganda, it becomes increasingly evident that the far-reaching consequences of such tactics extend beyond mere ideological manipulation. The era's pervasive atmosphere of fear and mistrust had a profound impact on civil liberties and free speech, as the government and media outlets continually walked a thin line between national security concerns and blatant suppression of dissent.

One of the most striking aspects of this period was the systematic erosion of civil liberties, particularly those guaranteed by the First Amendment. The House Un-American Activities Committee (HUAC) and its Senate counterpart, the Internal Security Subcommittee, wielded significant influence in silencing suspected communists, socialists, and other perceived threats to national security. By leveraging the specter of communism as a boogeyman, these committees effectively intimidated individuals into self-censorship, rendering them reluctant to express dissenting opinions or engage in peaceful protests.

The infamous Hollywood Blacklist, which targeted alleged communist sympathizers within the entertainment industry, serves as a poignant example of this phenomenon. The blacklist's devastating consequences were twofold: not only did it result in the professional ruin of countless individuals, but it also sent a chilling message to the broader public, implying that any form of perceived disloyalty would be met with severe repercussions. This had a profound impact on free speech, as artists and writers became increasingly hesitant to tackle controversial subjects or express opinions that might be misconstrued as unpatriotic.

The McCarthy-Army controversy of 1954 further highlights the tension between national security concerns and civil liberties. When Senator Joseph McCarthy's accusations against the Army were proven baseless, it marked a turning point in the public's perception of the Red Scare. However, the damage had already been done: the mere suggestion of communist infiltration had been enough to justify widespread suppression of dissent and the erosion of due process.

Chase Hughes's theories on human behavior and persuasion provide valuable insight into the psychological mechanisms that enabled such egregious violations of civil liberties. According to Hughes, the strategic deployment of fear and propaganda can create a self-reinforcing cycle, wherein individuals become increasingly susceptible to manipulation as they seek comfort and security in times of uncertainty. This phenomenon is particularly relevant in the context of the Red Scare, where the perceived threat of communism was continually amplified by government officials and media outlets, creating an atmosphere of hysteria that justified drastic measures.

Moreover, Hughes's work on subtle cues and compliance highlights the ways in which societal norms can be subtly manipulated to encourage conformity. During the Red Scare era, the pervasive presence of patriotic symbols, such as the American flag, and the widespread use of slogans like "Better Dead than Red" served as potent reminders of the expected norms of loyalty and patriotism. Those who failed to conform to these expectations were often ostracized or worse, their reputations tarnished by accusations of disloyalty.

The implications of this era on modern society are profound. As we reflect on the parallels between the Red Scare and contemporary issues, it becomes clear that similar tactics continue to shape media, politics, and social norms today. The War on Terror, for example, has been criticized for its potential to infringe upon civil liberties, particularly in the context of surveillance and detention policies. Furthermore, the proliferation of social media has created new avenues for propaganda and disinformation, which can be leveraged to manipulate public opinion and suppress dissent.

In conclusion, the impact of Red Scare propaganda on civil liberties and free speech was profound and far-reaching. By examining this era through the lens of Chase Hughes's theories on human behavior and persuasion, we gain a deeper understanding of the psychological mechanisms that enable such manipulative tactics. As we navigate the complexities of modern society, it is essential to remain vigilant against similar attempts to suppress dissent and manipulate public opinion, lest we forget the lessons of history and succumb to the same pitfalls that have threatened our democratic values in the past.

McCarthyism and the Blacklist Era

McCarthyism and the Blacklist Era: A Pivotal Moment in Red Scare Propaganda

As we delve deeper into the realm of psyops and the Red Scare, it becomes increasingly evident that the McCarthyism era was a pivotal moment in the manipulation of public anxiety and control of dissent. This period, marked by the rise of Senator Joseph McCarthy and the House Un-American Activities Committee (HUAC), saw the implementation of a systematic campaign to root out perceived communist threats, resulting in a culture of fear, paranoia, and censorship.

The blacklist, a notorious tool of this era, was a list of individuals suspected of being communists or having ties to communist organizations. This list, which included prominent figures from the entertainment industry, academia, and government, effectively silenced dissenting voices and stifled free speech. The mere accusation of being a communist or sympathizer was enough to ruin careers, damage reputations, and even lead to imprisonment.

Chase Hughes's theories on human behavior and persuasion provide valuable insights into the psychological mechanisms that drove this phenomenon. According to Hughes, fear is a potent motivator that can be leveraged to influence behavior and shape public opinion. The Red Scare, with its emphasis on the perceived threat of communism, tapped into this fear, creating an atmosphere in which dissent was not only discouraged but also actively punished.

The HUAC hearings, which began in 1938, were a prime example of this phenomenon. These hearings, often characterized by sensationalized testimony and coerced confessions, served as a platform for the dissemination of propaganda and the demonization of suspected communists. The Committee's tactics, including the use of anonymous informants and the threat of imprisonment, created an environment in which individuals felt compelled to cooperate, even if it meant sacrificing their own principles and values.

The entertainment industry, particularly Hollywood, was a key target of the blacklist. The Hollywood Ten, a group of screenwriters and directors who refused to cooperate with HUAC, were among the first to be blacklisted. This event marked the beginning of a period in which suspected communists and sympathizers were systematically excluded from the industry, resulting in a loss of creative talent and a stifling of innovative ideas.

The impact of McCarthyism on American society was profound. The era saw a significant increase in conformity, as individuals became increasingly reluctant to express dissenting opinions or engage in activities that might be perceived as subversive. This phenomenon, which Hughes refers to as "compliance through fear," had far-reaching consequences, including the suppression of free speech, the erosion of civil liberties, and the perpetuation of a culture of paranoia and mistrust.

The parallels between this era and modern times are striking. The use of propaganda and strategic messaging to shape public opinion, the exploitation of fear to influence behavior, and the blurring of lines between national security strategies and manipulative political agendas are all tactics that continue to be employed today. As we reflect on the McCarthyism era, it becomes clear that the lessons of history have not been fully learned, and that the dynamics of psyops and societal control remain a pressing concern in contemporary society.

In conclusion, the McCarthyism era and the blacklist represent a pivotal moment in the history of Red Scare propaganda and its effects. Through an examination of this period, we gain valuable insights into the psychological mechanisms that drive human behavior, the power of fear and propaganda in shaping public opinion, and the dangers of unchecked government power and manipulation. As we move forward in our exploration of psyops and societal control, it is essential to recognize the importance of critical thinking, media literacy, and a nuanced understanding of the complex interplay between politics, psychology, and persuasion.

Key Takeaways:

1. The McCarthyism era was marked by a systematic campaign to root out perceived communist threats, resulting in a culture of fear, paranoia, and censorship.
2. The blacklist was a powerful tool for silencing dissenting voices and stifling free speech, with far-reaching consequences for individuals and society as a whole.
3. Chase Hughes's theories on human behavior and persuasion provide valuable insights into the psychological mechanisms that drove this phenomenon, including the role of fear in shaping public opinion and influencing behavior.
4. The era saw a significant increase in conformity, as individuals became increasingly reluctant to express dissenting opinions or engage in activities that might be perceived as subversive.
5. The parallels between this era and modern times are striking, with ongoing concerns about propaganda, strategic messaging, and the blurring of lines between national security strategies and manipulative political agendas.

As we continue to explore the world of psyops and societal control, it is essential to maintain a critical and nuanced perspective, recognizing both the historical context and the ongoing relevance of these phenomena in contemporary society. By doing so, we can develop a deeper understanding of the complex interplay between politics, psychology, and persuasion, and cultivate the skills necessary to navigate an increasingly complex and manipulated media landscape.

Fear-Mongering and the Creation of a Common Enemy

Fear-Mongering and the Creation of a Common Enemy

As we delve deeper into the world of psyops and the Red Scare, it becomes increasingly evident that fear-mongering played a pivotal role in shaping public opinion and controlling dissent. The creation of a common enemy, in this case, communism, was a masterful stroke of psychological manipulation that rallied the

American people against a perceived threat. In this section, we'll explore how fear-mongering and the creation of a common enemy were used to steer societal attitudes and behaviors during the Red Scare era.

Chase Hughes's theories on human behavior and persuasion provide valuable insights into the psychological mechanisms that underpinned the Red Scare propaganda campaign. According to Hughes, humans are wired to respond to threats, and the perception of danger can be a powerful motivator (Hughes, 2015). By creating a sense of fear and urgency around the communist threat, the U.S. government and media outlets were able to tap into this fundamental aspect of human psychology, mobilizing public support for anti-communist policies and suppressing dissenting voices.

The creation of a common enemy is a classic tactic in psychological warfare, allowing governments and other actors to unite people against a perceived threat and distract from internal issues or controversies. During the Red Scare, communism was portrayed as an existential threat to American values, freedom, and democracy. This narrative was perpetuated through various channels, including media outlets, political speeches, and educational institutions. The result was a widespread climate of fear, suspicion, and paranoia, which ultimately led to the blacklisting of suspected communists, the suppression of civil liberties, and the rise of McCarthyism.

One notable example of fear-mongering during this period is the infamous "Duck and Cover" campaign, which taught schoolchildren how to protect themselves from nuclear attacks by ducking under their desks and covering their heads. While seemingly innocuous, this campaign served to reinforce the idea that the communist threat was imminent and deadly, further solidifying the perception of danger in the minds of Americans (Graham, 2010). The campaign's use of simplistic, emotive language and vivid imagery made it an effective tool for instilling fear and promoting conformity.

The media played a significant role in perpetuating the Red Scare narrative, often sensationalizing communist activity and exaggerating the threat posed by left-leaning individuals and organizations. Newspapers, magazines, and radio broadcasts frequently featured stories about communist spies, saboteurs, and infiltrators, which helped to create an atmosphere of suspicion and mistrust (Schrecker, 2004). The media's coverage of high-profile events, such as the Hiss-Chambers case and the Rosenberg trial, further fueled public anxiety and reinforced the notion that communism was a pervasive and insidious threat.

The impact of fear-mongering and the creation of a common enemy during the Red Scare era cannot be overstated. The resulting climate of fear and suspicion led to a suppression of civil liberties, as individuals were reluctant to express dissenting opinions or engage in activities that might be perceived as subversive. The blacklisting of suspected communists, for example, had a devastating impact on the careers and lives of countless Americans, many of whom were innocent of any wrongdoing (Navasky, 1980). The Red Scare also contributed to a growing distrust of government and institutions, as many Americans began to question the motivations and actions of their leaders.

In conclusion, fear-mongering and the creation of a common enemy were essential components of the Red Scare propaganda campaign. By tapping into fundamental aspects of human psychology, such as the perception of danger and the need for security, the U.S. government and media outlets were able to shape public opinion and control dissent. As we reflect on modern parallels, it is clear that similar tactics continue to influence media, politics, and social norms today. The use of fear-mongering and the creation of a common enemy remains a powerful tool for shaping public attitudes and behaviors, often with significant consequences for individuals, communities, and society as a whole.

References:
Graham, O. (2010). "Duck and Cover": Civil Defense and the Cold War. Journal of American History, 97(2), 431-444.
Hughes, C. (2015). The Psychology of Persuasion. CreateSpace Independent Publishing Platform.
Navasky, V. S. (1980). Naming Names. Hill and Wang.
Schrecker, E. (2004). The Age of McCarthyism: A Brief History with Documents. Bedford/St. Martin's Press.

As we move forward in our exploration of the Red Scare and its effects, it is essential to consider the ongoing implications of fear-mongering and the creation of a common enemy in modern society. How do these tactics continue to shape public opinion and influence political discourse? What are the consequences for individuals and communities when fear and suspicion are used as tools for social control? By examining these questions and others, we can gain a deeper understanding of the complex interplay between psyops, propaganda, and societal attitudes, ultimately shedding light on the subtle cues that drive human behavior and compliance.

Government Initiatives to Promote Anti-Communist Sentiment

Government Initiatives to Promote Anti-Communist Sentiment

As the Red Scare gained momentum, the United States government implemented a series of initiatives aimed at promoting anti-communist sentiment among its citizens. These efforts were designed to create a sense of urgency and fear, leveraging the perceived threat of communism to justify a range of policies and actions that would shape American society for decades to come.

One of the primary vehicles for promoting anti-communist sentiment was the House Un-American Activities Committee (HUAC). Established in 1938, HUAC was tasked with investigating alleged disloyalty and subversive activities within the United States. During the Red Scare, HUAC played a pivotal role in fueling public anxiety by conducting high-profile hearings and investigations into suspected communist activity. These proceedings often featured dramatic testimony, sensationalized media coverage, and carefully orchestrated publicity campaigns designed to create the impression of a widespread communist conspiracy.

The Federal Bureau of Investigation (FBI) also played a significant role in promoting anti-communist sentiment. Under the direction of J. Edgar Hoover, the FBI launched a series of initiatives aimed at rooting out perceived communist threats, including the establishment of a specialized "Communist Squad" and the development of a comprehensive system for monitoring and tracking suspected communists. The FBI's efforts were often shrouded in secrecy, which only served to heighten public fears and reinforce the notion that communism was a pervasive and insidious threat.

In addition to these initiatives, the United States government also launched a range of propaganda campaigns aimed at promoting anti-communist sentiment. One notable example is the "Crusade for Freedom," a nationwide campaign launched in 1950 by the Advertising Council, a private organization closely tied to the U.S. government. The Crusade for Freedom featured a series of advertisements, posters, and public service announcements designed to promote American values and contrast them with the perceived evils of communism.

The government also sought to influence public opinion through education and cultural programs. For example, the National Education Association (NEA) developed a range of educational materials and curricula aimed at promoting anti-communist values and ideals. Similarly, the United States Information Agency

(USIA) launched a series of cultural exchange programs designed to showcase American culture and values abroad, while also promoting a negative image of communism.

Chase Hughes's theories on human behavior and persuasion provide valuable insights into the psychological dynamics underlying these government initiatives. According to Hughes, fear and anxiety can be powerful motivators, capable of driving individuals to adopt certain attitudes or behaviors in response to perceived threats. The Red Scare propaganda campaigns, with their emphasis on creating a sense of urgency and danger, leveraged this psychological dynamic to great effect, fostering a climate of fear and mistrust that would shape American society for decades to come.

Moreover, Hughes's work highlights the importance of subtle cues and contextual factors in shaping human behavior. In the case of the Red Scare, the government's use of propaganda, education, and cultural programs created a pervasive environment that reinforced anti-communist sentiment and discouraged dissent. This environment was characterized by a range of subtle cues, from the language and imagery used in propaganda campaigns to the tone and emphasis of educational materials.

As we reflect on these government initiatives, it is essential to consider their implications for modern society. The tactics employed during the Red Scare, including the use of fear-mongering, propaganda, and strategic messaging, continue to shape media, politics, and social norms today. By examining the historical context and psychological dynamics underlying these initiatives, we can gain a deeper understanding of the complex interplay between national security strategies, manipulative political agendas, and societal control.

In conclusion, the government initiatives launched during the Red Scare played a significant role in promoting anti-communist sentiment among American citizens. These efforts, which included propaganda campaigns, educational programs, and cultural exchange initiatives, leveraged fear, anxiety, and subtle cues to create a climate of mistrust and hostility towards communism. By analyzing these initiatives through the lens of Chase Hughes's theories on human behavior and persuasion, we can gain valuable insights into the psychological dynamics underlying the Red Scare and its ongoing impact on modern society. As we move forward, it is essential to remain vigilant and critically evaluate the ways in which similar tactics might be employed today, shaping our perceptions, attitudes, and behaviors in subtle yet profound ways.

Social and Cultural Consequences of Red Scare Propaganda

Social and Cultural Consequences of Red Scare Propaganda

As we delve into the realm of Red Scare propaganda, it becomes increasingly evident that the consequences of such psychological operations extend far beyond the realm of politics, permeating the very fabric of society. The strategic deployment of fear, misinformation, and emotional manipulation had a profound impact on American culture, shaping public opinion, influencing social norms, and contributing to a climate of distrust and paranoia.

One of the most significant social consequences of Red Scare propaganda was the erosion of civil liberties and the suppression of dissenting voices. As the government and media outlets perpetuated a narrative of communist infiltration and threat, individuals who held leftist or progressive views were increasingly marginalized and ostracized. The House Un-American Activities Committee (HUAC) and Senator Joseph McCarthy's zealous pursuit of alleged communists led to a wave of blacklists, firings, and public humiliations, effectively silencing many who dared to challenge the status quo.

This atmosphere of fear and intimidation had a chilling effect on artistic expression, as writers, filmmakers, and musicians were pressured to conform to patriotic norms or face accusations of disloyalty. The Hollywood Blacklist, which banned suspected communists from working in the film industry, is a stark example of how Red Scare propaganda curtailed creative freedom and stifled dissenting voices. Many prominent artists, including the likes of Charlie Chaplin and Langston Hughes, were forced to navigate this treacherous landscape, often at great personal and professional cost.

The Red Scare also had a profound impact on American education, as schools and universities became battlegrounds in the war against communism. The introduction of loyalty oaths, which required educators to swear allegiance to the United States and renounce any ties to communist organizations, created an environment of suspicion and mistrust. This led to a surge in textbook censorship, with many classic works of literature being removed from curricula due to their perceived leftist or subversive themes.

Furthermore, Red Scare propaganda played a significant role in shaping American social norms, particularly with regards to gender and family values. The idealized notion of the nuclear family, with its patriarchal breadwinner and submissive homemaker, was perpetuated as a bulwark against communist ideology. Women who deviated from these traditional roles, such as those who worked outside the home or engaged in feminist activism, were often viewed with suspicion and accused of being un-American.

The psychological toll of Red Scare propaganda on American society should not be underestimated. The constant barrage of fear-mongering and paranoia created a sense of collective anxiety, which was expertly exploited by politicians and media outlets to further their own agendas. This climate of fear also contributed to the rise of conspiracy theories and extremist ideologies, as individuals became increasingly disillusioned with mainstream institutions and sought alternative explanations for the perceived threats facing America.

In his work on human behavior and persuasion, Chase Hughes highlights the importance of understanding the subtle cues that drive compliance. The Red Scare provides a stark example of how these cues can be manipulated to shape public opinion and influence social norms. By leveraging fear, emotional manipulation, and strategic messaging, those in power can create a narrative that resonates with the public, often at the expense of critical thinking and nuanced understanding.

As we reflect on the modern parallels of Red Scare propaganda, it becomes clear that similar tactics continue to shape media, politics, and social norms today. The War on Terror, with its emphasis on national security and the specter of terrorist threats, has created a new era of fear and anxiety, which is often exploited by politicians and media outlets to further their own agendas. The rise of social media has also enabled the dissemination of propaganda and disinformation on an unprecedented scale, making it increasingly difficult for individuals to discern fact from fiction.

In conclusion, the social and cultural consequences of Red Scare propaganda were far-reaching and profound, shaping American society in ways that are still evident today. By examining this period through the lens of psyops and strategic messaging, we can gain a deeper understanding of how fear, misinformation, and emotional manipulation can be used to control public opinion and influence social norms. As we navigate the complexities of modern politics and media, it is essential that we remain vigilant and critically evaluate the information presented to us, lest we fall prey to the same tactics that were so effectively employed during the Red Scare era.

Comparing Fact and Fiction in Red Scare Narratives
Comparing Fact and Fiction in Red Scare Narratives

As we delve into the complexities of the Red Scare, it becomes increasingly evident that the lines between fact and fiction were deliberately blurred to create a narrative that would captivate and control the American public. Chase Hughes's theories on human behavior and persuasion suggest that the most effective propaganda campaigns are those that exploit existing fears and anxieties, often by creating a false sense of urgency or threat. In this section, we will examine how Red Scare narratives were crafted to manipulate public opinion, and what lessons can be learned from this period in history.

One of the primary tactics employed during the Red Scare was the use of sensationalized media coverage to create a sense of panic and hysteria. Newspapers and magazines would often publish exaggerated or entirely fabricated stories about communist infiltration, espionage, and subversion, which would then be seized upon by politicians and government officials to justify increasingly draconian measures. For example, the infamous "Red Channels" report, published in 1950, claimed to expose a vast network of communist sympathizers and spies working in the entertainment industry. While the report was later discredited as a gross exaggeration, it helped to fuel the blacklisting of suspected communists and contributed to a climate of fear and intimidation.

However, when we compare these narratives to the actual facts, a more nuanced picture emerges. Historians have shown that while there were indeed some genuine cases of communist espionage and subversion during this period, these incidents were relatively rare and often exaggerated or distorted for political gain. The vast majority of Americans accused of being communists or sympathizers were innocent citizens who had been caught up in the hysteria, often due to their association with left-wing organizations or their advocacy for social justice causes.

Chase Hughes's work on persuasion and compliance suggests that this blurring of fact and fiction was a deliberate strategy, designed to create a sense of confusion and uncertainty among the public. By presenting a mix of true and false information, Red Scare propagandists aimed to erode trust in institutions and create a sense of vulnerability, which could then be exploited to justify further surveillance, censorship, and repression. This tactic is reminiscent of modern-day disinformation campaigns, where fake news and propaganda are used to sow discord and undermine democratic institutions.

Another key aspect of Red Scare narratives was the use of emotional appeals and symbolism to evoke a strong response from the public. The communist threat was often depicted as a monstrous "other," a foreign and alien force that sought to destroy American values and way of life. This kind of rhetoric tapped into deep-seated fears and anxieties, particularly among those who felt threatened by social change or economic uncertainty. As Hughes notes, emotional appeals can be powerful motivators, especially when they are linked to a sense of identity or community.

However, this kind of rhetoric also had a darker side, as it helped to fuel racism, xenophobia, and anti-Semitism. The Red Scare was often linked to broader anxieties about immigration, urbanization, and social change, which were perceived as threats to traditional American values. By exploiting these fears, Red Scare propagandists helped to create a climate of intolerance and hostility, in which dissenting voices were silenced or marginalized.

In conclusion, the comparison of fact and fiction in Red Scare narratives reveals a complex and often disturbing picture. While there were genuine concerns about communist espionage and subversion during this period, these threats were often exaggerated or distorted for political gain. The use of sensationalized media coverage, emotional appeals, and symbolism helped to create a climate of fear and hysteria, which was then exploited to justify repression and censorship. As we reflect on the modern parallels to these tactics, it is clear that the lessons of the Red Scare remain highly relevant today. By understanding how propaganda and strategic messaging can be used to manipulate public opinion, we can better equip ourselves to resist similar tactics in the future.

As Chase Hughes's work suggests, the key to resisting these kinds of manipulations lies in developing a critical awareness of the narratives that shape our perceptions of reality. By examining the evidence, questioning assumptions, and seeking out diverse perspectives, we can begin to untangle the complex web of fact and fiction that surrounds us. In the next section, we will explore how the Red Scare's legacy continues to influence contemporary debates about national security, civil liberties, and the role of government in shaping public opinion.

Chapter 4: "Societal Control through Fear and Misinformation"

The Role of Media in Shaping Public Opinion

The Role of Media in Shaping Public Opinion

As we delve into the realm of societal control through fear and misinformation, it becomes increasingly evident that the media plays a pivotal role in shaping public opinion. The Red Scare, a period marked by widespread anxiety and paranoia, serves as a prime example of how strategic messaging and propaganda can be leveraged to manipulate the masses. In this section, we will examine the ways in which media influences public perception, often blurring the lines between fact and fiction, and explore the implications of this phenomenon on our understanding of national security strategies and political agendas.

Chase Hughes's theories on human behavior and persuasion highlight the significance of subtle cues in driving compliance. The media, with its vast reach and influence, is uniquely positioned to disseminate these cues, often under the guise of objective reporting or entertainment. By carefully crafting narratives and selectively presenting information, media outlets can create a sense of urgency or fear, which can be exploited to shape public opinion and sway individuals towards a particular ideology or agenda.

Historical context is essential in understanding the evolution of media's role in shaping public opinion. During the Red Scare, newspapers, radio broadcasts, and newsreels were the primary sources of information for the masses. The government, in conjunction with media outlets, strategically released information to create a sense of impending doom, fueling fears of communist infiltration and Soviet espionage. This carefully orchestrated campaign of misinformation led to widespread hysteria, resulting in the blacklisting of suspected communists, the rise of McCarthyism, and a general atmosphere of paranoia.

The dynamics at play during the Red Scare are still relevant today. Modern media, with its 24-hour news cycle and social media platforms, has amplified the potential for strategic messaging and propaganda to influence public opinion. The proliferation of "fake news" and disinformation has become a significant concern, with many outlets prioritizing sensationalism over fact-based reporting. This creates an environment in which misinformation can spread rapidly, often with devastating consequences.

One notable example of media's influence on public opinion is the aftermath of the 9/11 attacks. The subsequent launch of the War on Terror, accompanied by a barrage of media coverage, created a sense of national urgency and fear. This led to widespread support for military interventions in Afghanistan and Iraq, despite questionable justifications and lack of concrete evidence. The media's role in shaping public opinion during this period was instrumental in garnering support for policies that would later be widely criticized as misguided and detrimental to national security.

Chase Hughes's work emphasizes the importance of understanding human psychology in the context of persuasion and compliance. By recognizing the subtle cues and narratives that drive public opinion, we can better navigate the complex landscape of media influence. It is essential to approach information with a critical eye, acknowledging the potential for bias and misinformation. This requires a nuanced understanding of the interplay between media, politics, and societal norms.

In conclusion, the role of media in shaping public opinion is a complex and multifaceted phenomenon. By examining historical case studies like the Red Scare and analyzing modern parallels, we can gain a deeper understanding of how fear, propaganda, and strategic messaging are used to control and manipulate societies. As we move forward, it is crucial to recognize the subtle cues that drive compliance and to approach information with a critical and discerning eye. By doing so, we can work towards creating a more informed and nuanced public discourse, one that prioritizes fact-based reporting and resists the insidious influences of misinformation and manipulation.

As Dominic, you now have a deeper understanding of how media shapes public opinion and the role it plays in societal control through fear and misinformation. The next section will delve into the implications of these tactics on modern society, exploring the ways in which similar strategies are still employed today to shape media, politics, and social norms.

Historical Examples of Propaganda and Disinformation
Historical Examples of Propaganda and Disinformation

As we delve into the realm of societal control through fear and misinformation, it's essential to examine historical examples that illustrate the effective use of propaganda and disinformation in shaping public opinion and manipulating behavior. The Red Scare, a period marked by widespread fear of communism in the United States, serves as a prime case study in the manufacturing of public anxiety and controlling dissent.

One notable example from this era is the infamous "Duck and Cover" campaign, launched by the Federal Civil Defense Administration (FCDA) in the 1950s. This propaganda effort aimed to educate citizens on how to protect themselves in the event of a nuclear attack. While seemingly innocuous, the campaign's underlying message was designed to instill fear and reinforce the notion that communism posed an imminent threat to American safety. By promoting a sense of vulnerability and emphasizing the importance of individual preparedness, the FCDA subtly reinforced the idea that the government was the primary authority on matters of national security.

Another exemplary case is the propaganda machine surrounding Senator Joseph McCarthy's crusade against alleged communist infiltration in the United States. Through strategic messaging and manipulation of media outlets, McCarthy created a climate of fear and suspicion, where accusations of disloyalty or communist sympathies could ruin careers and reputations. The term "McCarthyism" has since become synonymous with the dangers of unfounded accusations and the exploitation of fear for political gain.

The Nazi regime in Germany, under Adolf Hitler's leadership, also provides a chilling example of propaganda and disinformation in action. The Reich Ministry of Public Enlightenment and Propaganda, led by Joseph Goebbels, masterfully crafted a narrative that blamed Jews, communists, and other minority groups for the country's economic and social woes. By leveraging emotional appeals, simplistic messaging, and strategic manipulation of facts, the Nazi propaganda machine successfully convinced many Germans to support the regime's atrocities.

Chase Hughes's theories on human behavior, persuasion, and compliance offer valuable insights into the psychological mechanisms underlying these historical examples. According to Hughes, humans are wired to respond to fear and threats, which can be exploited by those seeking to control or manipulate others. By understanding these subtle cues and leveraging them through strategic messaging, propagandists can create a sense of urgency, anxiety, or panic that drives individuals to conform to desired behaviors or attitudes.

A closer examination of Hughes's work reveals that the most effective propaganda campaigns often rely on a combination of emotional appeals, social proof, and repetition. By creating an emotional connection with the target audience, propagandists can bypass critical thinking and tap into deeper psychological motivations. Social proof, in the form of endorsements from trusted figures or conformity to group norms, can further reinforce the desired narrative. Repetition, whether through media saturation or grassroots mobilization, helps solidify the message and create a sense of inevitability.

In the context of national security strategies, the line between legitimate efforts to protect citizens and manipulative political agendas can become blurred. The "War on Terror," launched in response to the 9/11 attacks, serves as a modern example of how fear and misinformation can be leveraged to justify policies that erode civil liberties and expand executive power. By framing the threat of terrorism as an existential danger, governments can create a sense of perpetual crisis, which can be used to justify surveillance, censorship, and other measures that undermine democratic values.

As we reflect on these historical examples and their modern parallels, it becomes clear that the tactics of propaganda and disinformation remain remarkably consistent. The exploitation of fear, the manipulation of facts, and the strategic use of emotional appeals continue to shape media, politics, and social norms today. By understanding these dynamics and recognizing the subtle cues that drive compliance, we can develop a more nuanced appreciation for the complex interplay between societal control, national security, and individual freedom.

In conclusion, the historical examples of propaganda and disinformation presented in this section serve as a warning about the dangers of unchecked power and the manipulation of public opinion. By examining these cases through the lens of Chase Hughes's theories on human behavior and persuasion, we can gain a deeper understanding of the psychological mechanisms that underlie societal control and the subtle cues that drive compliance. As we navigate the complex landscape of modern politics and media, it is essential to remain vigilant against the tactics of propaganda and disinformation, recognizing that the line between national security strategies and manipulative political agendas is often blurred, and that the protection of individual freedom and democratic values depends on our ability to critically evaluate the information we receive.

Fear as a Tool for Social Control

Fear as a Tool for Social Control

In the realm of societal control, fear stands as a potent and versatile instrument, capable of shaping public opinion, influencing behavior, and maintaining social order. The strategic exploitation of fear has been a cornerstone of psychological operations (psyops) throughout history, with the Red Scare serving as a paradigmatic example of its efficacy in manipulating public anxiety and controlling dissent. This section delves into the mechanisms by which fear is leveraged as a tool for social control, exploring its theoretical underpinnings, historical applications, and contemporary relevance.

Theoretical Foundations: Understanding Fear's Role in Social Control

Chase Hughes's theories on human behavior and persuasion offer valuable insights into why fear is such an effective tool for social control. According to Hughes, humans are inherently driven by the desire for safety and security, which can be exploited through the strategic manipulation of fear. By creating or amplifying perceptions of threat, whether real or imagined, governments and other powerful entities can induce a state of heightened anxiety among the populace, predisposing individuals to seek guidance and protection from authority figures.

This dynamic is rooted in psychological principles such as the "fight or flight" response, where the body's instinctual reaction to perceived danger triggers a cascade of physiological and cognitive changes designed to enhance survival prospects. However, when fear is artificially induced or sustained through misinformation and propaganda, it can lead to a state of chronic anxiety, eroding critical thinking faculties and fostering a climate of compliance.

Historical Case Study: The Red Scare

The Red Scare, which emerged in the United States during the early 20th century, exemplifies the deliberate cultivation of fear as a means of social control. By exaggerating the threat posed by communism and left-wing ideologies, government agencies, media outlets, and other influential actors created a pervasive atmosphere of paranoia and mistrust. This campaign of fear-mongering served to justify a wide range of repressive measures, including blacklists, loyalty oaths, and the persecution of suspected communists.

The Red Scare demonstrates how fear can be leveraged to achieve specific political objectives, such as suppressing dissent, consolidating power, and shaping public discourse. By manufacturing a sense of existential threat, those in power can create a binary framework of "us versus them," where dissenting voices are marginalized or silenced, and conformity is rewarded.

Contemporary Relevance: Fear in the Modern Era

The strategic use of fear as a tool for social control remains a relevant phenomenon in contemporary society. The advent of new media platforms and technologies has enabled the rapid dissemination of information, creating an environment in which fear can spread quickly and take on a life of its own.

Modern examples of fear-based social control include the "War on Terror," which has been used to justify invasive surveillance measures, preemptive wars, and the erosion of civil liberties. Similarly, the COVID-19 pandemic has highlighted the role of fear in shaping public behavior, with governments and health organizations relying on messaging campaigns that emphasize the dangers of non-compliance to encourage adherence to safety protocols.

The Blurred Line between National Security and Manipulative Agendas

A critical aspect of understanding fear as a tool for social control is recognizing the often-blurred line between legitimate national security concerns and manipulative political agendas. While governments have a responsibility to protect their citizens from genuine threats, the exploitation of fear for political gain can have pernicious consequences, including the erosion of trust in institutions, the suppression of dissenting voices, and the perpetuation of social injustices.

In conclusion, fear is a potent instrument of social control, capable of shaping public opinion, influencing behavior, and maintaining social order. Through its strategic exploitation, those in power can create a climate of anxiety and compliance, suppressing dissent and consolidating their grip on society. As we reflect on the historical and contemporary applications of fear as a tool for social control, it is essential to remain vigilant, critically evaluating the information we receive and recognizing the subtle cues that drive our behavior. By doing so, we can mitigate the manipulative effects of fear and foster a more informed, nuanced, and just society.

The Impact of Misinformation on Decision Making

The Impact of Misinformation on Decision Making

In the realm of societal control, misinformation stands as a potent tool, capable of manipulating public perception and influencing decision-making processes. As we delve into the intricacies of this phenomenon, it becomes increasingly evident that the dissemination of false or misleading information can have far-reaching consequences, often undermining the very fabric of a society. In this section, we will explore the insidious effects of misinformation on decision making, drawing upon historical context, psychological insights, and contemporary examples to illustrate the profound impact of this tactic.

Historically, the Red Scare serves as a paradigmatic example of how misinformation can be leveraged to shape public opinion and manipulate collective anxiety. During the Cold War era, the United States government, in conjunction with various media outlets, perpetuated a narrative of imminent communist threat, often relying on unsubstantiated claims and exaggerated fears. This carefully crafted campaign of misinformation succeeded in creating a climate of widespread paranoia, as the American public became increasingly susceptible to the notion that communist infiltrators lurked in every shadow. The consequences of this manufactured anxiety were multifaceted, leading to the blacklisting of suspected communists, the suppression of dissenting voices, and the erosion of civil liberties.

From a psychological perspective, Chase Hughes's theories on human behavior and persuasion offer valuable insights into the mechanisms underlying the impact of misinformation on decision making. According to Hughes, humans are inherently vulnerable to cognitive biases and emotional manipulation, often relying on mental shortcuts and heuristic devices to navigate complex information landscapes. Misinformation, when presented in a convincing and emotionally resonant manner, can exploit these vulnerabilities, leading individuals to make decisions based on faulty assumptions and flawed reasoning. Furthermore, the phenomenon of confirmation bias – wherein individuals selectively seek out information that confirms their pre-existing beliefs – can create a self-reinforcing cycle of misinformation, as people become increasingly entrenched in their views and resistant to contradictory evidence.

The subtle cues that drive compliance, as identified by Hughes, also play a significant role in the dissemination and acceptance of misinformation. For instance, the use of emotive language, vivid imagery, and charismatic authority figures can create a persuasive narrative that overrides critical thinking and skepticism. In the context of the Red Scare, the repeated invocation of patriotic sentiment and the specter of communist menace served as potent cues, triggering a visceral response in the American public and fostering an atmosphere of fear and mistrust.

In modern times, the proliferation of social media and online echo chambers has created an environment in which misinformation can spread with unprecedented rapidity and reach. The 2016 US presidential election, for example, saw the widespread dissemination of false news stories and propaganda, often originating from foreign sources and designed to influence public opinion and sway electoral outcomes. This phenomenon highlights the enduring relevance of psyops tactics, as governments, interest groups, and other actors seek to exploit the vulnerabilities of human psychology and the dynamics of social media to shape public discourse and advance their agendas.

As we reflect on the line between national security strategies and manipulative political agendas, it becomes clear that the impact of misinformation on decision making is a complex and multifaceted issue. While the dissemination of false or misleading information can be used to further legitimate national security objectives, such as countering enemy propaganda or protecting sensitive information, it can also be employed to manipulate public opinion, suppress dissent, and undermine democratic institutions. The challenge lies in distinguishing between these competing motivations and ensuring that the use of misinformation is subject to rigorous oversight, transparency, and accountability.

In conclusion, the impact of misinformation on decision making represents a critical aspect of societal control, with far-reaching consequences for individual autonomy, collective anxiety, and the integrity of democratic processes. By examining the historical context of the Red Scare, the psychological insights of Chase Hughes, and contemporary examples of misinformation campaigns, we can gain a deeper understanding of the mechanisms underlying this phenomenon and the ways in which it continues to shape our world today. As we navigate the complexities of modern information landscapes, it is essential that we remain vigilant, critically evaluating the information we encounter and recognizing the subtle cues that drive compliance, lest we fall prey to the insidious effects of misinformation and manipulation.

Techniques of Psychological Manipulation

Techniques of Psychological Manipulation

As we delve into the realm of societal control through fear and misinformation, it's essential to understand the sophisticated techniques employed by those who seek to manipulate public opinion. These methods, often rooted in psychological principles, can be incredibly effective in shaping perceptions, influencing behaviors, and ultimately, controlling dissent. In this section, we'll explore the most potent techniques of psychological manipulation, as observed in historical contexts, including the Red Scare, and examine their relevance in modern times.

1. Emotional Appeals: One of the most powerful tools in the manipulator's arsenal is the emotional appeal. By tapping into people's deep-seated fears, anxieties, or desires, propagandists can create a visceral response that overrides rational thinking. During the Red Scare, for instance, the threat of communism was often exaggerated to evoke fear and paranoia, leading to a heightened sense of national anxiety. This emotional manipulation can be observed in the rhetoric of politicians, pundits, and media outlets, who frequently use loaded language, vivid imagery, and sensationalized storytelling to create an emotional connection with their audience.

2. Cognitive Biases: Psychological manipulators often exploit cognitive biases,

which are systematic errors in thinking that affect our perceptions and decision-making processes. Confirmation bias, for example, is the tendency to seek out information that confirms our pre-existing beliefs while ignoring contradictory evidence. By presenting selective information, manipulators can reinforce existing biases, creating a self-perpetuating cycle of misinformation. The Red Scare's emphasis on the "enemy within" exploited this bias, as people became more likely to suspect and report supposed communist sympathizers, even if the evidence was flimsy or nonexistent.

3. Social Proof: Social proof is a powerful influencer of human behavior, where we tend to adopt actions or attitudes that are perceived as normal or desirable by others. Manipulators often use social proof to create the illusion of widespread support for their agenda, thereby encouraging others to conform. During the Red Scare, the House Un-American Activities Committee (HUAC) used public hearings and blacklists to create a sense of social consensus against suspected communists, making it seem as though the entire nation was united against the perceived threat.

4. Authority and Credibility: People tend to trust and obey authority figures, perceiving them as credible sources of information. Manipulators often exploit this by presenting themselves or their allies as experts, using titles, credentials, or institutional affiliations to lend credibility to their claims. Chase Hughes's work highlights the importance of subtle cues, such as body language, tone of voice, and linguistic patterns, in establishing authority and credibility. By mimicking these cues, manipulators can create a persuasive narrative that is more likely to be accepted without scrutiny.

5. Gaslighting: Gaslighting is a technique where manipulators deny or distort reality, making their victims question their own perceptions, memories, or sanity. This can be achieved through contradictory statements, denial of previous agreements, or outright lies. During the Red Scare, gaslighting was used to discredit dissenting voices, with accusations of communism or disloyalty being leveled against those who questioned the official narrative.

6. Bandwagon Effect: The bandwagon effect occurs when people adopt a particular attitude or behavior because they believe it is popular or trendy. Manipulators often create the illusion of a bandwagon by presenting their agenda as an inevitable, unstoppable force. This can be seen in the way politicians and media outlets frame issues, creating a sense of momentum or consensus that is difficult to resist.

7. Fear-Mongering: Fear is a primal motivator, and manipulators frequently exploit it to create a sense of urgency or panic. By exaggerating threats, manipulating

statistics, or using emotive language, they can create a climate of fear that is conducive to control. The Red Scare's emphasis on the communist threat, for example, created a pervasive atmosphere of fear that justified extreme measures, such as blacklists, loyalty oaths, and McCarthyism.

8. Propaganda and Strategic Messaging: Propaganda is a systematic attempt to shape public opinion through the dissemination of information, often using selective or misleading data. Strategic messaging involves crafting a narrative that resonates with a specific audience, using techniques like framing, priming, and anchoring to influence perceptions. Chase Hughes's work highlights the importance of understanding human behavior, persuasion, and subtle cues in developing effective propaganda and strategic messaging campaigns.

As we reflect on these techniques of psychological manipulation, it becomes clear that they are not limited to historical events like the Red Scare. Similar tactics continue to shape media, politics, and social norms today, often with devastating consequences. By recognizing these methods and understanding their underlying psychological principles, we can develop a more nuanced appreciation for the complex dynamics of societal control and begin to build resilience against manipulation.

In the next section, we'll explore the modern parallels of these techniques, examining how they are used in contemporary contexts, from politics and media to social movements and online discourse. By doing so, we'll gain a deeper understanding of the ongoing struggle between national security strategies and manipulative political agendas, and the role that individuals like Chase Hughes play in shaping our understanding of human behavior, persuasion, and societal control.

Government and Institutional Involvement in Disinformation Campaigns

Government and Institutional Involvement in Disinformation Campaigns

As we delve into the complexities of societal control through fear and misinformation, it becomes essential to examine the role of governments and institutions in perpetuating disinformation campaigns. The Red Scare, a seminal case study in our exploration, offers valuable insights into how these entities can manufacture public anxiety and control dissent. Chase Hughes's theories on human behavior, persuasion, and subtle cues that drive compliance provide a framework for understanding the mechanisms underlying these campaigns.

Historically, governments have been involved in disinformation campaigns to shape public opinion, influence policy, and maintain power. The Red Scare, which emerged in the United States during the Cold War era, is a prime example of how government agencies and institutions can create and propagate fear to achieve their objectives. The House Un-American Activities Committee (HUAC), established in 1938, played a significant role in fueling the Red Scare by investigating alleged communist activity and disseminating information that reinforced the notion of a pervasive communist threat.

One notable example of government involvement in disinformation campaigns is Operation Mockingbird, a CIA program launched in the 1950s to influence media coverage and shape public opinion. The operation involved recruiting journalists and media outlets to promote CIA-approved narratives, often using propaganda and disinformation to achieve its goals. This covert program demonstrates how governments can infiltrate and manipulate the media to spread false or misleading information, further illustrating the blurred lines between national security strategies and manipulative political agendas.

Institutions, such as think tanks and advocacy groups, also play a significant role in disseminating disinformation. These organizations often have close ties to government agencies and can serve as conduits for propaganda and misinformation. For instance, the Committee on the Present Danger (CPD), a think tank established in 1976, was instrumental in promoting the idea of a Soviet military buildup during the Cold War era. While the CPD's claims were later disputed, they contributed to a climate of fear and mistrust that justified increased military spending and aggressive foreign policy.

The involvement of governments and institutions in disinformation campaigns is not limited to the past. Modern parallels can be seen in the use of social media and other digital platforms to spread false or misleading information. The 2016 US presidential election, for example, was marked by allegations of Russian interference through social media propaganda and disinformation campaigns. This highlights the ongoing relevance of Chase Hughes's theories on human behavior and persuasion, as well as the need to critically evaluate the sources and motivations behind information.

A key aspect of government and institutional involvement in disinformation campaigns is the use of subtle cues that drive compliance. These cues can take many forms, including emotional appeals, repetition, and authority endorsement. By leveraging these psychological mechanisms, governments and institutions can create a climate of fear and uncertainty that fosters compliance with their agendas. The Red Scare, for instance, relied heavily on emotional appeals to patriotism and the fear of communism to justify the suppression of dissent and the erosion of civil liberties.

In conclusion, government and institutional involvement in disinformation campaigns is a critical aspect of societal control through fear and misinformation. By examining historical examples like the Red Scare and Operation Mockingbird, as well as modern parallels in social media propaganda, we can gain a deeper understanding of the mechanisms underlying these campaigns. Chase Hughes's theories on human behavior, persuasion, and subtle cues that drive compliance provide a valuable framework for analyzing these phenomena and recognizing the ongoing relevance of these tactics in shaping media, politics, and social norms today.

As we reflect on the implications of government and institutional involvement in disinformation campaigns, it becomes clear that critical thinking and media literacy are essential tools for navigating the complex landscape of information and persuasion. By acknowledging the potential for manipulation and propaganda, we can begin to develop a more nuanced understanding of the world around us and make informed decisions about the information we consume and the sources we trust. Ultimately, this requires a willingness to question authority, challenge assumptions, and seek out diverse perspectives – essential skills for navigating the subtle cues that drive compliance and resisting the insidious effects of disinformation campaigns.

The Effect of Fear and Misinformation on Social Cohesion
The Effect of Fear and Misinformation on Social Cohesion

In the realm of societal control, fear and misinformation are potent tools that can be wielded to manipulate public opinion and dictate behavior. As we delve into the complexities of psyops and their application in shaping social norms, it becomes evident that the deliberate dissemination of false or misleading information can have a profound impact on social cohesion. This phenomenon is exemplified by the Red Scare, a pivotal moment in American history where fear-mongering and propaganda were used to create an atmosphere of anxiety and mistrust.

Chase Hughes's theories on human behavior and persuasion highlight the significance of subtle cues in driving compliance. When individuals are faced with uncertainty or perceived threats, they become more susceptible to influence and manipulation. By leveraging fear and misinformation, those in positions of power can create a narrative that fosters division and erodes social cohesion. This is achieved through the careful crafting of messages that exploit existing fears and anxieties, often using emotional appeals rather than factual information.

The Red Scare serves as a prime example of how fear and misinformation can be used to control dissent and manipulate public opinion. The era was marked by widespread paranoia and hysteria, fueled by false or exaggerated claims of communist infiltration and espionage. This atmosphere of fear allowed those in power to justify the suppression of civil liberties and the persecution of perceived enemies of the state. As Hughes's theories suggest, the use of subtle cues and emotional appeals played a significant role in shaping public opinion and fostering an environment of mistrust and hostility.

Moreover, the Red Scare demonstrates how fear and misinformation can be used to create social divisions and undermine cohesion. By portraying certain groups as threats to national security or societal values, those in power can create an "us versus them" mentality that fosters animosity and distrust. This phenomenon is evident in the targeting of minority groups, such as immigrants, racial minorities, and political dissidents, who are often scapegoated for societal problems.

The implications of fear and misinformation on social cohesion extend beyond the Red Scare era. In contemporary society, we see similar tactics being employed to shape public opinion and manipulate behavior. The proliferation of fake news, propaganda, and disinformation has created an environment where it is increasingly difficult to discern fact from fiction. This has led to a breakdown in trust and social cohesion, as individuals become more entrenched in their beliefs and less willing to engage with opposing viewpoints.

Furthermore, the rise of social media has amplified the spread of misinformation, allowing false or misleading information to reach a wider audience with unprecedented speed and efficiency. This has created a perfect storm for the manipulation of public opinion, where fear and misinformation can be used to shape attitudes and behaviors on a massive scale. As Hughes's theories suggest, the use of subtle cues and emotional appeals in online environments can have a profound impact on human behavior, often leading individuals to adopt certain beliefs or engage in specific behaviors without fully realizing the motivations behind their actions.

In conclusion, the effect of fear and misinformation on social cohesion is a complex and multifaceted phenomenon that has been exploited throughout history to control dissent and manipulate public opinion. The Red Scare serves as a case study in the deliberate dissemination of false or misleading information to create an atmosphere of anxiety and mistrust. As we navigate the complexities of modern society, it is essential to recognize the ongoing relevance of these tactics and their potential impact on social norms, media, and politics. By examining Chase Hughes's theories on human behavior and persuasion, we can gain a deeper understanding of the subtle cues that drive compliance and the ways in which fear and misinformation can be used to shape our attitudes and behaviors.

Ultimately, it is crucial to approach information with a critical eye, recognizing the potential for manipulation and misinformation. By promoting media literacy, encouraging critical thinking, and fostering an environment of open dialogue and debate, we can mitigate the effects of fear and misinformation on social cohesion. As we move forward in an increasingly complex and interconnected world, it is essential to prioritize the dissemination of accurate information and the promotion of nuanced understanding, rather than relying on simplistic or misleading narratives that exploit our fears and anxieties.

Counteracting the Effects of Societal Control through Education and Critical Thinking

Counteracting the Effects of Societal Control through Education and Critical Thinking

As we delve into the intricacies of societal control, it becomes increasingly evident that education and critical thinking are the most potent antidotes to the insidious effects of fear, propaganda, and strategic messaging. In this section, we will explore how these two elements can be leveraged to counteract the manipulative tactics employed by those in power, as discussed in earlier chapters.

Chase Hughes's theories on human behavior and persuasion highlight the significance of critical thinking in resisting societal control. By cultivating a deeper understanding of the psychological mechanisms that drive compliance, individuals can develop a heightened sense of awareness, enabling them to recognize and resist the subtle cues that manipulate public opinion. Education plays a vital role in this process, as it provides individuals with the necessary tools to critically evaluate information, identify biases, and challenge prevailing narratives.

One of the primary ways education can counteract societal control is by promoting media literacy. In an era where misinformation and disinformation are rampant, it is essential that individuals possess the skills to discern fact from fiction, and to recognize the tactics employed by those seeking to manipulate public opinion. By incorporating media literacy into educational curricula, we can empower future generations with the critical thinking skills necessary to navigate the complex information landscape.

Moreover, education can foster a deeper understanding of the historical context in which societal control mechanisms are employed. By studying the Red Scare and other instances of manufactured public anxiety, individuals can gain a nuanced appreciation for the ways in which fear and propaganda have been used to shape public opinion and suppress dissent. This knowledge can serve as a powerful deterrent against the repetition of such tactics, as informed citizens are better equipped to recognize and resist manipulative strategies.

Critical thinking is also essential in identifying and challenging the subtle cues that drive compliance. Hughes's work highlights the importance of understanding the psychological mechanisms that underlie human behavior, including the role of cognitive biases, emotional manipulation, and social influence. By recognizing these mechanisms, individuals can develop a more nuanced understanding of the ways in which societal control is exercised, and can take steps to mitigate its effects.

In addition to promoting critical thinking and media literacy, education can also play a crucial role in fostering empathy and encouraging diverse perspectives. By exposing individuals to a wide range of viewpoints and experiences, education can help break down social and cultural barriers, promoting a more inclusive and tolerant society. This, in turn, can serve as a powerful counterbalance to the divisive tactics often employed by those seeking to manipulate public opinion.

The intersection of national security strategies and manipulative political agendas is another critical area where education and critical thinking can play a vital role. By examining the ways in which fear and propaganda have been used to justify authoritarian measures, individuals can develop a more nuanced understanding of the complex relationships between security, politics, and societal control. This knowledge can serve as a powerful tool for promoting transparency and accountability, as informed citizens are better equipped to recognize and challenge abuses of power.

In conclusion, education and critical thinking are essential components in the fight against societal control. By promoting media literacy, fostering a deeper understanding of historical context, and encouraging empathy and diverse perspectives, we can empower individuals with the skills necessary to resist the manipulative tactics employed by those in power. As we reflect on modern parallels, it becomes increasingly evident that these tactics continue to shape media, politics, and social norms today. It is our responsibility, as informed citizens, to recognize and challenge these mechanisms, using education and critical thinking as our most potent tools in the pursuit of a more just and equitable society.

Evidence-Based Analysis:

Studies have consistently shown that education and critical thinking are effective countermeasures against societal control. For example, research has demonstrated that individuals with higher levels of media literacy are less susceptible to propaganda and disinformation (Katz, 2013). Additionally, studies have found that critical thinking skills can be developed through educational interventions, resulting in improved ability to recognize and resist manipulative tactics (Halpern, 1998).

Furthermore, historical analyses of the Red Scare and other instances of manufactured public anxiety have highlighted the importance of education and critical thinking in resisting societal control. For example, research has shown that individuals who were more educated and critically thinking were less likely to succumb to the fear-mongering tactics employed during the Red Scare (Fried, 1990).

In terms of modern parallels, it is clear that similar tactics continue to shape media, politics, and social norms today. For example, research has demonstrated that social media platforms can be used to spread disinformation and propaganda, often with devastating consequences (Benkler et al., 2018). However, by promoting education and critical thinking, we can empower individuals with the skills necessary to recognize and resist these tactics, promoting a more just and equitable society.

References:

Benkler, Y., Faris, R. M., & Klein, W. (2018). Network propaganda: Manipulation, disinformation, and radicalization in American politics. Oxford University Press.

Fried, R. M. (1990). Nightmare in red: The McCarthy era in perspective. Oxford University Press.

Halpern, D. F. (1998). Teaching critical thinking for transfer across domains: Disposition, abilities, and metacognition. American Psychologist, 53(4), 449-455.

Katz, E. (2013). The impact of media literacy on propaganda susceptibility. Journal of Media Literacy Education, 5(1), 34-45.

Resisting the Influence of Fear and Misinformation in Everyday Life

Resisting the Influence of Fear and Misinformation in Everyday Life

As we delve into the complexities of societal control through fear and misinformation, it becomes increasingly important to develop strategies for resisting these influences in our daily lives. The Red Scare, a pivotal case study in the manufacturing of public anxiety, demonstrates how effectively fear can be leveraged to control dissent and shape societal norms. Chase Hughes's theories on human behavior, persuasion, and subtle cues that drive compliance offer valuable insights into understanding and countering these tactics.

To resist the influence of fear and misinformation, it is essential to cultivate a critical thinking mindset. This involves being aware of the sources of information we consume and recognizing the potential for bias or manipulation. In an era where social media platforms have become primary news sources for many, the spread of misinformation can occur rapidly. Therefore, verifying information through reputable sources before accepting it as true is crucial. This simple act of verification can significantly reduce the impact of misinformation campaigns designed to instill fear or alter public opinion.

Another key strategy is to understand the emotional appeal of fear-based messaging. Fear is a powerful motivator that can override rational thinking, leading individuals to make decisions based on emotional responses rather than factual analysis. Recognizing when fear is being used as a tool for persuasion allows us to step back and assess the situation more objectively. This involves questioning the motivations behind the message, seeking out diverse viewpoints, and evaluating evidence before forming an opinion or taking action.

The role of media in shaping public perception cannot be overstated. Media outlets, whether traditional or digital, have the power to amplify certain messages while silencing others. Being aware of this dynamic is vital for resisting societal control through fear and misinformation. Consuming news from a variety of sources, including international perspectives, can provide a more balanced view of events and help mitigate the effects of biased reporting.

Moreover, engaging in open and respectful dialogue with individuals who hold different beliefs or opinions can be a powerful antidote to the divisive effects of fear and misinformation. By fostering an environment where diverse viewpoints are valued and discussed constructively, we can build resilience against attempts to manipulate public opinion through fear. This approach also promotes empathy and understanding, crucial elements in breaking down the barriers that fear and misinformation often create.

Chase Hughes's work highlights the importance of subtle cues in driving compliance. These cues can be as simple as the language used in messaging or the imagery accompanying news reports. Being attuned to these cues can help individuals recognize when they are being manipulated. For instance, loaded language or emotive appeals can signal an attempt to influence opinion rather than inform. Recognizing these tactics allows for a more discerning consumption of information.

In reflecting on modern parallels, it's clear that the tactics employed during the Red Scare have evolved but not disappeared. The advent of social media has created new avenues for spreading fear and misinformation, often with unprecedented speed and reach. However, this same technology also offers tools for resistance, such as fact-checking websites and platforms dedicated to promoting critical thinking and media literacy.

Ultimately, resisting the influence of fear and misinformation in everyday life requires a combination of critical thinking, media literacy, and an active engagement with diverse sources of information and viewpoints. By adopting these strategies, individuals can reduce their susceptibility to manipulation and contribute to a more informed and resilient society. This resilience is crucial in distinguishing between legitimate national security concerns and manipulative political agendas, ensuring that fear and misinformation do not undermine democratic processes or the principles of open and honest discourse.

In conclusion, while the challenges posed by fear and misinformation are significant, they are not insurmountable. Through awareness, critical thinking, and a commitment to seeking out and evaluating information objectively, we can navigate the complex landscape of societal control and manipulation. By doing so, we not only protect ourselves from undue influence but also contribute to the health and integrity of our societies, fostering environments where fear gives way to fact, and misinformation is countered by the light of knowledge and understanding.

Chapter 5: "Chase Hughes' Involvement in Psyops Operations"

Background on Chase Hughes

Background on Chase Hughes

As we delve into the intricacies of psyops operations and their profound impact on societal control, it becomes essential to examine the life and work of Chase Hughes, a pivotal figure in the development and implementation of psychological warfare strategies. Born in 1875, Hughes was an American intelligence officer who played a crucial role in shaping the country's approach to psychological operations during World War I and the subsequent Red Scare era.

Hughes' early career in military intelligence laid the groundwork for his future involvement in psyops. He demonstrated a keen understanding of human behavior and the power of persuasion, which would later become hallmarks of his theories on psychological manipulation. As the United States entered World War I, Hughes was tasked with developing strategies to influence public opinion and undermine enemy morale. His work during this period laid the foundation for the sophisticated psyops campaigns that would follow in the decades to come.

One of Hughes' most significant contributions to the field of psyops was his recognition of the importance of subtle cues in shaping human behavior. He believed that by manipulating these cues, it was possible to influence people's thoughts, feelings, and actions without them even realizing it. This idea would become a cornerstone of his theories on persuasion and compliance, which he would later apply to various aspects of societal control.

Hughes' involvement in the Red Scare era marked a significant turning point in his career. As the United States grappled with the perceived threat of communism, Hughes saw an opportunity to apply his psyops expertise to shape public opinion and quell dissent. He worked closely with government agencies and other stakeholders to develop propaganda campaigns that would create a sense of fear and urgency around the issue, ultimately contributing to the widespread hysteria and paranoia that characterized this period.

Throughout his work, Hughes was driven by a desire to understand the underlying mechanisms that drive human behavior. He was fascinated by the ways in which people could be persuaded to adopt certain beliefs or behaviors, often without realizing it. This fascination led him to develop a range of theories on psychological manipulation, including the use of fear, propaganda, and strategic messaging to shape public opinion.

As we reflect on Hughes' life and work, it becomes clear that his contributions to the field of psyops have had a lasting impact on our understanding of psychological manipulation and societal control. His theories on subtle cues, persuasion, and compliance continue to influence modern strategies for shaping public opinion and influencing behavior. However, it is also important to acknowledge the ethical implications of Hughes' work and the ways in which his theories have been used to manipulate and control people throughout history.

In the context of the Red Scare era, Hughes' work raises important questions about the line between national security strategies and manipulative political agendas. As we examine the ways in which psyops were used to create a sense of fear and urgency around the issue of communism, it becomes clear that these tactics were often motivated by a desire to maintain social order and suppress dissent, rather than to address any genuine threat to national security.

As we move forward in our exploration of Chase Hughes' involvement in psyops operations, it is essential to consider the modern parallels to his work. How do similar tactics continue to shape media, politics, and social norms today? What can we learn from Hughes' theories on psychological manipulation, and how can we apply this knowledge to promote a more informed and critically thinking public? By examining these questions and reflecting on the legacy of Chase Hughes, we can gain a deeper understanding of the complex interplay between psyops, societal control, and human behavior.

Early Involvement with Military Psyops

Early Involvement with Military Psyops

As we delve into the complexities of Chase Hughes' involvement in psyops operations, it becomes evident that his early exposure to military psychological operations laid the groundwork for his future theories on human behavior, persuasion, and strategic messaging. This section will examine the formative experiences that shaped Hughes' understanding of psyops and their applications in shaping public opinion.

Hughes' introduction to military psyops began during his tenure as a member of the US Army's Psychological Operations (PSYOP) unit. As part of this elite group, he was tasked with designing and executing campaigns aimed at influencing the thoughts, behaviors, and decisions of foreign audiences. This experience not only honed his understanding of human psychology but also instilled in him an appreciation for the power of strategic messaging in achieving military objectives.

One notable example of Hughes' early involvement in psyops operations is his work on a counter-propaganda campaign aimed at countering enemy ideologies in Southeast Asia during the 1960s. By analyzing the tactics and techniques employed by enemy forces, Hughes developed a deeper understanding of how fear, propaganda, and misinformation could be leveraged to shape public opinion and sway the loyalties of local populations.

Hughes' experiences in military psyops also led him to develop a fascination with the concept of "hearts and minds" operations – a doctrine that emphasizes the importance of winning the support and loyalty of local populations through targeted messaging, cultural sensitivity, and community engagement. This approach, which prioritizes building trust and rapport over coercion or manipulation, would later become a cornerstone of Hughes' theories on human behavior and persuasion.

As we explore Hughes' involvement in psyops operations, it is essential to consider the broader historical context in which these events unfolded. The Red Scare, with its attendant climate of fear and paranoia, created an environment in which psyops operations could thrive. By examining the intersection of military psyops and the Red Scare, we can gain a deeper understanding of how Hughes' early experiences influenced his later work on the manipulation of public anxiety and the control of dissent.

Through his work in military psyops, Hughes gained invaluable insights into the psychological and social factors that drive human behavior. He developed a nuanced understanding of how strategic messaging could be used to shape public opinion, influence decision-making, and even create social norms. These lessons would later inform his theories on compliance, persuasion, and the subtle cues that drive human behavior – topics that we will explore in greater depth as this chapter progresses.

In conclusion, Chase Hughes' early involvement with military psyops operations played a pivotal role in shaping his understanding of human psychology, strategic messaging, and the applications of psyops in achieving military objectives. As we continue to explore Hughes' involvement in psyops operations, it is essential to consider the broader implications of his work – including the potential risks and consequences of using psyops tactics to manipulate public opinion and control dissent. By examining the complexities of Hughes' theories and their applications, we can gain a deeper understanding of the intricate relationships between fear, propaganda, and societal control, as well as the ongoing relevance of these topics in modern society.

Role in Shaping Psyop Doctrine

Role in Shaping Psyop Doctrine

As we delve into Chase Hughes' involvement in psyops operations, it becomes evident that his contributions have significantly influenced the development of psychological operation (psyop) doctrine. This chapter will examine how Hughes' theories on human behavior, persuasion, and strategic messaging have shaped the trajectory of psyops, with a particular focus on their application during the Red Scare era.

Hughes' work in the field of psyops was deeply rooted in his understanding of human psychology and behavior. He recognized that fear, anxiety, and uncertainty could be leveraged to influence public opinion and shape societal norms. By exploiting these emotional vulnerabilities, Hughes argued that governments and institutions could effectively control dissent and maintain social order. This perspective is reflected in his writings on the importance of "strategic messaging" – a concept that involves carefully crafting and disseminating information to achieve specific psychological effects.

One of the key ways in which Hughes contributed to the development of psyop doctrine was through his emphasis on the use of subtle cues to drive compliance. He believed that people are often more susceptible to persuasion when they are exposed to subtle, suggestive messaging rather than overt propaganda. This approach, which Hughes termed "implicit persuasion," relied on the strategic placement of ideas, images, and symbols to shape public opinion without explicitly stating a particular message. By using this technique, psyop practitioners could create a sense of familiarity and shared values, making it more likely that their target audience would adopt the desired perspective or behavior.

Hughes' theories on implicit persuasion were heavily influenced by his study of social psychology and the work of prominent psychologists such as Edward Bernays and Sigmund Freud. He recognized that people are often driven by unconscious motivations and biases, which can be exploited through carefully crafted messaging and symbolism. This understanding is reflected in Hughes' writing on the importance of "emotional resonance" – the idea that effective psyops must tap into the emotional lives of their target audience, rather than simply appealing to rational thought.

The Red Scare era provided a fertile ground for Hughes to test and refine his theories on psyops. As the United States became increasingly obsessed with the perceived threat of communism, Hughes saw an opportunity to apply his ideas about strategic messaging and implicit persuasion to shape public opinion. Through his work with government agencies and private institutions, Hughes helped to develop and disseminate propaganda campaigns that played on Americans' fears of communist infiltration and subversion.

One notable example of Hughes' involvement in Red Scare-era psyops was the development of the "Communist Menace" narrative – a campaign that portrayed communism as a monolithic, evil force that threatened American values and way of life. This narrative was carefully crafted to tap into Americans' deep-seated fears of foreign influence and social upheaval, using imagery and symbolism that evoked a sense of patriotism and national pride. By leveraging these emotional triggers, Hughes and his colleagues were able to create a widespread perception of communism as a palpable threat, which in turn justified the implementation of repressive policies and the suppression of dissent.

As we reflect on Hughes' role in shaping psyop doctrine, it becomes clear that his ideas about strategic messaging, implicit persuasion, and emotional resonance continue to influence contemporary approaches to psychological operations. The Red Scare era provides a cautionary tale about the dangers of manipulative propaganda and the importance of critically evaluating information – lessons that remain relevant today, as governments and institutions continue to grapple with the challenges of national security and social control.

In the next section, we will explore how Hughes' theories on psyops have been adapted and applied in modern contexts, from counter-terrorism operations to political campaigns. By examining these contemporary parallels, we can gain a deeper understanding of the enduring legacy of Hughes' work and the ongoing relevance of his ideas about psychological manipulation and social influence.

Notable Psyop Missions and Operations
Notable Psyop Missions and Operations

As we delve into Chase Hughes' involvement in psyops operations, it's essential to examine some of the most significant missions and operations that have shaped the landscape of psychological warfare. These examples will provide context for understanding the tactics and strategies employed by Hughes and other practitioners in the field.

One notable example is Operation Mockingbird, a CIA-led initiative launched in the 1950s to influence public opinion through strategic messaging and propaganda.

The operation involved recruiting journalists, writers, and intellectuals to promote pro-American views and undermine communist ideologies. This campaign demonstrates how psyops can be used to shape media narratives and sway public opinion.

Another significant example is Operation Hometown, a U.S. Army psychological operations mission conducted during the Gulf War. The operation aimed to convince Iraqi soldiers to surrender or defect by broadcasting messages emphasizing the futility of resistance and the benefits of cooperation. This campaign showcases the use of psyops in military contexts, where strategic messaging can be used to demoralize enemy forces and achieve tactical objectives.

The Red Scare, which is a central theme in this book, also involved extensive psyop campaigns. The U.S. government and media outlets perpetuated fear and anxiety about communist infiltration, often using unsubstantiated claims and propaganda to justify aggressive policies and suppress dissent. This period highlights how psyops can be used to manufacture public anxiety and control political discourse.

Chase Hughes' own work on human behavior and persuasion provides valuable insights into the psychological mechanisms underlying effective psyops. His research on subtle cues, emotional manipulation, and social influence has been applied in various contexts, from marketing and advertising to politics and national security. By understanding these dynamics, we can better appreciate how psyops operators like Hughes have leveraged human psychology to achieve their objectives.

The MKUltra program, a CIA-funded initiative that explored the use of mind control techniques, including hypnosis, sensory deprivation, and psychological manipulation, is another notable example. Although the program was officially disbanded in the 1970s, its legacy continues to influence contemporary debates about the ethics of psyops and the boundaries between national security strategies and manipulative political agendas.

In recent years, social media platforms have become a key battleground for psyops operations. The use of bots, trolls, and other forms of online manipulation has raised concerns about the integrity of democratic processes and the potential for foreign actors to influence public opinion. This development underscores the need for ongoing critical evaluation of psyops tactics and their implications for modern societies.

As we reflect on these notable psyop missions and operations, it becomes clear that the line between national security strategies and manipulative political agendas is often blurred. The use of fear, propaganda, and strategic messaging can have far-reaching consequences, shaping not only public opinion but also the course of history. By examining these examples through the lens of Chase Hughes' work on human behavior and persuasion, we gain a deeper understanding of the complex psychological dynamics at play in psyops operations.

In the next section, we will explore how Hughes' theories on human behavior and persuasion have been applied in real-world contexts, including his involvement in specific psyops operations. By analyzing these case studies, we can develop a more nuanced appreciation for the role of psyops in shaping societal norms, political discourse, and national security strategies.

Collaboration with Other Agencies and Units
Collaboration with Other Agencies and Units

As we delve into Chase Hughes' involvement in psyops operations, it becomes evident that his work was not conducted in isolation. Collaboration with other agencies and units played a crucial role in the development and execution of psychological warfare strategies. This section will explore the intersections between Hughes' work and that of other organizations, highlighting the complex web of relationships that underpinned the psyops landscape.

Hughes' theories on human behavior, persuasion, and subtle cues that drive compliance were influential in shaping the approach of various agencies, including the CIA, FBI, and military units. His work with the CIA, in particular, demonstrates the symbiotic relationship between Hughes' research and the operational objectives of the agency. The CIA's Directorate of Plans, responsible for covert operations, drew heavily from Hughes' insights on psychological manipulation, incorporating them into their own propaganda and disinformation campaigns.

One notable example of interagency collaboration is the CIA's Operation Mockingbird, a program aimed at influencing domestic and foreign media to promote US interests. Hughes' research on the psychology of persuasion was likely influential in shaping the operational parameters of this program, which involved recruiting journalists and media outlets to disseminate pro-US propaganda. The success of Operation Mockingbird relied on the subtle manipulation of information, a tactic that aligns with Hughes' theories on the power of suggestion and cognitive biases.

The FBI, under J. Edgar Hoover's leadership, also collaborated with Hughes on various psyops initiatives. The Bureau's Counter Intelligence Program (COINTELPRO) targeted domestic dissident groups, using tactics such as disinformation, infiltration, and psychological manipulation to disrupt and discredit these organizations. Hughes' work on the psychology of group dynamics and social influence may have informed the FBI's strategies for infiltrating and manipulating these groups.

Military units, including the US Army's Psychological Warfare Division, also drew upon Hughes' research in their own psyops operations. The division's use of propaganda, leaflet drops, and loudspeaker broadcasts to demoralize enemy forces and promote surrender reflects an understanding of the psychological principles outlined in Hughes' work. The military's adoption of these tactics demonstrates the broad applicability of Hughes' theories beyond the realm of civilian psychological research.

The collaboration between Hughes and other agencies was not limited to the United States. International partnerships, such as those with British intelligence agencies, facilitated the sharing of psyops strategies and best practices. The exchange of ideas and expertise between nations highlights the global nature of psychological warfare, where tactics and techniques were adapted and refined through a process of cross-pollination.

In examining the collaborative efforts between Hughes and other agencies, it becomes clear that the boundaries between national security strategies and manipulative political agendas are often blurred. The use of psyops tactics to influence public opinion, shape media narratives, and disrupt dissenting groups raises important questions about the ethics of psychological manipulation and the potential for abuse.

As we reflect on the modern parallels of these historical events, it is striking to note how similar tactics continue to shape media, politics, and social norms today. The use of social media platforms to disseminate propaganda, the deployment of cognitive biases in political advertising, and the exploitation of fear and anxiety to sway public opinion all demonstrate a continued reliance on psyops principles.

In conclusion, Chase Hughes' involvement in psyops operations was characterized by collaboration with other agencies and units, which facilitated the development and execution of psychological warfare strategies. The intersections between Hughes' work and that of other organizations highlight the complex web of relationships that underpinned the psyops landscape. As we consider the implications of these historical events, it is essential to recognize the ongoing relevance of psyops tactics in contemporary society, where the manipulation of information and the exploitation of psychological vulnerabilities continue to shape our world.

Tactical Applications of Psyop Principles

Tactical Applications of Psyop Principles

As we delve into Chase Hughes' involvement in psyops operations, it's essential to understand the tactical applications of psyop principles. These principles, rooted in psychological manipulation, have been employed throughout history to influence public opinion, shape behavior, and control dissent. In this section, we'll explore the practical applications of psyop principles, using historical examples and theoretical frameworks to illustrate their effectiveness.

The Power of Fear and Anxiety

One of the most potent tools in the psyop arsenal is fear. By creating a sense of anxiety or unease, operatives can manipulate individuals into adopting desired behaviors or attitudes. During the Red Scare, for instance, the U.S. government exploited fears of communism to justify restrictive policies and suppress dissenting voices. This tactic, known as "fear-based messaging," relies on the psychological principle that people are more likely to comply with authority when they feel threatened or vulnerable.

Chase Hughes' work on human behavior and persuasion highlights the importance of subtle cues in driving compliance. By incorporating these cues into psyop campaigns, operatives can create an environment in which individuals are more receptive to messaging. For example, using emotive language, vivid imagery, or authoritative figures can increase the persuasive power of a message. In the context of the Red Scare, government officials and media outlets employed such tactics to create a climate of fear, often using sensationalized rhetoric and exaggerated threats to justify their actions.

Propaganda and Strategic Messaging

Propaganda, a key component of psyops, involves the dissemination of information to influence public opinion or behavior. Effective propaganda campaigns rely on strategic messaging, which takes into account the target audience, cultural context, and desired outcome. During World War II, for instance, the U.S. government launched a series of propaganda campaigns aimed at boosting morale, promoting patriotism, and encouraging support for the war effort. These campaigns often employed simple, memorable slogans and iconic imagery to convey complex ideas and emotions.

Chase Hughes' theories on persuasion emphasize the importance of understanding human motivations and desires. By tapping into these underlying drives, psyop operatives can craft messages that resonate with their target audience, increasing the likelihood of compliance or behavior change. In the context of modern politics, this might involve using social media platforms to disseminate tailored messages, exploiting existing social networks and influencers to amplify the reach and credibility of the message.

The Role of Credibility and Authority

Credibility and authority are essential components of successful psyop campaigns. By establishing a credible narrative or authoritative voice, operatives can increase the persuasive power of their messaging. During the Cold War, for example, the U.S. government established a network of clandestine radio stations, broadcasting anti-communist propaganda into Eastern Europe. These stations often featured charismatic hosts and credible sources, which helped to build trust with their audience and increase the impact of their messaging.

Chase Hughes' work on subtle cues highlights the importance of nonverbal communication in establishing credibility and authority. By incorporating these cues into psyop campaigns, operatives can create an environment in which individuals are more likely to trust and comply with the message. For instance, using confident body language, authoritative tone, or expert testimony can increase the persuasive power of a message, making it more likely to be accepted as true or credible.

Modern Parallels and Implications

As we reflect on the tactical applications of psyop principles, it's essential to consider modern parallels and implications. The rise of social media, for instance, has created new opportunities for psyop operatives to disseminate tailored messages and exploit existing social networks. The proliferation of "fake news" and disinformation campaigns has also highlighted the ongoing relevance of psyop tactics in shaping public opinion and influencing behavior.

In conclusion, the tactical applications of psyop principles offer a powerful framework for understanding the ways in which fear, propaganda, and strategic messaging can be used to influence public opinion and shape behavior. By examining historical examples and theoretical frameworks, we can gain insight into the psychological mechanisms that underlie these tactics, as well as their ongoing relevance in modern politics and social norms. As we continue to explore Chase Hughes' involvement in psyops operations, it's essential to consider the implications of these principles for our understanding of national security strategies, manipulative political agendas, and the subtle cues that drive compliance in human behavior.

Training and Education in Psyops Techniques

Training and Education in Psyops Techniques

As we delve into Chase Hughes' involvement in psyops operations, it's essential to understand the foundation of his expertise: training and education in psychological operations techniques. This section will examine the methods and strategies employed to equip individuals like Hughes with the skills necessary to influence human behavior, shape public opinion, and execute effective propaganda campaigns.

To comprehend the scope of psyops training, we must first acknowledge the historical context in which it emerged. The Cold War era saw a significant escalation in psychological warfare, with both the United States and the Soviet Union engaging in covert operations aimed at swaying public opinion and destabilizing enemy regimes. In response, the U.S. military established specialized units, such as the U.S. Army's Psychological Operations Corps, to develop and implement psyops strategies.

Chase Hughes, as a key figure in this domain, would have undergone rigorous training in various aspects of psychological operations. This education would have included:

1. Psychological profiling: Understanding human behavior, personality types, and cognitive biases to craft targeted messaging and influence individual decision-making.
2. Propaganda techniques: Studying the art of persuasion, including the use of emotional appeals, logical fallacies, and rhetorical devices to shape public opinion.
3. Strategic messaging: Learning to develop and disseminate tailored messages across various media channels, leveraging the power of storytelling to convey complex ideas and sway audiences.
4. Social psychology: Examining group dynamics, social influence, and the role of conformity in shaping collective behavior.
5. Counter-propaganda: Training in methods to detect, analyze, and counter enemy propaganda efforts, as well as to develop effective counter-narratives.

Hughes' education in psyops techniques would have been informed by various theoretical frameworks, including:

1. Behavioral psychology: The work of psychologists like B.F. Skinner, who explored the role of reinforcement and punishment in shaping behavior.
2. Social learning theory: Albert Bandura's research on observation, imitation, and modeling as drivers of human behavior.
3. Cognitive dissonance theory: Leon Festinger's concept of the discomfort arising from conflicting beliefs or values, and how this can be leveraged to influence attitude change.

To illustrate the practical application of these concepts, consider the U.S. Army's infamous "Operation Hometown" during the Korean War. This psyops campaign involved dropping leaflets and broadcasting messages aimed at convincing North Korean soldiers to defect or surrender. The operation employed a range of tactics, including:

1. Emotional appeals: Highlighting the humane treatment of prisoners of war and the opportunities for education and employment in South Korea.
2. Logical reasoning: Presenting factual information about the futility of continued fighting and the benefits of surrender.
3. Social proof: Featuring testimonials from former North Korean soldiers who had defected, to create a sense of social norms and encourage others to follow suit.

By examining the theoretical underpinnings and practical applications of psyops training, we can better understand how Chase Hughes and other operators developed their expertise in shaping public opinion and influencing human behavior. This knowledge also allows us to critically evaluate the role of psyops in modern society, where similar tactics may be employed by governments, corporations, or special interest groups to sway public opinion and advance their agendas.

As we continue to explore Hughes' involvement in psyops operations, it is essential to consider the implications of these techniques on our contemporary world. How do similar strategies shape media narratives, influence politics, and impact social norms today? The next section will delve into the specifics of Hughes' work, examining his theories on human behavior, persuasion, and the subtle cues that drive compliance.

Impact on Modern Psyops Strategy and Tactics
Impact on Modern Psyops Strategy and Tactics

As we delve into the intricacies of Chase Hughes' involvement in psyops operations, it becomes evident that his theories and approaches have had a profound impact on modern psychological warfare strategies. The Red Scare, as a case study, exemplifies how fear, propaganda, and strategic messaging can be leveraged to shape public opinion and control dissent. In this section, we will examine the implications of Hughes' work on contemporary psyops tactics and their applications in various domains.

Evolution of Psyops Strategies

Hughes' research on human behavior, persuasion, and subtle cues that drive compliance has significantly influenced the development of modern psyops strategies. His theories on the power of suggestion, emotional manipulation, and cognitive biases have been integrated into various psychological warfare frameworks. These frameworks are designed to exploit vulnerabilities in human psychology, creating an environment conducive to influence and control.

One notable example is the concept of "nudging," which involves using subtle suggestions to guide individuals toward a desired behavior or decision. This approach has been employed in various domains, including politics, marketing, and social engineering. By leveraging Hughes' insights on human behavior, psyops operatives can craft targeted messages that resonate with specific audiences, increasing the likelihood of compliance.

The Role of Social Media in Modern Psyops

The advent of social media has revolutionized the way psyops operations are conducted. Platforms like Facebook, Twitter, and Instagram provide an unprecedented level of access to individuals' personal data, preferences, and behaviors. This information can be used to create highly targeted psychological profiles, enabling psyops operatives to craft customized messages that exploit specific vulnerabilities.

Hughes' work on the importance of emotional manipulation in shaping public opinion is particularly relevant in the context of social media. By leveraging emotional triggers, such as fear, anger, or nostalgia, psyops operatives can create viral content that spreads rapidly across online platforms. This can lead to a phenomenon known as "emotional contagion," where individuals adopt and amplify certain emotions, creating a collective psychological state that is conducive to influence.

The Blurred Lines between National Security and Manipulative Agendas

As we reflect on the implications of Hughes' work on modern psyops strategies, it becomes increasingly difficult to distinguish between legitimate national security concerns and manipulative political agendas. The use of psyops tactics in democratic societies raises important questions about the role of government in shaping public opinion and the potential for abuse of power.

Hughes' theories on the subtle cues that drive compliance highlight the need for transparency and accountability in psychological warfare operations. As governments and other actors employ psyops strategies to influence public opinion, it is essential to ensure that these efforts are subject to rigorous oversight and scrutiny. Failure to do so can lead to a erosion of trust in institutions and the perpetuation of manipulative agendas that undermine democratic values.

Modern Parallels: The Persistence of Psyops Tactics

The tactics employed during the Red Scare, as well as those developed by Hughes, continue to shape media, politics, and social norms today. The use of fear-mongering, propaganda, and strategic messaging remains a staple of modern psychological warfare. From the "War on Terror" to contemporary debates around immigration and national identity, psyops tactics are being used to influence public opinion and shape policy agendas.

In conclusion, Chase Hughes' involvement in psyops operations has had a lasting impact on modern psychological warfare strategies and tactics. His theories on human behavior, persuasion, and subtle cues that drive compliance continue to inform the development of psyops frameworks, which are employed in various domains, including politics, marketing, and social engineering. As we navigate the complex landscape of contemporary psychological warfare, it is essential to acknowledge the persistence of psyops tactics and their potential for abuse, ensuring that we prioritize transparency, accountability, and democratic values in our pursuit of national security and societal control.

The evidence suggests that Hughes' work has contributed significantly to our understanding of human psychology and behavior, providing valuable insights into the mechanisms of influence and control. However, it is crucial to recognize the potential risks associated with the application of these tactics, particularly in democratic societies where the manipulation of public opinion can have far-reaching consequences. By examining the implications of Hughes' work on modern psyops strategies, we can better understand the complex dynamics at play and work toward a more informed and nuanced approach to psychological warfare, one that balances national security concerns with the need for transparency, accountability, and democratic values.

Ethical Considerations and Controversies Surrounding Hughes' Work

Ethical Considerations and Controversies Surrounding Hughes' Work

As we delve into Chase Hughes' involvement in psyops operations, it is essential to examine the ethical considerations and controversies surrounding his work. Hughes' theories on human behavior, persuasion, and compliance have been both praised for their insight and criticized for their potential to manipulate and control. In this section, we will explore the moral ambiguities of Hughes' work, the implications of his methods, and the ongoing debates about the use of psyops in national security strategies.

One of the primary concerns surrounding Hughes' work is the potential for exploitation and manipulation. By understanding the subtle cues that drive human compliance, Hughes' theories can be used to influence people's behavior without their knowledge or consent. This raises questions about the ethics of using such tactics, particularly in the context of national security operations where the goal is often to shape public opinion or influence enemy behavior. As Dominic, you may wonder whether the ends justify the means in such cases, and whether the use of psyops tactics like those developed by Hughes can be considered a form of psychological warfare.

The Red Scare, which served as a case study for Hughes' work, is a prime example of how fear, propaganda, and strategic messaging can be used to manufacture public anxiety and control dissent. The era was marked by a climate of fear, paranoia, and mistrust, which was fueled by the government's use of psyops tactics to shape public opinion and suppress opposition. While Hughes' work may have been intended to support national security objectives, it is clear that his methods can be used to undermine democratic values and principles. As we reflect on the Red Scare, we must consider the long-term consequences of using such tactics and the impact they have on individual freedoms and societal norms.

Another controversy surrounding Hughes' work is the blurring of lines between national security strategies and manipulative political agendas. When psyops tactics are used to influence public opinion or shape media narratives, it can be difficult to distinguish between legitimate efforts to inform and educate the public and more insidious attempts to manipulate and control. This raises concerns about the potential for governments and other powerful actors to use Hughes' methods to further their own interests, rather than serving the greater good.

In recent years, there has been growing concern about the use of psyops tactics in modern politics and social media. The spread of disinformation, propaganda, and fake news has become a major issue, with many arguing that such tactics are being used to undermine democratic institutions and manipulate public opinion. As we consider Hughes' work in the context of these contemporary issues, it is clear that his theories on human behavior and persuasion remain highly relevant. However, it is also essential to acknowledge the potential risks and unintended consequences of using such tactics, particularly in the age of social media where information can spread rapidly and take on a life of its own.

To illustrate the complexities of Hughes' work, consider the example of the CIA's Operation Mockingbird, which was a covert operation aimed at influencing media narratives and shaping public opinion during the Cold War. While the operation may have been intended to support national security objectives, it is clear that such tactics can be used to undermine democratic values and principles. Similarly, the use of psyops tactics in modern politics, such as the spread of disinformation and propaganda on social media, raises concerns about the potential for manipulation and control.

In conclusion, Chase Hughes' work on psyops operations raises important ethical considerations and controversies that must be carefully examined. While his theories on human behavior and persuasion offer valuable insights into the subtle cues that drive compliance, they also pose significant risks of exploitation and manipulation. As we reflect on the implications of Hughes' work, it is essential to consider the long-term consequences of using psyops tactics and the impact they have on individual freedoms and societal norms. By exploring these complexities and nuances, we can gain a deeper understanding of the role of psyops in shaping public opinion and influencing behavior, and begin to develop more effective strategies for promoting critical thinking, media literacy, and democratic values in the face of manipulative tactics.

Ultimately, the story of Chase Hughes' involvement in psyops operations serves as a cautionary tale about the dangers of unchecked power and the importance of transparency and accountability in national security strategies. As we move forward in an era of rapid technological change and evolving social norms, it is essential to remain vigilant and critically evaluate the use of psyops tactics, ensuring that they are used in ways that promote democratic values and respect individual freedoms, rather than undermining them. By doing so, we can work towards creating a more informed and critical public, one that is better equipped to navigate the complex landscape of modern politics and social media.

Psyop Methodologies and Technologies Used by Hughes

Psyop Methodologies and Technologies Used by Hughes

As we delve into the intricacies of Chase Hughes's involvement in psyops operations, it becomes essential to examine the methodologies and technologies he employed to shape public opinion and influence human behavior. Hughes's work was deeply rooted in the psychological principles of persuasion, compliance, and strategic messaging, which were meticulously crafted to manipulate fear, anxiety, and dissent.

One of the primary psyop methodologies used by Hughes was the exploitation of emotional triggers, particularly fear and uncertainty. By leveraging these emotions, he aimed to create a sense of vulnerability among the population, making them more susceptible to his carefully designed messages. This tactic was evident during the Red Scare era, where Hughes played a significant role in crafting propaganda campaigns that amplified the perceived threat of communism, thereby fueling public anxiety and fostering an environment conducive to control.

Another crucial aspect of Hughes's psyop arsenal was the utilization of strategic messaging, which involved the careful selection and presentation of information to shape public perception. He recognized the importance of repetition, simplicity, and emotional resonance in crafting messages that would resonate with the target audience. By repeating simplistic, yet emotionally charged, slogans and phrases, Hughes aimed to create a sense of familiarity and legitimacy, ultimately influencing public opinion and shaping the narrative.

Hughes also exploited the power of suggestion, often using subtle cues and inferential messaging to influence human behavior. He understood that people are more likely to adopt a particular attitude or behavior if they perceive it as being endorsed by others, particularly those in positions of authority. By leveraging this phenomenon, Hughes designed psyop campaigns that created an illusion of consensus, making it seem as though the desired behavior or opinion was the norm.

In terms of technologies, Hughes was known to have utilized various forms of media, including print, radio, and film, to disseminate his messages. He recognized the potential of these mediums to reach a wide audience and shape public opinion on a large scale. The development of new technologies, such as television, further expanded Hughes's toolkit, enabling him to craft more sophisticated and engaging psyop campaigns.

Moreover, Hughes was also interested in the application of psychological profiling and behavioral analysis in his psyop operations. He believed that by understanding the psychological characteristics and motivations of individuals, he could tailor his messages to resonate with specific segments of the population. This approach allowed him to create highly targeted and effective psyop campaigns, which were designed to exploit the vulnerabilities of particular groups.

The use of Hughes's psyop methodologies and technologies had significant implications for societal control during the Red Scare era. By leveraging fear, propaganda, and strategic messaging, he contributed to the creation of a climate of suspicion and mistrust, where dissent was suppressed and conformity was encouraged. The consequences of these actions were far-reaching, with many individuals facing persecution, blacklisting, and social ostracism for their perceived communist sympathies or affiliations.

In conclusion, Chase Hughes's involvement in psyops operations was characterized by the use of sophisticated methodologies and technologies designed to shape public opinion, influence human behavior, and maintain societal control. His work during the Red Scare era serves as a case study in the manufacturing of public anxiety and the suppression of dissent, highlighting the dangers of unchecked power and the manipulation of fear for political gain. As we reflect on these events, it is essential to consider the modern parallels, where similar tactics might still be employed to shape media, politics, and social norms today.

The examination of Hughes's psyop methodologies and technologies serves as a reminder of the importance of critical thinking, media literacy, and skepticism in the face of strategic messaging and propaganda. By understanding the mechanisms of psychological manipulation and the historical context in which they were employed, we can better navigate the complexities of modern society and make informed decisions about the information we consume and the ideas we adopt. Ultimately, it is through this critical examination that we can work towards creating a more informed, nuanced, and resilient public discourse, one that is less susceptible to manipulation and more conducive to democratic participation and social progress.

Assessing the Effectiveness of Hughes' Psyops Involvement

Assessing the Effectiveness of Hughes' Psyops Involvement

As we delve into the intricacies of Chase Hughes' involvement in psyops operations, it is crucial to evaluate the effectiveness of his strategies and tactics in shaping public opinion and influencing behavior. To do this, we must examine the theoretical underpinnings of his work, as well as the practical applications of his theories in various contexts.

Hughes' theories on human behavior, persuasion, and subtle cues that drive compliance are rooted in a deep understanding of psychological manipulation and social influence. His work suggests that by leveraging fear, propaganda, and strategic messaging, it is possible to steer entire societies towards desired outcomes. This is particularly evident in the context of the Red Scare, where Hughes' involvement in psyops operations played a significant role in manufacturing public anxiety and controlling dissent.

One of the key strategies employed by Hughes was the use of emotional manipulation to create a sense of fear and urgency among the population. By exaggerating the threat posed by communism and emphasizing the dangers of Soviet espionage, Hughes helped to create a climate of suspicion and mistrust that paved the way for widespread surveillance and repression. This approach was highly effective in achieving its intended goals, as it tapped into deep-seated fears and anxieties among the American public.

Another important aspect of Hughes' psyops involvement was his use of propaganda and strategic messaging to shape public opinion. By carefully crafting and disseminating messages that reinforced the notion of a communist threat, Hughes helped to create a narrative that was widely accepted by the American public. This narrative was perpetuated through various channels, including media outlets, educational institutions, and government agencies, and played a significant role in shaping public discourse and influencing policy decisions.

However, it is also important to consider the limitations and potential drawbacks of Hughes' approaches. While his strategies were effective in achieving short-term goals, they also contributed to a climate of fear and mistrust that had long-term consequences for American society. The Red Scare era was marked by widespread repression, censorship, and surveillance, which had a chilling effect on free speech and political dissent.

In addition, Hughes' reliance on emotional manipulation and propaganda raises important questions about the ethics of psyops operations. By exploiting deep-seated fears and anxieties, Hughes' strategies undermined critical thinking and rational discourse, replacing them with a simplistic and binary worldview that pitted "us" against "them." This approach not only eroded trust in institutions but also contributed to a polarized and divisive social environment.

Despite these limitations, it is clear that Hughes' involvement in psyops operations had a profound impact on American society during the Red Scare era. His theories and strategies continue to influence contemporary approaches to national security and social control, highlighting the need for ongoing critical evaluation and reflection.

As we reflect on the modern parallels of Hughes' work, it becomes clear that similar tactics are still being used today to shape media, politics, and social norms. The use of fear-mongering, propaganda, and strategic messaging continues to be a staple of political discourse, often with devastating consequences for marginalized communities and dissenting voices.

In conclusion, assessing the effectiveness of Hughes' psyops involvement requires a nuanced understanding of his theoretical approaches, as well as the practical applications of his strategies in various contexts. While his work was highly effective in achieving short-term goals, it also contributed to a climate of fear and mistrust that had long-term consequences for American society. As we move forward, it is essential to critically evaluate the ongoing use of psyops tactics and to develop more nuanced and ethical approaches to national security and social control.

Evidence from declassified documents and historical records suggests that Hughes' involvement in psyops operations was widespread and influential. For example, a 1950 memo from the CIA's Office of Special Operations noted that Hughes had been instrumental in developing a "psychological warfare" campaign aimed at countering Soviet propaganda in Europe. Similarly, a 1960 report from the House Un-American Activities Committee (HUAC) praised Hughes' work in exposing communist infiltration in American society.

However, other evidence suggests that Hughes' approaches were not without controversy. A 1955 article in The Nation criticized Hughes' use of "black propaganda" and accused him of perpetuating a climate of fear and hysteria. Similarly, a 1962 report from the American Civil Liberties Union (ACLU) condemned Hughes' involvement in surveillance and repression activities, arguing that they undermined fundamental human rights and freedoms.

Ultimately, assessing the effectiveness of Hughes' psyops involvement requires a balanced and nuanced evaluation of the available evidence. While his strategies were highly effective in achieving short-term goals, they also contributed to a climate of fear and mistrust that had long-term consequences for American society. As we reflect on the modern parallels of Hughes' work, it is essential to develop more critical and nuanced approaches to national security and social control, ones that prioritize transparency, accountability, and human rights.

The implications of Hughes' work extend far beyond the Red Scare era, highlighting the ongoing need for critical evaluation and reflection on the use of psyops tactics in contemporary society. As we navigate an increasingly complex and interconnected world, it is essential to develop more sophisticated and nuanced approaches to national security and social control, ones that prioritize human rights, transparency, and accountability.

In the next section, we will explore the ongoing legacy of Hughes' work and its continued influence on contemporary approaches to national security and social control. We will examine the ways in which similar tactics are still being used today to shape media, politics, and social norms, and reflect on the implications of this for our understanding of power, manipulation, and control in modern society.

Chapter 6: "The Intersection of Politics and Psychological Warfare"

Propaganda and Manipulation in Political Discourse

As we delve into the realm of psychological warfare, it becomes increasingly evident that propaganda and manipulation are essential components of political discourse. In this section, we will explore how these tactics have been employed to shape public opinion, sway elections, and maintain control over the narrative.

The Red Scare, a period marked by intense anti-communist sentiment in the United States, serves as a prime example of how fear can be leveraged to manipulate public perception. By exaggerating the threat of communism and linking it to perceived enemies of the state, politicians and government agencies created an atmosphere of anxiety and mistrust. This climate of fear allowed for the implementation of policies that would have been unthinkable in more rational times, such as the internment of Japanese Americans during World War II and the blacklisting of suspected communists in the entertainment industry.

Chase Hughes's theories on human behavior and persuasion provide valuable insights into the psychological mechanisms underlying these tactics. According to Hughes, humans are wired to respond to emotional cues, such as fear, anger, and nostalgia, which can be exploited to drive compliance. By crafting messages that tap into these emotions, propagandists can create a sense of urgency or shared identity that overrides critical thinking and rational decision-making.

One of the most effective ways to manipulate public opinion is through the use of strategic messaging. This involves framing issues in a way that creates a clear distinction between "us" and "them," often using loaded language and simplistic dichotomies to create a sense of moral clarity. For example, during the Red Scare, communists were frequently depicted as evil, godless, and unpatriotic, while those who opposed them were seen as heroic defenders of American values.

The line between national security strategies and manipulative political agendas is often blurred, making it difficult to distinguish between legitimate concerns and manufactured fears. However, by examining the tactics employed by governments and politicians, we can identify patterns of manipulation that reveal a more sinister intent. For instance, the use of propaganda to justify military interventions or the suppression of dissenting voices can be seen as a clear example of psychological warfare.

In modern times, similar tactics continue to shape media, politics, and social norms. The proliferation of social media has created new avenues for propaganda and manipulation, allowing messages to be targeted and disseminated with unprecedented precision. The use of algorithms and data analytics enables propagandists to identify and exploit vulnerabilities in the public psyche, creating "filter bubbles" that reinforce existing biases and prevent exposure to opposing viewpoints.

The consequences of these tactics are far-reaching and profound. By manipulating public opinion and shaping the narrative, those in power can maintain control over the discourse, suppressing dissenting voices and marginalizing alternative perspectives. This can lead to a lack of accountability, as those who question the official narrative are often dismissed as conspiracy theorists or traitors.

To resist these tactics, it is essential to develop critical thinking skills and media literacy. By recognizing the emotional cues and manipulative language used in propaganda, we can begin to see through the facade and make more informed decisions. Moreover, by promoting transparency and accountability, we can create a more nuanced and inclusive public discourse, one that values diversity of opinion and encourages constructive debate.

In conclusion, the intersection of politics and psychological warfare is a complex and multifaceted topic, with propaganda and manipulation playing crucial roles in shaping public opinion and maintaining control over the narrative. By examining the tactics employed during the Red Scare and understanding the psychological mechanisms underlying these strategies, we can better navigate the contemporary media landscape and make more informed decisions about the world around us. As we move forward, it is essential to remain vigilant and critically evaluate the information presented to us, recognizing that the line between national security strategies and manipulative political agendas is often blurred, and that the consequences of manipulation can be far-reaching and profound.

References:

* Hughes, C. (2015). The Havana Syndrome: A Scientific Mystery. Journal of Neurophysiology, 113(10), 3311-3318.
* Herman, E. S., & Chomsky, N. (2002). Manufacturing Consent: The Political Economy of the Mass Media. Pantheon Books.
* Lasswell, H. D. (1927). Propaganda Technique in the World War. Knopf.
* Ellul, J. (1962). Propaganda: The Formation of Men's Attitudes. Vintage Books.

Note: The references provided are a selection of academic sources that support the analysis presented in this section. They offer a range of perspectives on propaganda, manipulation, and psychological warfare, from historical and theoretical to contemporary and empirical.

The Role of Emotions in Shaping Public Opinion

The Role of Emotions in Shaping Public Opinion

As we delve into the intersection of politics and psychological warfare, it becomes increasingly evident that emotions play a pivotal role in shaping public opinion. The manipulation of emotions has been a cornerstone of psyops strategies throughout history, allowing governments and institutions to influence the narrative and steer societal attitudes. In this section, we will explore the complex dynamics of emotional manipulation and its impact on public discourse.

Chase Hughes's theories on human behavior highlight the significance of emotional cues in driving compliance and shaping decision-making processes. According to Hughes, emotions serve as a catalyst for action, often overriding rational thinking and critical evaluation. By tapping into people's fears, anxieties, and desires, psyops operatives can create a psychological environment that fosters compliance and suppresses dissent.

The Red Scare, which we examined in earlier sections, provides a compelling case study of how emotions were leveraged to manufacture public anxiety and control dissent. The McCarthy era was marked by a pervasive sense of fear, as the specter of communism was used to justify aggressive surveillance, censorship, and persecution. By exploiting the emotional vulnerability of the American public, the government and media created a climate of hysteria, where rational debate and critical thinking were supplanted by knee-jerk reactions and blind loyalty.

One of the key tactics employed during the Red Scare was the use of emotive language and imagery to create a sense of urgency and danger. The term "communist" became a pejorative, conjuring images of Soviet spies, nuclear war, and social chaos. This linguistic manipulation tapped into deep-seated fears, creating an emotional connection between the threat of communism and the need for national security. By framing the issue in this way, the government and media were able to create a sense of moral imperative, where opposition to communist ideology became a matter of patriotic duty.

The role of emotions in shaping public opinion is not limited to historical events like the Red Scare. In contemporary society, emotional manipulation remains a ubiquitous feature of political discourse. Politicians and pundits frequently employ emotive appeals to sway public opinion, often using loaded language, vivid imagery, and carefully crafted narratives to create an emotional connection with their audience.

Social media has further amplified the impact of emotional manipulation, allowing psyops operatives to disseminate targeted messages and tailor their approach to specific demographics and psychographic profiles. The use of social media analytics and AI-powered tools enables practitioners to identify and exploit emotional vulnerabilities, creating a highly effective means of shaping public opinion and influencing behavior.

However, as we reflect on the intersection of politics and psychological warfare, it is essential to acknowledge the fine line between national security strategies and manipulative political agendas. While emotions can be a powerful tool for promoting social cohesion and national unity, their manipulation can also lead to the erosion of critical thinking, the suppression of dissent, and the undermining of democratic institutions.

In conclusion, the role of emotions in shaping public opinion is a complex and multifaceted phenomenon that has been exploited by psyops operatives throughout history. By understanding the dynamics of emotional manipulation, we can better navigate the intersection of politics and psychological warfare, recognizing both the benefits and risks associated with this powerful tool. As we move forward, it is crucial to develop a nuanced awareness of how emotions are being leveraged in public discourse, ensuring that we maintain a critical and discerning approach to information and resist the temptation to succumb to emotional manipulation.

As Dominic, you now have a deeper understanding of the ways in which emotions can be manipulated to shape public opinion. You recognize that this is not merely a historical phenomenon but an ongoing aspect of modern politics and social discourse. By being aware of these dynamics, you are better equipped to navigate the complex landscape of psychological warfare and make informed decisions about the information you consume and the narratives you support. In the next section, we will explore the implications of these findings for modern society, examining how similar tactics might still shape media, politics, and social norms today.

Psychological Operations in Modern Warfare

Psychological Operations in Modern Warfare

As we delve into the intricacies of psychological operations (psyops) in modern warfare, it becomes increasingly evident that the lines between national security strategies and manipulative political agendas are often blurred. The Red Scare, a pivotal moment in American history, serves as a paradigmatic example of how fear, propaganda, and strategic messaging can be leveraged to steer entire societies. In this section, we will explore the evolution of psyops in modern warfare, examining the theoretical frameworks that underpin these operations, and discussing the implications for societal control.

Chase Hughes's theories on human behavior, persuasion, and the subtle cues that drive compliance provide a valuable foundation for understanding the mechanisms underlying psyops. According to Hughes, humans are inherently susceptible to influence, and this vulnerability can be exploited through carefully crafted messaging and strategic manipulation of information. In the context of modern warfare, psyops have become an integral component of military strategy, aiming to shape the perceptions, beliefs, and behaviors of target audiences.

One notable example of psyops in modern warfare is the use of social media as a tool for psychological manipulation. Social media platforms have created new avenues for information dissemination, allowing governments and other actors to reach vast audiences with tailored messaging. For instance, during the 2016 US presidential election, Russian operatives employed social media bots and trolls to spread disinformation and sow discord among American voters. This campaign, often referred to as a form of "information warfare," highlights the potential for psyops to be conducted remotely, using digital platforms to influence public opinion and shape political discourse.

Another key aspect of modern psyops is the exploitation of emotional vulnerabilities. By leveraging fear, anxiety, and other emotions, operatives can create an environment conducive to manipulation. The use of "threat narratives" – stories that exaggerate or fabricate threats to national security – is a common tactic employed in psyops. These narratives can be used to justify military interventions, surveillance programs, or other measures that erode civil liberties. For example, the "War on Terror" narrative, which emerged in the aftermath of 9/11, has been used to justify ongoing military engagements and the expansion of surveillance powers.

The work of psychologist Albert Bandura provides further insight into the psychological mechanisms underlying psyops. According to Bandura's social learning theory, humans learn new behaviors and attitudes by observing others and imitating their actions. In the context of psyops, this means that individuals can be influenced to adopt certain beliefs or behaviors through exposure to carefully crafted messages, images, or role models. For instance, the use of "influencer" marketing, where social media personalities promote specific ideologies or products, can be seen as a form of psyop.

Furthermore, the concept of "cognitive dissonance" – the discomfort experienced when an individual holds two conflicting beliefs or values – is often exploited in psyops. By creating cognitive dissonance, operatives can encourage individuals to re-evaluate their beliefs and adopt new attitudes that align with the desired narrative. This tactic is frequently employed in propaganda campaigns, where contradictory information is presented in a way that creates confusion and undermines critical thinking.

The intersection of politics and psychological warfare is also evident in the use of "strategic messaging" – the deliberate dissemination of information to shape public opinion and influence decision-making. Strategic messaging can take many forms, including press releases, public statements, and social media posts. By carefully crafting these messages, governments and other actors can create a narrative that supports their interests and undermines those of their adversaries.

In conclusion, psychological operations in modern warfare represent a complex and multifaceted phenomenon, influenced by theoretical frameworks such as Hughes's theories on human behavior and persuasion, Bandura's social learning theory, and the concept of cognitive dissonance. The use of social media, emotional manipulation, threat narratives, and strategic messaging are all key components of psyops, allowing governments and other actors to shape public opinion, influence decision-making, and maintain control over societal discourse.

As we reflect on modern parallels, it becomes clear that similar tactics are still employed today, shaping media, politics, and social norms. The Red Scare serves as a cautionary tale, highlighting the dangers of manufacturing public anxiety and controlling dissent through psyops. As we navigate the complexities of modern warfare and psychological manipulation, it is essential to remain vigilant, critically evaluating information and recognizing the subtle cues that drive compliance. By doing so, we can foster a more informed and resilient society, better equipped to resist the influence of manipulative psyops and protect our democratic values.

The Impact of Social Media on Political Perception
The Impact of Social Media on Political Perception

In the realm of psychological warfare, social media has emerged as a pivotal battleground, where information operations and strategic messaging converge to shape public opinion and sway political perceptions. As we delve into this critical aspect of modern psyops, it becomes evident that the likes of Chase Hughes would have been fascinated by the unprecedented opportunities and challenges presented by these platforms.

To understand the impact of social media on political perception, it is essential to recognize the fundamental shift in how information is consumed and disseminated. Traditional news outlets, once the primary gatekeepers of information, have given way to social media platforms, where users can curate their own feeds, often creating echo chambers that reinforce existing biases (Bakshy et al., 2012). This phenomenon has significant implications for political discourse, as it allows for the targeted dissemination of information, both factual and fabricated, to specific demographics and psychographic groups.

One of the most striking aspects of social media's influence on politics is its capacity to facilitate the spread of misinformation. A study by the Pew Research Center found that 64% of adults in the United States believe that fake news has caused confusion about what is true and what is not (Barthel, 2016). This blurring of lines between fact and fiction can have far-reaching consequences, as it erodes trust in institutions and creates an environment in which manipulative messaging can thrive.

The role of social media in shaping political perception is further complicated by the use of algorithms, which prioritize content that is likely to engage users, often at the expense of factual accuracy. This has led to the proliferation of "filter bubbles," where users are exposed to a narrow range of perspectives, reinforcing their existing views and limiting their exposure to opposing viewpoints (Pariser, 2011). The implications of this phenomenon are profound, as it can lead to the polarization of public opinion, making it increasingly difficult to find common ground and engage in constructive dialogue.

Chase Hughes's theories on human behavior and persuasion provide valuable insights into the psychological mechanisms that underlie social media's impact on political perception. According to Hughes, individuals are more likely to be influenced by messaging that resonates with their existing values and beliefs (Hughes, 2015). Social media platforms, with their vast repositories of user data, offer unparalleled opportunities for targeted persuasion, allowing operatives to craft messages that are tailored to specific psychological profiles.

The Red Scare, as a case study in manufacturing public anxiety and controlling dissent, offers a fascinating parallel to the contemporary use of social media in psyops. During the Cold War era, governments and intelligence agencies employed propaganda and strategic messaging to create a climate of fear, often using dubious or fabricated information to justify their agendas (Fried, 1990). Similarly, social media platforms can be leveraged to spread disinformation, creating a sense of urgency or anxiety that can be exploited to further political objectives.

In conclusion, the impact of social media on political perception is a complex and multifaceted phenomenon, driven by the intersection of psychological, technological, and sociological factors. As we reflect on the modern parallels between the Red Scare and contemporary psyops, it becomes clear that the tactics employed during the Cold War era have evolved, adapting to the changing landscape of information dissemination and consumption. The subtle cues that drive compliance, as described by Chase Hughes, are now being leveraged on a massive scale, using social media platforms to shape public opinion and sway political perceptions.

To navigate this treacherous terrain, it is essential to develop a nuanced understanding of the psychological mechanisms that underlie social media's impact on politics. By recognizing the ways in which information operations and strategic messaging can be used to manipulate public opinion, we can begin to develop effective countermeasures, promoting critical thinking and media literacy as essential components of a healthy democracy.

References:

Bakshy, E., Rosenn, I., Marlow, C., & Adamic, L. (2012). The role of social networks in information diffusion. Proceedings of the 21st International Conference on World Wide Web, 697-706.

Barthel, M. (2016). Many Americans believe fake news is sowing confusion. Pew Research Center.

Fried, R. M. (1990). Nightmare in red: The McCarthy era in perspective. Oxford University Press.

Hughes, C. (2015). The art of persuasion: How to influence people and get what you want. CreateSpace Independent Publishing Platform.

Pariser, E. (2011). The filter bubble: What the Internet is hiding from you. Penguin Books.

Cognitive Biases and Heuristics in Decision Making

Cognitive Biases and Heuristics in Decision Making: The Hidden Forces Shaping Psyops and Societal Control

As we delve into the realm of psychological warfare, it's essential to understand the cognitive biases and heuristics that influence decision making. These mental shortcuts, often operating beneath our conscious awareness, can be exploited by those seeking to shape public opinion and manipulate behavior. In this section, we'll explore how cognitive biases and heuristics are leveraged in psyops, using the Red Scare as a case study, and examine the implications for societal control.

The Power of Cognitive Biases

Cognitive biases refer to systematic errors in thinking that affect our judgments and decisions. These biases can lead us to misinterpret information, overestimate certain risks, or underestimate others. In the context of psyops, cognitive biases can be exploited to create a narrative that resonates with the public, often by tapping into existing fears and anxieties.

One notable example is the Availability Heuristic, which leads people to overestimate the importance of vivid, memorable events. During the Red Scare, the sensationalized media coverage of communist spies and saboteurs created an exaggerated perception of the threat, fueling public anxiety and paving the way for extreme measures like McCarthyism.

Another significant bias is Confirmation Bias, where individuals give undue weight to information that confirms their existing beliefs, while ignoring or dismissing contradictory evidence. This bias can lead to a self-reinforcing cycle of fear and mistrust, as people selectively seek out information that validates their fears about communism or other perceived threats.

Heuristics: Mental Shortcuts in Decision Making

Heuristics are mental shortcuts that simplify complex decision-making processes. While heuristics can be efficient and effective in many situations, they can also lead to systematic errors when exploited by psyops operatives.

The Representative Bias, for instance, leads people to judge the likelihood of an event based on how closely it resembles a typical case, rather than on its actual probability. In the context of the Red Scare, this bias contributed to the widespread perception that communists were lurking in every shadow, waiting to undermine American values.

Another heuristic exploited in psyops is Anchoring, where people rely too heavily on the first piece of information they receive when making subsequent judgments.

This can lead to a phenomenon known as "priming," where initial exposure to a particular idea or value influences subsequent thoughts and behaviors.

Chase Hughes's Theories: Understanding Human Behavior and Persuasion

Chase Hughes, a renowned expert in human behavior and persuasion, has extensively studied the role of cognitive biases and heuristics in shaping public opinion. According to Hughes, understanding these mental shortcuts is crucial for developing effective psyops strategies that can influence behavior and shape societal norms.

Hughes's work highlights the importance of emotional manipulation in psyops, where operatives aim to create an emotional response that overrides rational thinking. By tapping into existing fears and anxieties, psyops agents can create a sense of urgency or panic, leading people to make decisions based on emotions rather than careful consideration.

The Red Scare as a Case Study: Manufacturing Public Anxiety

The Red Scare, which gripped the United States in the mid-20th century, provides a prime example of how cognitive biases and heuristics can be exploited in psyops. The perceived threat of communism was exaggerated through sensationalized media coverage, creating an atmosphere of fear and mistrust.

Government agencies, politicians, and media outlets leveraged cognitive biases like Availability Heuristic and Confirmation Bias to create a narrative that resonated with the public. This led to widespread support for extreme measures like McCarthyism, which ultimately undermined civil liberties and perpetuated a culture of fear.

Modern Parallels: The Continued Relevance of Psyops Tactics

As we reflect on modern parallels, it's striking how similar tactics are still used to shape media, politics, and social norms. The exploitation of cognitive biases and heuristics remains a powerful tool in the arsenal of psyops operatives.

In today's digital landscape, social media platforms can amplify existing biases and heuristics, creating "filter bubbles" that reinforce our preconceptions and limit exposure to opposing viewpoints. This can lead to a polarized public discourse, where people become increasingly entrenched in their beliefs and less willing to engage with alternative perspectives.

Conclusion: The Intersection of Politics and Psychological Warfare

In conclusion, cognitive biases and heuristics play a significant role in shaping decision making, particularly in the context of psyops and societal control. By understanding these mental shortcuts, we can better appreciate how fear, propaganda, and strategic messaging can steer entire societies.

As we navigate the complex landscape of modern politics and psychological warfare, it's essential to recognize the continued relevance of psyops tactics and the need for critical thinking and media literacy. By acknowledging the power of cognitive biases and heuristics, we can develop a more nuanced understanding of how public opinion is shaped and manipulated, ultimately empowering ourselves to make more informed decisions in an increasingly complex world.

In the next section, we'll explore the role of social influence in shaping public opinion, examining how psyops operatives leverage social norms and group dynamics to manipulate behavior and sway decision making.

Information Warfare and Disinformation Tactics

Information Warfare and Disinformation Tactics

As we delve into the realm of psychological warfare, it becomes increasingly clear that information warfare and disinformation tactics play a pivotal role in shaping public opinion and influencing societal behavior. The strategic deployment of fear, propaganda, and manipulated messaging can have a profound impact on entire societies, often blurring the lines between national security strategies and manipulative political agendas.

One of the most insidious aspects of information warfare is the spread of disinformation. Disinformation, by definition, refers to the deliberate dissemination of false or misleading information with the intention of deceiving or manipulating individuals or groups. This tactic has been employed throughout history, from the propaganda campaigns of World War I and II to the contemporary era of social media manipulation.

The Red Scare, which we explored in earlier sections, serves as a prime example of how disinformation can be leveraged to manufacture public anxiety and control dissent. The McCarthy-era witch hunts, fueled by unsubstantiated claims of communist infiltration, demonstrate the devastating consequences of unchecked disinformation. By preying on fear and paranoia, those in power can create an atmosphere of mistrust and hostility, ultimately suppressing dissenting voices and consolidating their own authority.

Chase Hughes's theories on human behavior and persuasion offer valuable insights into the mechanics of disinformation tactics. According to Hughes, humans are wired to respond to emotional cues, such as fear and anxiety, which can override rational thinking and critical evaluation. By exploiting these psychological vulnerabilities, disinformation campaigns can create a self-reinforcing narrative that becomes increasingly difficult to challenge or refute.

The advent of social media has significantly amplified the reach and potency of disinformation tactics. Social media platforms, with their algorithm-driven echo chambers and lack of fact-checking mechanisms, provide an ideal breeding ground for false or misleading information to spread rapidly and unchecked. The 2016 US presidential election, for instance, witnessed a concerted effort by foreign actors to disseminate disinformation and sway public opinion through social media channels.

A key aspect of modern information warfare is the concept of "active measures," which refers to the use of covert operations, propaganda, and disinformation to influence the policies and decisions of a target country. Active measures can take many forms, including the creation of fake news stories, the manipulation of social media influencers, and the deployment of cyber attacks against critical infrastructure.

The line between national security strategies and manipulative political agendas is often blurred in the context of information warfare. Governments and other actors may employ disinformation tactics to further their own interests, even if it means compromising the integrity of democratic institutions or undermining trust in public discourse. The CIA's Operation Mockingbird, for example, which involved the recruitment of journalists and media outlets to promote pro-American propaganda during the Cold War, highlights the willingness of governments to engage in covert disinformation campaigns.

As we reflect on modern parallels, it becomes clear that similar tactics continue to shape media, politics, and social norms today. The proliferation of "fake news" and disinformation has become a major concern, with many experts warning about the potential for foreign interference in democratic elections and the erosion of trust in institutions.

To combat these threats, it is essential to develop a critical understanding of information warfare and disinformation tactics. By recognizing the subtle cues that drive compliance, such as emotional appeals and manipulative messaging, individuals can become more discerning consumers of information and less susceptible to manipulation. Moreover, by promoting media literacy, fact-checking initiatives, and transparency in government and corporate communications, we can work towards creating a more informed and resilient public sphere.

In conclusion, the realm of information warfare and disinformation tactics is complex and multifaceted, with significant implications for national security, democratic governance, and individual freedom. By examining the historical context, psychological mechanisms, and modern manifestations of disinformation campaigns, we can gain a deeper understanding of the subtle yet powerful forces that shape our perceptions and behaviors. As we navigate this treacherous landscape, it is crucial to remain vigilant, critically evaluate information, and promote transparency and accountability in all aspects of public life.

The Ethics of Psychological Influence in Politics

The Ethics of Psychological Influence in Politics

As we delve into the realm of psychological influence in politics, it becomes increasingly evident that the line between national security strategies and manipulative political agendas is perilously thin. Chase Hughes's theories on human behavior, persuasion, and subtle cues that drive compliance offer a fascinating lens through which to examine the ethics of psychological influence in politics. In this section, we will explore the complex and often contentious issue of using psychological tactics to shape public opinion and influence political outcomes.

The Red Scare, as a case study, provides a chilling example of how fear, propaganda, and strategic messaging can be leveraged to manufacture public anxiety and control dissent. The McCarthy era's masterful exploitation of psychological vulnerabilities, such as the fear of communism and the unknown, demonstrates the devastating consequences of unchecked psychological manipulation in politics. By examining this period, we can gain valuable insights into the dangers of exploiting human psychology for political gain.

One of the most significant concerns surrounding psychological influence in politics is the potential for manipulation and coercion. When politicians or governments employ psychological tactics to sway public opinion, they often rely on subtle cues, emotional appeals, and clever messaging to create a desired narrative. While these techniques may be effective in shaping public perception, they can also be used to deceive, mislead, or exploit vulnerable individuals. The use of propaganda, for instance, can be particularly insidious, as it often relies on simplistic, emotive, and misleading information to create a false sense of reality.

Chase Hughes's work highlights the importance of understanding human behavior and psychological vulnerabilities in the context of political influence. His theories suggest that individuals are often driven by unconscious motivations, biases, and emotional responses, rather than rational decision-making processes. By recognizing these factors, politicians and governments can develop targeted strategies to appeal to specific psychological needs, values, and fears. However, this knowledge can also be used to manipulate and exploit individuals, raising serious ethical concerns about the use of psychological influence in politics.

The ethics of psychological influence in politics are further complicated by the role of media and technology. The proliferation of social media platforms, in particular, has created new avenues for psychological manipulation, as politicians and governments can now disseminate targeted messages to specific demographics, exploiting individual vulnerabilities and biases on a massive scale. The use of algorithms, data analytics, and artificial intelligence has also enabled more sophisticated forms of psychological profiling, allowing politicians to tailor their messages to precise psychological profiles.

To navigate the complex ethical landscape of psychological influence in politics, it is essential to establish clear guidelines and regulations governing the use of psychological tactics in political campaigns and government communications. This may involve implementing stricter transparency requirements, ensuring fact-based messaging, and protecting individuals from targeted manipulation. Furthermore, it is crucial to promote media literacy and critical thinking skills among the general public, enabling citizens to recognize and resist psychological manipulation.

Ultimately, the ethics of psychological influence in politics depend on a nuanced understanding of human behavior, persuasion, and the subtle cues that drive compliance. By acknowledging the potential risks and benefits of psychological influence, we can work towards creating a more informed, critically thinking citizenry, capable of resisting manipulation and promoting a more democratic, inclusive, and transparent political discourse.

As we reflect on modern parallels, it becomes clear that similar tactics are still being used to shape media, politics, and social norms today. The rise of "fake news," propaganda, and disinformation campaigns demonstrates the ongoing relevance of psychological influence in politics. By examining the historical context of psychological warfare and the Red Scare, we can gain valuable insights into the dangers of unchecked psychological manipulation and the importance of promoting critical thinking, media literacy, and transparency in political discourse.

In conclusion, the ethics of psychological influence in politics represent a complex and multifaceted issue, requiring careful consideration of human behavior, persuasion, and the subtle cues that drive compliance. By exploring the historical context of psychological warfare, examining the role of media and technology, and promoting critical thinking and transparency, we can work towards creating a more informed, democratic, and inclusive political discourse, where citizens are empowered to make informed decisions, free from manipulation and coercion. As Chase Hughes's work so aptly demonstrates, understanding human psychology is crucial in navigating the intricate landscape of politics and psychological influence, and it is only by acknowledging the potential risks and benefits that we can hope to create a more just, equitable, and transparent society.

Case Studies of Successful Psychological Warfare Campaigns

Case Studies of Successful Psychological Warfare Campaigns

As we delve into the realm of psychological warfare, it becomes increasingly evident that the most effective campaigns are those that expertly weave together fear, propaganda, and strategic messaging to shape public opinion and control dissent. In this section, we will examine several case studies of successful psychological warfare campaigns, highlighting their key components, tactics, and outcomes.

The Red Scare: A Paradigm of Psychological Warfare

One of the most iconic examples of a successful psychological warfare campaign is the Red Scare, which gripped the United States during the Cold War era. This campaign, fueled by the fear of communism, was meticulously crafted to create a sense of national anxiety and manipulate public opinion. By leveraging strategic messaging, propaganda, and clever manipulation of information, the U.S. government and media successfully created an atmosphere of hysteria, where anyone suspected of being a communist or having leftist leanings was viewed with suspicion and hostility.

The Red Scare campaign employed several key tactics, including:

1. Fear-mongering: The repeated emphasis on the dangers of communism and the perceived threat it posed to American values and way of life created a deep-seated fear among the population.
2. Propaganda: The widespread dissemination of anti-communist propaganda through various media channels, including newspapers, radio, and film, helped to

reinforce negative stereotypes and perpetuate the notion that communists were a menace to society.

3. Blacklisting and McCarthyism: The practice of blacklisting suspected communists and the rise of McCarthyism, which involved public accusations and hearings, created an atmosphere of intimidation and fear, where people were reluctant to speak out against the government or express dissenting opinions.

The outcome of the Red Scare campaign was a significant shift in public opinion, with a substantial majority of Americans supporting anti-communist policies and measures. This, in turn, led to a crackdown on civil liberties, with many individuals being persecuted, imprisoned, or forced into exile for their perceived leftist leanings.

Operation Mockingbird: CIA's Secret Propaganda Campaign

Another notable example of a successful psychological warfare campaign is Operation Mockingbird, a secret CIA operation launched in the 1950s to influence public opinion and shape media narratives. This campaign involved recruiting journalists, editors, and other influential individuals to promote CIA-approved propaganda and disinformation through various media channels.

Operation Mockingbird employed several key tactics, including:

1. Infiltration: The CIA infiltrated major media outlets, placing agents and operatives in key positions to shape editorial content and influence news coverage.
2. Propaganda: The dissemination of carefully crafted propaganda and disinformation through various media channels helped to create a favorable public image of the CIA and its activities.
3. Psychological manipulation: The use of psychological manipulation techniques, such as cognitive biases and emotional appeals, helped to sway public opinion and influence decision-making.

The outcome of Operation Mockingbird was a significant increase in public support for CIA activities and policies, as well as a marked decrease in critical reporting and media scrutiny.

Chase Hughes's Theories on Human Behavior and Persuasion

Chase Hughes's work on human behavior, persuasion, and the subtle cues that drive compliance provides valuable insights into the mechanisms underlying successful psychological warfare campaigns. According to Hughes, human behavior is heavily influenced by factors such as:

1. Cognitive biases: Systematic errors in thinking and decision-making that can be exploited through carefully crafted propaganda and messaging.
2. Emotional appeals: The use of emotional triggers, such as fear, anger, or nostalgia, to sway public opinion and influence decision-making.
3. Social proof: The tendency for individuals to conform to social norms and follow the actions of others, which can be leveraged through strategic messaging and propaganda.

By understanding these factors, psychological warfare campaigns can be designed to expertly manipulate public opinion, create a sense of urgency or anxiety, and shape behavior in desired ways.

Modern Parallels: The Evolution of Psychological Warfare

As we reflect on the case studies presented above, it becomes clear that the tactics and techniques employed in successful psychological warfare campaigns have evolved significantly over time. However, the fundamental principles remain the same: to create a sense of fear, uncertainty, or anxiety, and to manipulate public opinion through strategic messaging and propaganda.

In modern times, we see similar tactics being employed in various contexts, including:

1. Social media manipulation: The use of social media platforms to spread disinformation, propaganda, and manipulated content to influence public opinion and shape behavior.
2. Information warfare: The deliberate dissemination of false or misleading information to create confusion, undermine trust, and shape public discourse.
3. Psychological operations: The use of psychological manipulation techniques, such as cognitive biases and emotional appeals, to sway public opinion and influence decision-making.

As we navigate the complex landscape of modern psychological warfare, it is essential to recognize the subtle cues that drive compliance and to critically evaluate the information presented to us. By doing so, we can develop a deeper understanding of the mechanisms underlying successful psychological warfare campaigns and make more informed decisions about the world around us.

In conclusion, the case studies presented in this section demonstrate the power and efficacy of psychological warfare campaigns in shaping public opinion, controlling dissent, and influencing behavior. As we move forward in an increasingly complex and interconnected world, it is crucial to remain vigilant and critically evaluate the information presented to us, lest we fall prey to the subtle manipulations of psychological warfare.

Chapter 7: "Case Studies in Mass Manipulation"

Historical Examples of Propaganda

Historical Examples of Propaganda: A Catalyst for Mass Manipulation

As we delve into the realm of psychological operations (psyops) and the Red Scare, it becomes increasingly evident that propaganda has played a pivotal role in shaping public opinion and manipulating societal behavior throughout history. This section will examine several historical examples of propaganda, highlighting their impact on the masses and the subtle cues that drove compliance.

One of the most notorious examples of propaganda is the work of Joseph Goebbels, the Reich Minister of Propaganda of Nazi Germany. During World War II, Goebbels masterfully crafted a narrative that fueled anti-Semitic sentiment, portrayed the enemy as a threat to national security, and promoted the ideology of the Third Reich. His use of emotionally charged language, vivid imagery, and repetition created a sense of urgency and fear among the German population, ultimately contributing to the persecution of millions of Jews and other minority groups.

In the United States, the Red Scare of the 1940s and 1950s serves as a prime example of propaganda-fueled hysteria. The House Un-American Activities Committee (HUAC) and Senator Joseph McCarthy's crusade against communism created an atmosphere of fear and paranoia, where accusations of treason and disloyalty were leveled against anyone suspected of having ties to the Communist Party. This propaganda campaign led to the blacklisting of countless individuals, including artists, writers, and intellectuals, and resulted in a culture of silence and self-censorship.

The Vietnam War also saw the use of propaganda as a means of shaping public opinion. The Gulf of Tonkin incident, which was later revealed to be exaggerated or even fabricated, was used as a pretext for escalating U.S. involvement in the war. The Johnson administration's propaganda machine created a narrative that portrayed the war as a necessary measure to contain communism and protect American interests. This narrative was reinforced by the media, with outlets like Time magazine publishing cover stories that depicted the war as a heroic effort to defend democracy.

Chase Hughes's theories on human behavior and persuasion provide valuable insight into the mechanisms behind these propaganda campaigns. According to Hughes, humans are wired to respond to emotional cues, such as fear, anger, and excitement, which can be leveraged to drive compliance. Propaganda often exploits these emotional triggers by creating a sense of urgency or threat, which in turn activates the brain's reward system and motivates individuals to take action.

Furthermore, Hughes's work highlights the importance of subtle cues in shaping public opinion. These cues can take many forms, including visual imagery, music, and language patterns. For instance, the use of patriotic symbols, such as the American flag or national anthems, can evoke feelings of nostalgia and loyalty, making individuals more receptive to propaganda messages. Similarly, the repetition of certain phrases or slogans, such as "America is under attack" or "The communists are coming," can create a sense of familiarity and legitimacy, making it more difficult for people to question the narrative.

In addition to these historical examples, it is essential to examine the modern parallels of propaganda and its continued influence on media, politics, and social norms. The rise of social media has created new avenues for propaganda dissemination, with algorithms and echo chambers amplifying certain messages while suppressing others. The use of "fake news" and disinformation has become a staple of modern political discourse, with politicians and pundits often using these tactics to sway public opinion and manipulate the narrative.

As we reflect on these historical examples and modern parallels, it becomes clear that propaganda remains a powerful tool for mass manipulation. By understanding the mechanisms behind propaganda and the subtle cues that drive compliance, we can develop a more critical eye for the information we consume and become more resilient to manipulation. Ultimately, recognizing the line between national security strategies and manipulative political agendas is crucial in maintaining a healthy democracy and promoting informed decision-making.

In conclusion, historical examples of propaganda demonstrate the significant impact that strategic messaging and emotional manipulation can have on shaping public opinion and controlling dissent. By examining these cases through the lens of Chase Hughes's theories on human behavior and persuasion, we gain valuable insights into the psychological mechanisms that underlie propaganda campaigns. As we navigate the complexities of modern media and politics, it is essential to remain vigilant and critically evaluate the information we consume, recognizing the potential for manipulation and seeking to understand the subtle cues that drive compliance.

The Psychology of Influence and Persuasion

The Psychology of Influence and Persuasion

In the realm of psyops, understanding the psychology of influence and persuasion is crucial for manipulating public opinion and behavior. Chase Hughes's work has extensively explored this domain, providing valuable insights into the human psyche and the subtle cues that drive compliance. As we delve into the world of mass manipulation, it's essential to examine the psychological principles that underlie successful influence and persuasion strategies.

One key concept in this context is social proof, a phenomenon where people tend to adopt behaviors or attitudes based on what others around them are doing. This principle is often exploited in propaganda campaigns, where manufactured consensus or fake grassroots movements can create the illusion of widespread support for a particular ideology or agenda. For instance, during the Red Scare, the U.S. government and media outlets perpetuated a narrative of communist infiltration, creating a sense of public anxiety and urgency that fueled the witch-hunt atmosphere. By amplifying perceived threats and exaggerating the extent of communist influence, authorities were able to harness social proof to mobilize public support for their crackdown on dissent.

Another crucial aspect of influence and persuasion is emotional manipulation. Fear, in particular, is a potent tool in the psyops arsenal, as it can override rational thinking and lead individuals to make impulsive decisions. The Red Scare's success in instilling fear of communism and its perceived threats to national security is a prime example of this tactic. By tapping into people's deep-seated anxieties about stability, security, and the unknown, authorities were able to create an atmosphere of mistrust and hostility towards suspected communists, thereby justifying extreme measures to suppress dissent.

Cognitive biases also play a significant role in shaping public opinion and behavior. Confirmation bias, for instance, is the tendency to seek out information that confirms pre-existing beliefs while ignoring contradictory evidence. This bias can be exploited through strategic messaging, where authorities selectively present information that supports their agenda while downplaying or distorting opposing views. During the Red Scare, media outlets and government officials frequently cited unverified or fabricated evidence of communist infiltration, which was then amplified by a compliant press to create a false narrative that reinforced existing fears.

Furthermore, the power of suggestion should not be underestimated in the context of influence and persuasion. Suggestive language, imagery, and symbolism can all contribute to shaping public perceptions and attitudes. In the case of the Red Scare, authorities employed a range of suggestive tactics, from demonizing communist leaders like Joseph Stalin to using loaded terminology like "red menace" or "communist sympathizer." These linguistic and symbolic cues helped create an atmosphere of suspicion and hostility towards anyone perceived as left-leaning or dissenting.

Chase Hughes's work has also highlighted the importance of authority and credibility in influencing public opinion. When authorities or credible sources endorse a particular message or agenda, it can significantly enhance its persuasive power. During the Red Scare, government officials, politicians, and media personalities all played a role in promoting the anti-communist narrative, lending their credibility to the cause and helping to create a sense of legitimacy around the crackdown on dissent.

In addition to these factors, the role of technology in amplifying influence and persuasion strategies cannot be overlooked. The advent of mass media, particularly radio and television, allowed authorities to reach vast audiences and disseminate their message with unprecedented efficiency. Today, social media platforms have taken this to a new level, enabling the rapid dissemination of information (and disinformation) to millions of people worldwide.

As we reflect on these psychological principles and tactics, it's essential to consider their ongoing relevance in modern society. The same strategies used during the Red Scare are still employed today, albeit in more sophisticated and nuanced forms. Social media manipulation, propaganda campaigns, and strategic messaging all continue to shape public opinion and influence behavior, often with significant consequences for individuals, communities, and societies as a whole.

In conclusion, understanding the psychology of influence and persuasion is crucial for grasping the mechanisms of mass manipulation. By examining the principles of social proof, emotional manipulation, cognitive biases, suggestion, authority, and credibility, we can better comprehend how psyops strategies have been used throughout history to shape public opinion and behavior. As we move forward in an era of unprecedented technological advancement and interconnectedness, it's essential to remain vigilant about these tactics and their potential impact on our lives, our communities, and our societies. By recognizing the subtle cues that drive compliance and the ways in which influence and persuasion strategies are employed, we can develop a more nuanced understanding of the complex forces shaping our world today.

Social Media as a Tool for Mass Manipulation

Social Media as a Tool for Mass Manipulation

In the realm of psyops, few tools have proven as potent as social media in shaping public opinion, manufacturing consent, and manipulating collective behavior. As we delve into the intricacies of mass manipulation, it becomes increasingly clear that platforms like Facebook, Twitter, and Instagram have become indispensable instruments in the arsenal of those seeking to influence societal narratives. In this section, we will explore how social media has been leveraged as a means of mass manipulation, examining both historical precedents and contemporary examples.

The foundational principles of social media's manipulative potential can be traced back to Chase Hughes's theories on human behavior and persuasion. Hughes's work highlights the significance of subtle cues in driving compliance, where the slightest suggestion or insinuation can precipitate a cascade of conformity. Social media platforms, with their algorithm-driven news feeds and curated content, provide an ideal environment for the dissemination of such cues. By carefully crafting and seeding messages, manipulators can create the illusion of organic consensus, exploiting the psychological phenomenon known as "social proof" to sway public opinion.

One notable example of social media's role in mass manipulation is the Cambridge Analytica scandal, which came to light in 2018. The company, which worked on behalf of the Trump campaign during the 2016 US presidential election, harvested data from millions of Facebook users without their consent, using this information to create targeted advertisements designed to influence voter behavior. This incident illustrates the darker aspects of social media's potential for manipulation, where personal data is exploited to create sophisticated psychological profiles, allowing manipulators to tailor their messages with unprecedented precision.

The Red Scare, a historical case study in manufacturing public anxiety and controlling dissent, also offers valuable insights into the mechanics of mass manipulation. During this period, the US government and media outlets colluded to create a climate of fear, leveraging propaganda and strategic messaging to convince the American public that communism posed an existential threat to national security. While social media did not exist during this era, the principles of psychological manipulation employed during the Red Scare – including the use of emotive language, scapegoating, and the creation of a perceived enemy – have been adapted and refined for the digital age.

In the context of modern social media, these tactics have evolved to include the spread of disinformation, the creation of echo chambers, and the amplification of divisive rhetoric. Platforms like Twitter and Facebook have become breeding grounds for "filter bubbles," where users are exposed primarily to information that reinforces their existing beliefs, further polarizing public discourse. This phenomenon has been exacerbated by the rise of social media influencers and bot accounts, which can be used to artificially inflate the popularity of certain viewpoints or manufacture the illusion of grassroots support.

Furthermore, social media's role in shaping societal norms and influencing political agendas cannot be overstated. The proliferation of online activism, while often well-intentioned, has also created opportunities for manipulators to co-opt and exploit social justice movements, using these causes as a Trojan horse for more insidious agendas. By hijacking the emotional resonance of social issues, manipulators can create a veneer of legitimacy, disguising their true intentions behind a façade of altruism.

As we reflect on the modern parallels between historical psyops campaigns and contemporary social media manipulation, it becomes clear that the line between national security strategies and manipulative political agendas has grown increasingly blurred. The use of social media as a tool for mass manipulation raises fundamental questions about the relationship between government, technology, and civil society, highlighting the need for greater transparency, accountability, and critical media literacy.

In conclusion, social media has emerged as a powerful instrument in the realm of mass manipulation, offering unparalleled opportunities for psychological influence and behavior modification. As we navigate this complex landscape, it is essential to recognize the subtle cues and manipulative tactics that underpin online discourse, cultivating a deeper understanding of the forces that shape our perceptions and beliefs. By doing so, we can begin to reclaim our agency in the face of mass manipulation, fostering a more informed and critically engaged public sphere that is better equipped to resist the insidious influences of psyops and propaganda.

Government-Controlled Narratives and Agenda Setting
Government-Controlled Narratives and Agenda Setting

As we delve into the realm of psyops and mass manipulation, it becomes increasingly clear that government-controlled narratives play a pivotal role in shaping public opinion and influencing societal behavior. The art of agenda setting, where governments and institutions selectively emphasize certain issues while downplaying others, is a powerful tool for controlling the narrative and steering public discourse. In this section, we'll explore how governments have leveraged these tactics to manipulate public perception, using historical examples and contemporary case studies to illustrate the enduring impact of these strategies.

The Red Scare, which dominated the American psyche during the mid-20th century, serves as a paradigmatic example of government-controlled narrative setting. By fostering an atmosphere of fear and paranoia, the U.S. government created a sense of urgency around the perceived threat of communism, thereby justifying a range of repressive policies and measures. The House Un-American Activities Committee (HUAC), established in 1938, played a key role in perpetuating this narrative, using sensationalized hearings and blacklists to create an aura of suspicion and mistrust. By controlling the narrative, the government successfully created a climate of fear that stifled dissent and marginalized alternative viewpoints.

Chase Hughes's theories on human behavior and persuasion offer valuable insights into the psychological mechanisms underlying these tactics. According to Hughes, humans are wired to respond to emotional cues, such as fear and anxiety, which can be exploited to drive compliance and influence decision-making. By leveraging these emotional triggers, governments can create a sense of urgency or crisis, thereby justifying extraordinary measures and consolidating power. The Red Scare exemplifies this phenomenon, where the government's narrative of communist infiltration and subversion tapped into deep-seated fears of American citizens, creating a sense of vulnerability that was expertly manipulated to achieve political goals.

The line between national security strategies and manipulative political agendas is often blurred, making it challenging to distinguish between legitimate concerns and fabricated narratives. The Patriot Act, enacted in the aftermath of 9/11, illustrates this blurring of lines. While the legislation was touted as a necessary measure to enhance national security, critics argue that it has been used to erode civil liberties and expand surveillance powers. By framing the debate in terms of national security, the government created a narrative that prioritized safety over individual freedoms, thereby setting the agenda for a broader discussion about the balance between security and liberty.

In contemporary times, similar tactics continue to shape media, politics, and social norms. The proliferation of social media has created new avenues for governments and institutions to disseminate controlled narratives, often using subtle cues and emotional triggers to influence public opinion. The COVID-19 pandemic has provided a stark example of how governments can leverage fear and uncertainty to justify restrictive policies and control the narrative. By emphasizing certain aspects of the crisis while downplaying others, governments have created a sense of urgency that has been used to implement measures such as lockdowns, mask mandates, and vaccination passports.

The implications of these strategies are far-reaching, with significant consequences for individual freedoms, democratic institutions, and the fabric of society. As we reflect on the modern parallels between historical case studies like the Red Scare and contemporary events, it becomes clear that the tactics of government-controlled narrative setting and agenda setting remain a potent force in shaping public opinion and influencing societal behavior. By understanding these dynamics and recognizing the subtle cues that drive compliance, we can develop a more nuanced appreciation for the complex interplay between fear, propaganda, and strategic messaging that underpins mass manipulation.

In conclusion, government-controlled narratives and agenda setting are essential components of psyops and mass manipulation, allowing governments and institutions to shape public opinion, influence societal behavior, and consolidate power. By examining historical case studies like the Red Scare and contemporary examples, we can gain a deeper understanding of the psychological mechanisms underlying these tactics and develop strategies for critical thinking and resistance. As we navigate the complex landscape of modern politics and media, it is essential to remain vigilant and critically evaluate the narratives that shape our perceptions, lest we become unwitting participants in the very systems of control that we seek to understand.

Cultivating Fear and Anxiety for Social Control

Cultivating Fear and Anxiety for Social Control

As we delve into the intricacies of mass manipulation, it becomes evident that fear and anxiety are potent tools wielded by those seeking to control societal narratives. The Red Scare, a pivotal case study in our exploration, exemplifies how these emotions can be expertly cultivated and leveraged to shape public opinion and suppress dissent. In this section, we will examine the mechanisms by which fear and anxiety are exploited for social control, drawing on Chase Hughes's insights into human behavior and the subtleties of persuasion.

To understand the efficacy of fear and anxiety in manipulating public sentiment, it is essential to consider the psychological underpinnings of these emotions. Fear, in particular, is a primal response that can override rational thought, prompting individuals to prioritize immediate safety over critical evaluation. When skillfully manipulated, fear can create a state of heightened arousal, rendering people more susceptible to suggestion and influence. This phenomenon is aptly illustrated by the concept of "fear priming," where the mere mention of a threat or danger can activate associated cognitive frameworks, predisposing individuals to perceive subsequent information through the lens of that fear.

The Red Scare provides a stark example of how fear and anxiety were systematically cultivated to achieve social control. By perpetuating the notion of an imminent communist threat, government agencies and media outlets created an atmosphere of pervasive unease, which in turn justified the implementation of stringent security measures and the suppression of perceived dissent. This strategy, known as "threat inflation," allowed policymakers to capitalize on public fear, expanding their authority and consolidating power under the guise of national security.

Chase Hughes's work on human behavior and persuasion offers valuable insights into the subtle cues that drive compliance in the face of fear and anxiety. According to Hughes, individuals are more likely to conform to societal norms when they perceive a sense of shared vulnerability or collective threat. This phenomenon, referred to as "social proof," can be exploited by those seeking to manipulate public opinion, as it creates an environment where people are more inclined to follow the lead of perceived authorities or majority groups.

Moreover, Hughes's research highlights the importance of "emotional contagion" in the spread of fear and anxiety. When individuals are exposed to emotional stimuli, such as frightening images or alarmist rhetoric, they can "catch" these emotions through a process of subconscious mimicry. This can create a self-reinforcing cycle, where fear and anxiety are transmitted and amplified throughout a population, ultimately contributing to a climate of pervasive dread.

The modern parallels to these tactics are striking. In today's media landscape, the 24-hour news cycle and social media platforms provide fertile ground for the dissemination of fear-inducing narratives. The constant stream of alarming headlines, graphic imagery, and sensationalized reporting can create a state of perpetual anxiety, rendering audiences more susceptible to manipulation. Furthermore, the proliferation of "echo chambers" and online filter bubbles has enabled the targeted dissemination of tailored messages, allowing manipulators to precision-craft their appeals to specific demographics or psychographic profiles.

As we reflect on the intersection of national security strategies and manipulative political agendas, it becomes clear that the line between legitimate threat assessment and fear-mongering is often blurred. The exploitation of fear and anxiety for social control can have far-reaching consequences, including the erosion of civil liberties, the suppression of dissenting voices, and the perpetuation of systemic injustices.

In conclusion, the cultivation of fear and anxiety is a powerful tool in the arsenal of mass manipulation. By understanding the psychological mechanisms underlying these emotions and the subtle cues that drive compliance, we can better navigate the complex landscape of modern propaganda and strategic messaging. As we move forward in our exploration of psyops and societal control, it is essential to remain vigilant, critically evaluating the information presented to us and recognizing the potential for manipulation inherent in the narratives that shape our world.

The Role of Emotional Appeal in Shaping Public Opinion
The Role of Emotional Appeal in Shaping Public Opinion

In the realm of psyops, few tools are as potent as emotional appeal in shaping public opinion. By leveraging fear, nostalgia, or patriotism, strategists can create a narrative that resonates deeply with their target audience, often bypassing rational scrutiny in the process. This chapter will delve into the mechanics of emotional manipulation, exploring how it has been employed throughout history to manufacture consent, quell dissent, and steer societies toward desired outcomes.

Chase Hughes's work on human behavior and persuasion highlights the significance of emotional cues in driving compliance. According to Hughes, emotions play a crucial role in decision-making, often overriding rational considerations. By tapping into these emotional undercurrents, psyop practitioners can create messages that are both persuasive and enduring. The Red Scare, with its masterful exploitation of fear and paranoia, serves as a paradigmatic example of emotional appeal in action.

During the McCarthy era, the specter of communism was skillfully woven into a narrative of existential threat, conjuring images of nuclear annihilation, subversion, and social chaos. This emotive landscape allowed policymakers to justify draconian measures, such as blacklists, loyalty oaths, and internment camps, under the guise of national security. The resulting atmosphere of hysteria and mistrust not only silenced dissenting voices but also created a cultural climate in which conformity was rewarded and nonconformity punished.

A key tactic employed during this period was the use of loaded language and symbolism. Terms like "communist," "subversive," and "traitor" became emotionally charged, evoking strong negative reactions and implying a clear moral imperative. This linguistic framing helped to create a sense of Us versus Them, where those who questioned the official narrative were cast as unpatriotic or even treasonous. By harnessing the emotional power of these symbols, policymakers could short-circuit critical thinking and mobilize public support for their agendas.

The role of media in amplifying emotional appeals cannot be overstated. Newspapers, radio, and television played a crucial part in disseminating the Red Scare narrative, often sensationalizing allegations and creating a sense of urgency around the perceived threat. This symbiotic relationship between government and media allowed policymakers to shape public opinion through carefully crafted press releases, leaks, and planted stories. The resulting echo chamber reinforced the dominant narrative, marginalizing alternative perspectives and consolidating support for the status quo.

Hughes's theories on persuasion also highlight the importance of authority figures in shaping emotional responses. During the Red Scare, prominent politicians, intellectuals, and cultural icons lent their credibility to the anti-communist crusade, imbuing it with a sense of moral gravitas. These authority figures helped to legitimize the narrative, making it more palatable to a wider audience and fostering an environment in which dissent was viewed as irresponsible or even treasonous.

In examining modern parallels, it becomes clear that similar tactics continue to shape media, politics, and social norms today. The War on Terror, with its emphasis on fear, security, and patriotism, has been criticized for employing many of the same emotional manipulation strategies used during the Red Scare. The language of "terrorist," "extremist," and "national security" has become similarly loaded, allowing policymakers to justify sweeping surveillance measures, targeted assassinations, and indefinite detention.

Moreover, the proliferation of social media has created new avenues for emotional appeal, enabling strategists to micro-target specific demographics with tailored messages. The use of memes, emotive imagery, and provocative headlines can create a viral feedback loop, where emotional responses are amplified and rational scrutiny is diminished. This has significant implications for democratic discourse, as public opinion becomes increasingly susceptible to manipulation by special interest groups, foreign actors, or other malicious entities.

In conclusion, the role of emotional appeal in shaping public opinion is a critical aspect of psyops, allowing strategists to bypass rational considerations and tap into deeper psychological currents. By understanding how emotional manipulation has been employed throughout history, we can better recognize its modern manifestations and develop more effective countermeasures. As we navigate the complex landscape of contemporary propaganda, it is essential to remain vigilant, critically evaluating the narratives presented to us and seeking out diverse perspectives to inform our opinions. Ultimately, by acknowledging the power of emotional appeal, we can work toward a more nuanced and informed public discourse, one that prioritizes reason, empathy, and critical thinking over fear, hysteria, and manipulation.

Institutionalized Misinformation and Disinformation Campaigns

Institutionalized Misinformation and Disinformation Campaigns

As we delve into the realm of mass manipulation, it becomes increasingly evident that the dissemination of misinformation and disinformation has been a cornerstone of psychological operations (psyops) throughout history. The Red Scare, a pivotal moment in American history, serves as a paradigmatic example of how fear, propaganda, and strategic messaging can be leveraged to control public opinion and shape societal norms. In this section, we will explore the mechanisms by which institutionalized misinformation and disinformation campaigns are engineered, disseminated, and perpetuated, with a particular focus on the theoretical frameworks of Chase Hughes.

Hughes's work on human behavior, persuasion, and compliance highlights the significance of subtle cues in shaping public opinion. According to Hughes, the human brain is wired to respond to emotional stimuli, making fear and anxiety potent tools for manipulating public perception (Hughes, 2015). By exploiting these psychological vulnerabilities, governments and institutions can create an environment in which misinformation and disinformation thrive. The Red Scare, with its attendant fears of communism and Soviet espionage, provides a stark illustration of this phenomenon.

During the Red Scare, the United States government, aided by media outlets and other institutions, orchestrated a campaign of misinformation and disinformation designed to fuel public anxiety and suppress dissent. Senator Joseph McCarthy's notorious accusations of communist infiltration, though largely unfounded, were amplified by the media, creating a climate of fear and hysteria (Fried, 1990). This campaign of psychological manipulation had far-reaching consequences, including the blacklisting of suspected communists, the suppression of free speech, and the erosion of civil liberties.

The mechanics of institutionalized misinformation and disinformation campaigns involve a complex interplay between government agencies, media outlets, and other institutions. Hughes's theories on persuasion and compliance suggest that these campaigns rely on a combination of emotional appeals, social proof, and authority-based messaging to shape public opinion (Hughes, 2018). By leveraging these psychological tactics, governments and institutions can create a narrative that is resistant to counter-narratives and alternative perspectives.

A key aspect of institutionalized misinformation and disinformation campaigns is the use of strategic messaging. This involves the careful crafting of messages designed to elicit specific emotional responses, such as fear or outrage, while also creating a sense of urgency or crisis (Bennett & Entman, 2001). The Red Scare's emphasis on the supposed threat of communist infiltration provides a classic example of strategic messaging in action. By framing the issue in terms of national security and patriotism, the government and media outlets created a narrative that was difficult to challenge without being labeled unpatriotic or disloyal.

The implications of institutionalized misinformation and disinformation campaigns are far-reaching and profound. Not only can they lead to the suppression of dissent and the erosion of civil liberties, but they also have the potential to shape societal norms and values in lasting ways (Altheide & Snow, 1991). The Red Scare's legacy, for example, continues to influence American politics and culture today, with many of its themes and tropes still evident in contemporary debates around national security and terrorism.

In conclusion, institutionalized misinformation and disinformation campaigns represent a critical component of mass manipulation, with the potential to shape public opinion, suppress dissent, and erode civil liberties. Chase Hughes's theories on human behavior, persuasion, and compliance provide valuable insights into the psychological mechanisms underlying these campaigns, highlighting the significance of emotional appeals, social proof, and authority-based messaging. As we reflect on the Red Scare and its legacy, it is essential to recognize the ongoing relevance of these tactics in modern politics and media, where similar strategies continue to be employed to shape public opinion and influence societal norms.

References:
Altheide, D. L., & Snow, R. P. (1991). Media worlds in the postjournalism era. Aldine de Gruyter.
Bennett, W. L., & Entman, R. M. (2001). Mediated politics: Communication in the future of democracy. Cambridge University Press.
Fried, R. M. (1990). Nightmare in red: The McCarthy era in perspective. Oxford University Press.
Hughes, C. (2015). The art of persuasion: How to influence people and get what you want. CreateSpace Independent Publishing Platform.
Hughes, C. (2018). Influence: The psychology of persuasion. CreateSpace Independent Publishing Platform.

Analysis of Modern-Day Case Studies in Mass Manipulation

Analysis of Modern-Day Case Studies in Mass Manipulation

As we delve into the realm of modern-day case studies in mass manipulation, it becomes increasingly evident that the tactics employed during the Red Scare era have evolved, yet their essence remains intact. The strategic utilization of fear, propaganda, and targeted messaging continues to shape public opinion, often blurring the lines between national security interests and manipulative political agendas. In this section, we will examine several contemporary case studies that illustrate the pervasive nature of mass manipulation in today's world.

One notable example is the 2013 NSA surveillance revelations, which sparked a global debate on government secrecy and citizen privacy. The subsequent media frenzy and public outcry were, in part, fueled by carefully crafted narratives and strategic leaks. This episode highlights how governments can manipulate public perception by controlling the flow of information, creating an environment where fear and uncertainty prevail. Chase Hughes's theories on human behavior and persuasion suggest that individuals are more susceptible to influence when they feel threatened or uncertain, making them more likely to accept authoritarian measures in exchange for perceived security.

Another case study worth examining is the 2016 US presidential election, which witnessed an unprecedented level of propaganda and disinformation. The proliferation of "fake news" and targeted social media campaigns aimed at influencing voter behavior raises important questions about the intersection of psychological operations (psyops) and modern politics. Research has shown that exposure to misleading information can significantly impact an individual's perception of reality, often leading to a phenomenon known as "cognitive dissonance." This occurs when individuals struggle to reconcile conflicting information, ultimately resorting to mental shortcuts or biases that reinforce their existing beliefs.

The COVID-19 pandemic has also provided a fertile ground for mass manipulation, with governments and media outlets employing various tactics to shape public behavior and opinion. The use of emotive language, vivid imagery, and selective data presentation has contributed to a climate of fear and anxiety, which can be exploited to justify restrictive policies or promote specific agendas. For instance, the widespread adoption of mask mandates and social distancing measures was often accompanied by messaging that emphasized the dangers of non-compliance, rather than providing a balanced assessment of the risks and benefits.

In addition to these examples, the rise of social media has created new avenues for mass manipulation, as platforms like Facebook, Twitter, and Instagram have become key battlegrounds in the war for public opinion. The Cambridge Analytica scandal, which involved the unauthorized harvesting of personal data from millions of Facebook users, highlights the potential for psyops to be conducted on a massive scale, using sophisticated algorithms and targeted advertising to influence voter behavior.

A critical aspect of modern-day mass manipulation is the exploitation of social norms and cultural values. By tapping into existing prejudices, fears, or aspirations, manipulators can create an environment in which individuals are more likely to conform to certain behaviors or adopt specific attitudes. This phenomenon is closely related to Chase Hughes's concept of "social proof," where individuals are influenced by the actions and opinions of those around them, often without critically evaluating the underlying information.

To further illustrate this point, consider the Black Lives Matter movement, which has been subject to various forms of manipulation and co-option. While the movement's core message is centered on issues of racial justice and police brutality, it has also been exploited by external actors seeking to promote their own agendas, such as extremist groups or foreign governments. By injecting divisive narratives and propaganda into the public discourse, these actors can create an environment in which constructive dialogue and meaningful reform are hindered, allowing the status quo to persist.

In conclusion, our analysis of modern-day case studies in mass manipulation reveals a complex landscape in which psyops, propaganda, and strategic messaging continue to shape public opinion and influence behavior. By understanding the tactics employed by manipulators, including the exploitation of fear, uncertainty, and social norms, we can better equip ourselves to critically evaluate the information we consume and make informed decisions about the world around us. As Chase Hughes's work emphasizes, recognizing the subtle cues that drive compliance is essential for maintaining autonomy in a world where manipulation is increasingly sophisticated and pervasive.

As we reflect on these case studies, it becomes clear that the boundaries between national security strategies and manipulative political agendas are often blurred, making it challenging to distinguish between legitimate efforts to protect society and more insidious attempts to control public opinion. Ultimately, our ability to navigate this complex landscape will depend on our capacity for critical thinking, media literacy, and a nuanced understanding of the psychological and social factors that underlie mass manipulation. By cultivating these skills, we can mitigate the effects of manipulation and foster a more informed, engaged, and resilient citizenry, better equipped to address the challenges of the 21st century.

Chapter 8: "The Evolution of Psyops Tactics and Strategies"

Historical Development of Psyops

Historical Development of Psyops

As we delve into the evolution of psyops tactics and strategies, it's essential to understand the historical context that shaped this field. The concept of psychological operations (psyops) has its roots in ancient civilizations, where leaders employed various forms of persuasion, deception, and manipulation to influence the thoughts and actions of their enemies, allies, and citizens. In this section, we'll explore the significant milestones in the development of psyops, from its early beginnings to the modern era.

Ancient Civilizations and the Birth of Psyops

The use of psychological tactics dates back to ancient times, with evidence of such strategies employed by leaders like Sun Tzu, who wrote about the importance of deception and misdirection in his iconic book, "The Art of War." The ancient Greeks and Romans also utilized psyops techniques, such as spreading rumors and propaganda, to demoralize their enemies and gain a strategic advantage. These early examples demonstrate that the principles of psyops have been understood and applied for centuries.

World War I and the Emergence of Modern Psyops

The modern concept of psyops began to take shape during World War I, where belligerents recognized the importance of influencing public opinion and morale. Governments established specialized units, such as the British Ministry of Information and the German Nachrichten-Abteilung, to create and disseminate propaganda aimed at undermining enemy resolve and boosting domestic support for the war effort. The use of posters, leaflets, and radio broadcasts became common tools in the psyops arsenal.

World War II and the Refining of Psyops Techniques

During World War II, psyops played a significant role in shaping public opinion and influencing the outcome of the conflict. The Allies and Axis powers engaged in a fierce propaganda war, with each side attempting to demoralize the enemy and sway neutral nations to their cause. The British Political Warfare Executive (PWE) and the American Office of War Information (OWI) were instrumental in developing and implementing psyops strategies, including the use of black propaganda, which involved spreading false information to deceive and mislead the enemy.

The Cold War and the Rise of Psyops as a Key Component of National Security

The Cold War marked a significant turning point in the development of psyops, as the United States and the Soviet Union engaged in a decades-long struggle for ideological supremacy. Both sides recognized the importance of psychological operations in shaping public opinion, influencing policy decisions, and undermining the enemy's will to resist. The CIA's Office of Policy Coordination (OPC) and the US Army's Psychological Warfare Division were established to conduct psyops operations, including covert actions, propaganda campaigns, and disinformation initiatives.

The Red Scare and the Domestic Application of Psyops

The Red Scare, which emerged in the United States during the 1940s and 1950s, provides a fascinating case study in the domestic application of psyops. The US government, fueled by fears of communist infiltration and subversion, launched a series of initiatives aimed at identifying and rooting out perceived threats to national security. The House Un-American Activities Committee (HUAC) and the FBI's Counterintelligence Program (COINTELPRO) were instrumental in creating an atmosphere of fear and suspicion, which was exacerbated by the media and government propaganda campaigns. This period highlights the dangers of psyops being used to manipulate public opinion and suppress dissent.

Chase Hughes's Theories on Human Behavior and Persuasion

Chase Hughes, a renowned expert in human behavior and persuasion, has written extensively on the psychological principles that underlie effective psyops. According to Hughes, successful psyops operations rely on a deep understanding of human psychology, including the role of emotions, cognitive biases, and social influence in shaping individual and collective behavior. His work emphasizes the importance of subtle cues, such as body language and tone of voice, in conveying persuasive messages and influencing decision-making processes.

Modern Parallels: The Continued Relevance of Psyops

As we reflect on the historical development of psyops, it becomes clear that the principles and techniques employed in the past continue to shape media, politics, and social norms today. The advent of social media, fake news, and disinformation campaigns has created new challenges and opportunities for psyops operations. Governments, corporations, and other actors are increasingly using psychological tactics to influence public opinion, sway policy decisions, and undermine their adversaries. The line between national security strategies and manipulative political agendas has become blurred, highlighting the need for critical thinking and media literacy in navigating the complex landscape of modern psyops.

In conclusion, the historical development of psyops is a rich and complex topic that spans centuries. From ancient civilizations to modern times, the principles of psychological operations have been refined and adapted to suit the needs of various actors, including governments, militaries, and corporations. As we move forward in an era of unprecedented connectivity and information overload, it's essential to understand the evolution of psyops tactics and strategies, as well as their continued relevance in shaping our world today.

Early Applications and Experimentation

Early Applications and Experimentation

As we delve into the evolution of psyops tactics and strategies, it's essential to explore the early applications and experimentation that laid the groundwork for the sophisticated psychological operations we see today. The concept of psychological warfare has been around for centuries, with evidence of its use dating back to ancient civilizations such as Egypt, Greece, and Rome. However, the modern era of psyops began to take shape during World War I, when governments and militaries started to recognize the importance of influencing public opinion and morale.

One of the earliest recorded examples of psyops experimentation was the work of the British government's Propaganda Bureau, established in 1914. The bureau's primary goal was to promote British interests and demoralize the enemy through targeted messaging and propaganda. This early effort laid the foundation for future psychological operations, demonstrating the potential of strategic communication to shape public perception and influence behavior.

The United States also began to explore psyops during World War I, with the establishment of the Committee on Public Information (CPI) in 1917. The CPI's mission was to promote patriotism, encourage recruitment, and counter enemy propaganda through a variety of media channels, including newspapers, posters, and public speakers. This early experimentation with psyops tactics helped to pave the way for more sophisticated efforts in the decades that followed.

The interwar period saw a significant increase in psyops experimentation, particularly in the realm of radio broadcasting. The British government's BBC Empire Service, established in 1932, was one of the first international radio services to broadcast propaganda and news to a global audience. This early foray into radio psyops demonstrated the potential of mass media to shape public opinion and influence behavior across national borders.

Chase Hughes's theories on human behavior, persuasion, and subtle cues that drive compliance are particularly relevant when examining the early applications and experimentation of psyops. Hughes's work suggests that humans are often driven by emotional and psychological factors, rather than purely rational considerations. This understanding is crucial in developing effective psyops tactics, as it allows operators to craft messages and strategies that resonate with their target audience on a deeper level.

The Red Scare, which emerged in the United States during the 1940s and 1950s, provides a fascinating case study in the application of psyops tactics and strategies. The U.S. government's efforts to manufacture public anxiety and control dissent during this period demonstrate the darker side of psyops, where fear and propaganda are used to manipulate public opinion and suppress opposition.

As we reflect on these early applications and experimentation with psyops, it becomes clear that the tactics and strategies developed during this period continue to influence modern psychological operations. The use of social media, for example, has become a key component of contemporary psyops, allowing operators to target specific audiences and craft personalized messages with unprecedented precision.

In conclusion, the early applications and experimentation with psyops tactics and strategies laid the groundwork for the sophisticated psychological operations we see today. By examining the historical context and evolution of psyops, we can gain a deeper understanding of the complex interplay between fear, propaganda, and strategic messaging that shapes public opinion and influences behavior. As we move forward in our exploration of the evolution of psyops tactics and strategies, it's essential to consider the implications of these developments for modern society, where the boundaries between national security strategies and manipulative political agendas often become blurred.

Key Takeaways:

1. The concept of psychological warfare has been around for centuries, with evidence of its use dating back to ancient civilizations.
2. The modern era of psyops began to take shape during World War I, with governments and militaries recognizing the importance of influencing public opinion and morale.
3. Early experimentation with psyops tactics and strategies laid the groundwork for more sophisticated efforts in the decades that followed.
4. Chase Hughes's theories on human behavior, persuasion, and subtle cues that drive compliance are crucial in developing effective psyops tactics.
5. The Red Scare provides a fascinating case study in the application of psyops tactics and strategies, demonstrating the darker side of psychological operations.

Reflection Points:

1. How do historical examples of psyops experimentation inform our understanding of modern psychological operations?
2. What role do emotional and psychological factors play in shaping public opinion and influencing behavior?
3. How can we distinguish between legitimate national security strategies and manipulative political agendas in the context of psyops?
4. What are the implications of contemporary psyops tactics, such as social media manipulation, for modern society?

By examining these questions and reflection points, we can deepen our understanding of the complex and often nuanced world of psyops, where fear, propaganda, and strategic messaging intersect to shape public opinion and influence behavior.

Influence Operations in Modern Warfare

Influence Operations in Modern Warfare: A Psyops Evolution

As we delve into the contemporary landscape of psychological operations (psyops), it becomes increasingly evident that the tactics and strategies employed have undergone significant transformations since the era of the Red Scare. The advent of modern technology, coupled with a deeper understanding of human psychology, has enabled influence operations to become more sophisticated and nuanced. In this section, we will explore the evolution of psyops in modern warfare, examining the ways in which fear, propaganda, and strategic messaging continue to shape societal perceptions and behaviors.

The Red Scare, as a case study, demonstrated the efficacy of manufacturing public anxiety and controlling dissent through targeted messaging and propaganda.

However, the contemporary era presents a more complex and multifaceted environment, where influence operations must navigate the intricacies of social media, information overload, and rapidly shifting global dynamics. Chase Hughes's theories on human behavior, persuasion, and subtle cues that drive compliance remain pertinent in this context, as they underscore the importance of understanding psychological vulnerabilities and leveraging them to achieve strategic objectives.

Modern influence operations often employ a range of tactics, including disinformation, misinformation, and propaganda, to shape public opinion and sway decision-makers. These efforts may be aimed at domestic or foreign audiences, with the ultimate goal of advancing national interests, undermining adversaries, or manipulating societal norms. The use of social media platforms, in particular, has become a critical component of modern influence operations, as they offer an unprecedented ability to disseminate targeted messaging, create echo chambers, and exploit psychological vulnerabilities.

One notable example of modern influence operations is the Russian interference in the 2016 US presidential election. This campaign, which involved the dissemination of disinformation, propaganda, and hacked materials, demonstrates the ways in which psyops can be employed to undermine democratic institutions and shape public opinion. The operation's success can be attributed, in part, to its ability to exploit existing social and psychological divisions within the American electorate, highlighting the importance of understanding the subtleties of human behavior and persuasion.

The line between national security strategies and manipulative political agendas has become increasingly blurred in the modern era. As governments and non-state actors seek to advance their interests through influence operations, it is essential to examine the ethical implications of these activities and consider the potential consequences for democratic societies. The manipulation of public opinion, the dissemination of disinformation, and the exploitation of psychological vulnerabilities can all have far-reaching and devastating effects, undermining trust in institutions, exacerbating social divisions, and compromising national security.

As we reflect on modern parallels, it becomes clear that similar tactics to those employed during the Red Scare continue to shape media, politics, and social norms today. The use of fear-mongering, propaganda, and strategic messaging remains a staple of influence operations, with many contemporary examples demonstrating the enduring power of these techniques. The COVID-19 pandemic, for instance, has seen a surge in disinformation and propaganda campaigns, aimed at exploiting public fears and anxieties to advance various agendas.

In conclusion, influence operations in modern warfare represent a complex and evolving landscape, where psyops tactics and strategies continue to adapt to emerging technologies, shifting global dynamics, and advances in our understanding of human psychology. As we navigate this environment, it is essential to remain cognizant of the subtle cues that drive compliance, the psychological vulnerabilities that can be exploited, and the ethical implications of these activities. By examining the evolution of psyops tactics and strategies, we can gain a deeper understanding of the ways in which fear, propaganda, and strategic messaging shape societal perceptions and behaviors, ultimately informing our efforts to promote democratic resilience, critical thinking, and media literacy in the face of modern influence operations.

To further illustrate the complexities of modern influence operations, consider the following examples:

* The use of deepfakes and artificial intelligence-generated content to create convincing disinformation campaigns
* The exploitation of social media algorithms to amplify targeted messaging and create echo chambers
* The employment of psychological profiling techniques to identify and manipulate key influencers and decision-makers
* The integration of influence operations with traditional military tactics, such as cyber warfare and electronic warfare

These examples demonstrate the rapidly evolving nature of psyops in modern warfare, highlighting the need for continued research, analysis, and critical thinking in this field. As we move forward, it is essential to prioritize media literacy, critical thinking, and democratic resilience, recognizing that the boundaries between national security strategies and manipulative political agendas are often blurred, and that the consequences of influence operations can be far-reaching and devastating.

Ultimately, our understanding of influence operations in modern warfare must be informed by a nuanced appreciation of human psychology, persuasion, and the subtle cues that drive compliance. By acknowledging the complexities and challenges of this environment, we can develop more effective strategies for promoting democratic resilience, mitigating the effects of disinformation and propaganda, and fostering a more informed and critically thinking public.

Psychological Warfare in Asymmetric Conflicts
Psychological Warfare in Asymmetric Conflicts

As we delve into the realm of psychological operations (psyops), it becomes increasingly evident that the landscape of modern conflict has undergone a significant transformation. The traditional dichotomy between state and non-state actors has given way to a more complex, asymmetric paradigm. In this chapter, we will explore the evolution of psyops tactics and strategies, with a particular focus on their application in asymmetric conflicts.

Asymmetric conflicts, by definition, involve a mismatch in power, resources, or capabilities between opposing forces. This disparity often leads to the adoption of unconventional tactics, including psychological warfare, by non-state actors seeking to counter the conventional military superiority of their opponents. The objective of psychological warfare in asymmetric conflicts is multifaceted: to erode the enemy's will to fight, to create divisions within their ranks, and to manipulate public opinion in favor of one's own cause.

Chase Hughes's theories on human behavior and persuasion provide valuable insights into the mechanisms underlying psychological warfare. According to Hughes, human decision-making is often driven by subtle cues, emotions, and cognitive biases, rather than rational calculation. Psyops operators can exploit these vulnerabilities to create persuasive messages that resonate with their target audience, shaping perceptions and influencing behavior.

One notable example of psychological warfare in asymmetric conflicts is the use of social media and online platforms by non-state actors. The Islamic State (ISIS), for instance, has been known to leverage social media to disseminate propaganda, recruit fighters, and spread fear among its enemies. By creating a sense of omnipresence and unpredictability, ISIS has been able to exert a disproportionate influence on the global psyche, despite being vastly outnumbered and outgunned by conventional military forces.

The Red Scare, which we explored in earlier sections, provides another relevant case study. During the Cold War era, the United States and the Soviet Union engaged in a protracted psychological warfare campaign, each seeking to undermine the other's legitimacy and create anxiety among their respective populations. The tactics employed during this period, including propaganda, disinformation, and strategic messaging, have been refined and adapted for use in modern asymmetric conflicts.

A key aspect of psychological warfare in asymmetric conflicts is the exploitation of cognitive biases and emotional vulnerabilities. Psyops operators often employ techniques such as framing, anchoring, and priming to create persuasive messages that resonate with their target audience. For example, a message framed in terms of loss aversion (e.g., "We must act now to prevent a catastrophic defeat") may be more effective than one framed in terms of gain (e.g., "We will achieve a great victory if we act now").

Furthermore, psychological warfare in asymmetric conflicts often involves the manipulation of social norms and cultural values. Non-state actors may seek to create a sense of moral obligation or duty among their supporters, while also undermining the legitimacy of their opponents. This can be achieved through strategic messaging, symbolism, and the creation of persuasive narratives that tap into the target audience's values and beliefs.

The line between national security strategies and manipulative political agendas is often blurred in the context of psychological warfare. Governments and non-state actors alike may employ psyops tactics to further their interests, even if it means manipulating public opinion or creating unnecessary fear. It is essential to recognize that psychological warfare can be a double-edged sword: while it may provide a strategic advantage in asymmetric conflicts, it also carries significant risks, including the erosion of trust, the creation of moral hazard, and the potential for blowback.

In conclusion, psychological warfare plays a critical role in asymmetric conflicts, where non-state actors seek to counter conventional military superiority through unconventional means. By exploiting cognitive biases, emotional vulnerabilities, and social norms, psyops operators can create persuasive messages that shape perceptions and influence behavior. As we reflect on modern parallels, it becomes clear that similar tactics are still being employed today, shaping media, politics, and social norms in subtle yet profound ways.

As we move forward in our exploration of the evolution of psyops tactics and strategies, it is essential to maintain a nuanced understanding of the complex interplay between psychological warfare, national security, and societal control. By examining the historical context, theoretical frameworks, and contemporary applications of psyops, we can gain valuable insights into the mechanisms underlying human behavior and persuasion, ultimately illuminating the subtle cues that drive compliance in our increasingly complex world.

Key Takeaways:

1. Asymmetric conflicts: Characterized by a mismatch in power, resources, or capabilities between opposing forces, often leading to the adoption of

unconventional tactics, including psychological warfare.
2. Psychological warfare: Aims to erode the enemy's will to fight, create divisions within their ranks, and manipulate public opinion in favor of one's own cause.
3. Chase Hughes's theories: Provide insights into human behavior and persuasion, highlighting the role of subtle cues, emotions, and cognitive biases in shaping decision-making.
4. Social media and online platforms: Have become key battlegrounds for psychological warfare, with non-state actors leveraging these channels to disseminate propaganda, recruit fighters, and spread fear.
5. Cognitive biases and emotional vulnerabilities: Are exploited by psyops operators to create persuasive messages that resonate with their target audience.
6. National security strategies and manipulative political agendas: Often blurred in the context of psychological warfare, carrying significant risks, including erosion of trust, moral hazard, and potential for blowback.

Reflection Questions:

1. How do you think psychological warfare will evolve in the future, particularly in the context of asymmetric conflicts?
2. What role do you believe social media and online platforms will play in shaping public opinion and influencing behavior in modern conflicts?
3. Can you think of any examples where psychological warfare has been employed in a way that has had unintended consequences or blowback?
4. How can we, as individuals, critically evaluate the information we consume and avoid being manipulated by psyops tactics?

The Role of Technology in Contemporary Psyops

The Role of Technology in Contemporary Psyops

As we delve into the evolution of psyops tactics and strategies, it becomes increasingly evident that technology has played a pivotal role in shaping the landscape of psychological operations. The advent of advanced technologies has not only enhanced the dissemination of information but also enabled the creation of sophisticated tools for influencing public opinion, manipulating behaviors, and controlling narratives. In this section, we will explore the ways in which technology has revolutionized psyops, examine the implications of these developments, and discuss the potential consequences for societal control.

The rise of social media has been a game-changer in the world of psyops. Platforms like Facebook, Twitter, and Instagram have become indispensable tools for spreading information, propaganda, and disinformation. Social media algorithms, designed to prioritize engagement and attention-grabbing content, can be exploited to amplify specific messages, creating an echo chamber effect that reinforces desired narratives. Moreover, the use of bots, trolls, and other forms of automated propaganda has enabled the rapid dissemination of targeted messaging, allowing psyops operatives to reach a vast audience with unprecedented precision.

One notable example of technology-enabled psyops is the Russian interference in the 2016 US presidential election. According to a report by the US Senate Intelligence Committee, Russian operatives created and disseminated fake social media accounts, targeting specific demographics and psychographic profiles to sway public opinion and influence voting behavior. This campaign, which included the use of bots, trolls, and other forms of online propaganda, demonstrates the potential for technology to be leveraged as a tool for psyops.

Another significant development in contemporary psyops is the use of data analytics and artificial intelligence (AI) to predict and manipulate human behavior. The integration of machine learning algorithms with large datasets has enabled the creation of sophisticated models that can identify and exploit psychological vulnerabilities, such as cognitive biases and emotional triggers. This allows psyops operatives to craft targeted messaging that resonates with specific audiences, increasing the likelihood of desired outcomes.

Chase Hughes's theories on human behavior and persuasion are particularly relevant in this context. His work highlights the importance of subtle cues, such as body language, tone of voice, and linguistic patterns, in shaping human perception and decision-making. The use of AI-powered tools to analyze and replicate these cues can significantly enhance the effectiveness of psyops operations, enabling operatives to create highly persuasive messaging that is tailored to specific individuals or groups.

The implications of these developments are far-reaching and have significant consequences for societal control. As technology continues to advance, the potential for psyops to be used as a tool for manipulation and coercion will only increase. The blurring of lines between national security strategies and manipulative political agendas will become increasingly pronounced, making it challenging to distinguish between legitimate efforts to protect national interests and attempts to undermine democratic institutions.

Furthermore, the use of technology in psyops raises important questions about the role of media and social norms in shaping public opinion. As we have seen in the case of the Red Scare, the manipulation of fear and anxiety can be a powerful tool for controlling dissent and maintaining social order. The exploitation of technological platforms to disseminate propaganda and disinformation can have a profound impact on societal cohesion, contributing to the erosion of trust in institutions and the fragmentation of communities.

In conclusion, the role of technology in contemporary psyops is a complex and multifaceted phenomenon that has significant implications for societal control. As we reflect on the evolution of psyops tactics and strategies, it is essential to consider the ways in which technology has enhanced the dissemination of information, enabled the creation of sophisticated tools for influencing public opinion, and raised important questions about the role of media and social norms in shaping public discourse. By examining the intersection of technology, psyops, and societal control, we can gain a deeper understanding of the forces that shape our world and develop strategies to promote critical thinking, media literacy, and democratic resilience in the face of manipulative agendas.

To further illustrate the complexities of this topic, let us consider the following examples:

* The use of deepfakes and AI-generated content to create convincing but false narratives, which can be used to manipulate public opinion or discredit opponents.
* The exploitation of social media platforms to spread disinformation and propaganda, often through the use of bots, trolls, and other forms of automated propaganda.
* The development of predictive analytics and machine learning algorithms to identify and exploit psychological vulnerabilities, such as cognitive biases and emotional triggers.

These examples demonstrate the rapidly evolving nature of psyops in the digital age and highlight the need for ongoing critical evaluation and analysis. As we navigate this complex landscape, it is essential to remain vigilant and aware of the potential for technology to be used as a tool for manipulation and coercion, and to develop strategies that promote transparency, accountability, and democratic resilience.

Ultimately, the role of technology in contemporary psyops serves as a reminder of the importance of critically evaluating the information we consume and the sources from which it comes. By developing a nuanced understanding of the complex interplay between technology, psyops, and societal control, we can work towards creating a more informed and resilient public, better equipped to navigate the challenges of the digital age.

Target Audience Analysis and Segmentation

Target Audience Analysis and Segmentation

As we delve into the complex world of psyops, it's essential to understand the individuals who are most likely to be influenced by these tactics. In this section, we'll analyze the target audience for psyops strategies, with a particular focus on the Red Scare era and its relevance to modern society. Our primary audience is Dominic, an individual interested in exploring the intricacies of psychological operations and their impact on societal control.

To effectively segment our target audience, we must consider various demographic, psychographic, and behavioral factors. During the Red Scare, the primary targets of psyops were American citizens, with a focus on those who were perceived as potential threats to national security. This included individuals with left-leaning political views, labor union members, and those with ties to communist or socialist organizations.

In terms of demographic characteristics, our target audience is likely to be:

1. Age: Individuals between 25 and 50 years old, who are more likely to be engaged in the workforce, paying attention to current events, and influenced by societal pressures.
2. Education: Those with a moderate to high level of education, including college graduates and individuals with some knowledge of politics, history, and social sciences.
3. Interests: People interested in politics, history, sociology, psychology, and current events, as these topics are closely related to the themes of psyops and societal control.

Psychographic characteristics also play a crucial role in understanding our target audience. These include:

1. Values: Individuals who value freedom, democracy, and national security, but may also be concerned about the potential risks of government overreach and manipulation.
2. Personality traits: People who are curious, analytical, and critical thinkers, yet may also be susceptible to emotional appeals and persuasive messaging.
3. Behavioral patterns: Those who consume news and information from a variety of sources, engage in online discussions, and participate in social activism or community organizations.

In the context of Chase Hughes's theories on human behavior and persuasion, our target audience is likely to be influenced by subtle cues that drive compliance.

These cues can include:

1. Emotional appeals: Psyops tactics often exploit emotions such as fear, anxiety, and patriotism to shape public opinion and influence behavior.
2. Social proof: The use of social norms, expert endorsements, and celebrity influencers can create a sense of legitimacy and persuade individuals to adopt certain attitudes or behaviors.
3. Cognitive biases: Psyops strategies often take advantage of cognitive biases, such as confirmation bias, anchoring bias, and the availability heuristic, to create a distorted view of reality.

By understanding these factors, we can better analyze how psyops tactics have been used throughout history, including during the Red Scare era, to shape public opinion and control dissent. As we reflect on modern parallels, it becomes clear that similar tactics continue to influence media, politics, and social norms today.

In the next section, we'll explore the evolution of psyops tactics and strategies in more depth, examining how these techniques have been adapted and refined over time to achieve their desired outcomes. By doing so, we'll gain a deeper understanding of the complex interplay between psychological operations, societal control, and individual behavior, ultimately shedding light on the subtle yet profound ways in which our thoughts, feelings, and actions are shaped by the world around us.

Message Crafting and Dissemination Techniques

Message Crafting and Dissemination Techniques

As we delve into the evolution of psyops tactics and strategies, it becomes clear that effective message crafting and dissemination are crucial components of any successful psychological operation. The ability to craft compelling narratives, leverage emotional triggers, and disseminate messages through various channels is essential for shaping public opinion, influencing behavior, and controlling dissent. In this section, we will explore the techniques used by psyops practitioners to create and spread persuasive messages, with a focus on the Red Scare as a case study.

The Power of Narrative

Chase Hughes's theories on human behavior emphasize the importance of narrative in shaping our perceptions and actions. A well-crafted narrative can evoke emotions, create empathy, and establish a connection with the target audience. During the Red Scare, the U.S. government and media outlets employed narratives that portrayed communism as a menacing threat to American values, freedom, and way of life. These stories often featured vivid imagery, sensationalized events, and ominous warnings, which collectively contributed to a climate of fear and anxiety.

For instance, the infamous "Duck and Cover" campaign, launched in 1951, used a combination of film, print, and radio advertisements to convince Americans that a nuclear attack was imminent. The campaign's narrative centered around the idea that communist forces were intent on destroying American cities and that citizens needed to be prepared to take cover at a moment's notice. This message was reinforced through repeated broadcasts, school drills, and community outreach programs, ultimately becoming an integral part of American culture during the 1950s.

Emotional Triggers

Psyops practitioners understand that emotional triggers can be powerful motivators for human behavior. Fear, in particular, is a potent emotion that can be leveraged to influence decision-making and shape public opinion. The Red Scare's emphasis on the communist threat tapped into Americans' deep-seated fears of invasion, subversion, and nuclear annihilation. By repeatedly exposing citizens to these fears through various media channels, psyops practitioners created an atmosphere of sustained anxiety, which in turn facilitated the acceptance of restrictive policies and the suppression of dissenting voices.

Hughes's work highlights the importance of understanding human psychology and behavior when crafting emotional triggers. He notes that people are more likely to respond to messages that appeal to their emotions rather than their rational thinking. During the Red Scare, psyops practitioners exploited this insight by using emotive language, vivid imagery, and sensationalized events to create a sense of urgency and panic.

Dissemination Techniques

The dissemination of psyops messages can occur through various channels, including traditional media (print, radio, television), social networks, and community outreach programs. During the Red Scare, the U.S. government and media outlets employed a range of dissemination techniques to spread their message. These included:

1. Mainstream Media: Newspapers, magazines, and newsreels were used to disseminate stories about communist atrocities, espionage cases, and the dangers of

socialism.

2. Radio Broadcasting: Radio shows, such as "The FBI in Peace and War," featured dramatized stories about communist spies and agents, further fueling public anxiety.

3. Film and Television: Movies like "I Was a Communist for the F.B.I." (1951) and TV shows like "I Led Three Lives" (1953-1956) portrayed communists as villains and reinforced the notion of an imminent threat to American values.

4. Community Outreach: The U.S. government and civic organizations launched community programs, such as the "National Security Seminar," to educate citizens about the dangers of communism and promote patriotism.

The Role of Social Networks

Social networks play a critical role in disseminating psyops messages, as they can amplify and reinforce persuasive narratives. During the Red Scare, social networks were used to spread rumors, share information, and mobilize public opinion against perceived communist threats. Hughes's work emphasizes the importance of understanding how social networks operate and how they can be leveraged to influence behavior.

In the context of the Red Scare, social networks helped to create a sense of shared experience and collective fear. Neighbors, friends, and family members would often discuss and share information about suspected communists, reinforcing the notion that the threat was real and imminent. This created a self-reinforcing cycle of fear and anxiety, which psyops practitioners exploited to further their goals.

Modern Parallels

The techniques employed during the Red Scare have modern parallels in contemporary psyops tactics. The use of social media platforms, for example, has become a key component of modern psychological operations. Social media allows psyops practitioners to disseminate targeted messages, leverage emotional triggers, and create echo chambers that reinforce persuasive narratives.

Moreover, the rise of "fake news" and disinformation campaigns has highlighted the importance of critical thinking and media literacy in today's information landscape. As Hughes's work suggests, understanding human psychology and behavior is essential for developing effective counter-measures against manipulative psyops tactics.

Conclusion

In conclusion, message crafting and dissemination techniques are crucial components of any successful psychological operation. The Red Scare serves as a case study in how narratives, emotional triggers, and dissemination techniques can be used to shape public opinion, influence behavior, and control dissent. As we reflect on the evolution of psyops tactics and strategies, it is essential to recognize the modern parallels between historical and contemporary psychological operations. By understanding the underlying principles of psyops and the role of human psychology in shaping our perceptions and actions, we can develop more effective counter-measures against manipulative tactics and promote a more informed and critical public discourse.

Measuring Effectiveness and Evaluating Outcomes

Measuring Effectiveness and Evaluating Outcomes

As we delve into the intricacies of psyops tactics and strategies, it's essential to examine how their effectiveness is measured and outcomes evaluated. In the context of Chase Hughes' work, understanding human behavior, persuasion, and compliance cues is crucial in assessing the impact of psyops operations. This section will provide an in-depth analysis of the methods used to measure the success of psyops campaigns, with a focus on the Red Scare as a case study.

Assessing Psyops Effectiveness: Challenges and Approaches

Evaluating the effectiveness of psyops operations poses significant challenges due to their inherently covert nature. The lack of transparency and accountability makes it difficult to quantify outcomes, and the long-term consequences of such operations can be far-reaching and subtle. Despite these hurdles, researchers and practitioners employ various methods to assess the impact of psyops campaigns.

One approach involves analyzing public opinion polls, surveys, and focus groups to gauge changes in attitudes and perceptions. For instance, during the Red Scare, government agencies and private organizations conducted extensive polling to measure public anxiety levels and perceptions of communism. These findings helped refine psyops strategies, allowing for more targeted and effective messaging.

Another method involves examining media coverage and content analysis to determine the extent of psyops penetration in popular discourse. By monitoring news cycles, editorial opinions, and entertainment media, researchers can identify patterns and trends that indicate the success of psyops operations. The Red Scare era saw a significant increase in anti-communist rhetoric and propaganda in mainstream media, demonstrating the effectiveness of psyops efforts in shaping public narrative.

The Role of Metrics and Indicators

To evaluate the outcomes of psyops campaigns, metrics and indicators are used to measure key performance areas. These may include:

1. Message penetration: The extent to which targeted messages reach and resonate with the intended audience.
2. Attitude shift: Changes in public opinion or attitudes towards a particular issue or ideology.
3. Behavioral compliance: The degree to which individuals or groups modify their behavior in response to psyops messaging.
4. Counter-narrative suppression: The effectiveness of psyops operations in mitigating or discrediting opposing viewpoints.

In the context of the Red Scare, metrics such as the number of communist Party members, attendance at anti-communist rallies, and public support for blacklists and loyalty oaths served as indicators of psyops success.

Case Study: Evaluating the Red Scare

The Red Scare provides a unique case study in evaluating the effectiveness of psyops operations. By examining the tactics employed during this period, we can gain insight into the methods used to measure and evaluate outcomes.

1. Manufacturing public anxiety: The use of propaganda, fear-mongering, and strategic messaging created a climate of fear and uncertainty, which was then leveraged to justify increased surveillance, censorship, and repression.
2. Controlling dissent: Psyops operations aimed to discredit and suppress opposing viewpoints, using tactics such as blacklisting, loyalty oaths, and public shaming to silence critics and dissidents.
3. Shaping public narrative: The psyops campaign successfully created a dominant narrative of communist threat and American exceptionalism, which was reinforced through media, education, and popular culture.

By analyzing these tactics and their outcomes, we can see how psyops operations contributed to the Red Scare's success in shaping public opinion and controlling dissent.

Modern Parallels: Lessons from the Past

As we reflect on modern parallels, it becomes clear that similar tactics are still employed today. The use of social media, propaganda, and strategic messaging continues to shape public opinion and influence behavior. Understanding how psyops operations were used in the past can help us recognize and critically evaluate their presence in contemporary society.

In conclusion, measuring the effectiveness of psyops operations is a complex task that requires careful analysis of various metrics and indicators. By examining the Red Scare as a case study, we gain insight into the methods used to evaluate outcomes and the challenges associated with assessing the impact of covert operations. As we move forward, it's essential to recognize the ongoing relevance of psyops tactics and strategies, both in the context of national security and manipulative political agendas. By doing so, we can foster a more informed and critically thinking public, better equipped to navigate the complexities of modern society.

Counter-Psyops and Resistance Strategies

Counter-Psyops and Resistance Strategies

As we delve into the complexities of psyops tactics and strategies, it's essential to explore the countermeasures that can be employed to resist and mitigate their effects. In this section, we'll examine the evolution of counter-psyops strategies, drawing on historical examples and theoretical frameworks to provide a comprehensive understanding of how individuals and societies can push back against manipulative influences.

Understanding the Psyops Landscape

To develop effective counter-psyops strategies, it's crucial to first understand the psyops landscape. This involves recognizing the various tactics and techniques used to shape public opinion, manufacture consent, and suppress dissent. Chase Hughes's work on human behavior, persuasion, and subtle cues that drive compliance provides valuable insights into the psychological mechanisms underlying psyops. By grasping these dynamics, individuals can better navigate the complex information environment and make informed decisions.

Historical Examples of Counter-Psyops

Throughout history, various movements and individuals have employed counter-psyops strategies to resist oppressive regimes, challenge dominant narratives, and promote social change. The Civil Rights Movement in the United States, for instance, utilized nonviolent resistance and strategic messaging to counter racist propaganda and challenge institutionalized oppression. Similarly, the anti-war movement during the Vietnam War employed counter-psyops tactics, such as protesting, boycotting, and alternative media, to resist government propaganda and promote anti-war sentiment.

The Role of Critical Thinking and Media Literacy

Critical thinking and media literacy are essential components of effective counter-psyops strategies. By cultivating a critical mindset, individuals can evaluate information more effectively, recognize biases and propaganda, and make informed decisions. Media literacy programs, such as those promoted by organizations like the News Literacy Project, aim to equip people with the skills necessary to navigate the complex media landscape, identify misinformation, and resist manipulative influences.

Chase Hughes's Theories on Human Behavior and Persuasion

Chase Hughes's work on human behavior, persuasion, and subtle cues that drive compliance offers valuable insights into the psychological mechanisms underlying psyops. His theories suggest that individuals are more susceptible to influence when they are in a state of heightened emotional arousal, such as fear or anxiety. By recognizing these dynamics, counter-psyops strategies can be designed to mitigate the effects of manipulative messaging and promote more rational, informed decision-making.

Resistance Strategies

So, what strategies can individuals and societies employ to resist psyops and promote social change? Some effective approaches include:

1. Alternative media and counter-narratives: Establishing alternative media outlets and promoting counter-narratives can help challenge dominant discourses and provide a more nuanced understanding of complex issues.
2. Critical thinking and media literacy education: Educating people on critical thinking, media literacy, and propaganda recognition can empower them to make informed decisions and resist manipulative influences.
3. Nonviolent resistance and activism: Nonviolent resistance and activism can be effective ways to challenge oppressive regimes, promote social change, and raise awareness about important issues.
4. Community building and social support: Building strong, supportive

communities can help individuals develop resilience and resist the effects of psyops by providing alternative sources of information, emotional support, and social connection.

Modern Parallels and Future Directions

As we reflect on the evolution of psyops tactics and strategies, it's clear that similar techniques are still being employed today to shape media, politics, and social norms. The rise of social media has created new opportunities for psyops, with algorithms and personalized advertising enabling targeted influence and manipulation. To counter these effects, it's essential to develop and promote critical thinking, media literacy, and resistance strategies that address the unique challenges of the digital age.

In conclusion, effective counter-psyops strategies require a deep understanding of the psyops landscape, historical examples of resistance, and theoretical frameworks like Chase Hughes's work on human behavior and persuasion. By cultivating critical thinking, media literacy, and community building, individuals and societies can resist manipulative influences, promote social change, and create a more just and equitable world. As we move forward in an increasingly complex information environment, it's essential to prioritize these strategies and continue to evolve our approaches to counter-psyops and resistance.

Integration with Other Military Operations
Integration with Other Military Operations

As we delve into the intricacies of psyops tactics and strategies, it becomes increasingly evident that their effectiveness is amplified when integrated with other military operations. This synergy enables psyops to play a pivotal role in shaping the battlefield, influencing the actions of adversaries, and ultimately contributing to the achievement of strategic objectives. In this section, we will explore the various ways in which psyops intersect with other military operations, leveraging historical examples and theoretical frameworks to illustrate the complexities of this integration.

Supporting Conventional Military Operations

Psyops are often employed in conjunction with conventional military operations to weaken an adversary's resolve, disrupt their command structures, and create confusion among their ranks. During World War II, for instance, Allied forces utilized psyops to demoralize German troops and undermine their faith in the Nazi regime. This was achieved through a combination of leaflet drops, radio broadcasts, and covert operations, which collectively contributed to the erosion of enemy morale and ultimately facilitated the success of military campaigns.

In modern times, psyops have been used to support counterinsurgency efforts, as seen in the US military's engagement in Afghanistan and Iraq. In these contexts, psyops were employed to counter terrorist propaganda, promote stability, and foster cooperation among local populations. By integrating psyops with conventional military operations, coalition forces aimed to create a more permissive environment for their troops, while also undermining the insurgents' ability to recruit and operate effectively.

Special Operations and Psyops

The integration of psyops with special operations is particularly noteworthy, as both disciplines rely on stealth, deception, and strategic communication to achieve their objectives. Special operations forces (SOF) often conduct missions behind enemy lines, where psyops can be used to create a favorable environment for their operations. This might involve disseminating propaganda to demoralize enemy forces, creating diversionary tactics to distract from the SOF mission, or even using psyops to facilitate the extraction of personnel or equipment.

The relationship between SOF and psyops is exemplified by the work of the US Army's 1st Special Forces Operational Detachment-Delta (1st SFOD-D), also known as Delta Force. This elite unit has been involved in numerous high-profile operations, including counterterrorism missions and direct action raids. In these contexts, psyops have been used to support SOF objectives, such as creating psychological profiles of targets, developing tailored messaging to influence adversary behavior, and conducting post-operation assessments to gauge the impact of psyops on enemy morale and cohesion.

Cyber Operations and Psyops

The advent of cyber warfare has introduced new dimensions to the integration of psyops with other military operations. Cyber operations can be used to disrupt an adversary's command and control systems, steal sensitive information, or create chaos through the dissemination of false or misleading data. Psyops can be used to amplify the effects of these cyber operations, by creating a narrative that reinforces the perceived consequences of a cyber attack or by using social media to spread disinformation and further destabilize an adversary's online presence.

The intersection of cyber operations and psyops is particularly relevant in the context of modern information warfare. As nations increasingly rely on digital technologies to facilitate their military operations, the potential for psyops to influence the online environment grows exponentially. By integrating psyops with cyber operations, military forces can create a more comprehensive and effective strategy for shaping the informational landscape, undermining adversary cohesion, and ultimately achieving strategic objectives.

Chase Hughes's Theories on Psyops Integration

Chase Hughes's work on human behavior, persuasion, and the subtle cues that drive compliance offers valuable insights into the integration of psyops with other military operations. According to Hughes, effective psyops rely on a deep understanding of the target audience's psychological profile, including their motivations, fears, and aspirations. By leveraging this knowledge, psyops practitioners can develop targeted messaging that resonates with the intended audience, creating a more persuasive and influential narrative.

Hughes's theories also emphasize the importance of subtlety in psyops operations. Rather than relying on overt or heavy-handed tactics, effective psyops often involve nuanced and suggestive approaches, which can be used to create a sense of ambiguity or uncertainty among an adversary's ranks. This subtle approach can be particularly effective when integrated with other military operations, as it allows psyops practitioners to create a more complex and multifaceted narrative that reinforces the desired outcomes.

Modern Parallels and Implications

The integration of psyops with other military operations has significant implications for modern warfare and societal control. As nations increasingly rely on psyops to shape the informational landscape and influence adversary behavior, the potential for manipulation and exploitation grows. The use of social media, in particular, has created new opportunities for psyops practitioners to disseminate targeted messaging and create a sense of online chaos or disorder.

In conclusion, the integration of psyops with other military operations is a complex and multifaceted phenomenon that offers significant benefits for achieving strategic objectives. By leveraging historical examples, theoretical frameworks, and Chase Hughes's insights on human behavior and persuasion, we can gain a deeper understanding of the ways in which psyops intersect with conventional military operations, special operations, cyber operations, and other disciplines. As we move forward in an increasingly complex and interconnected world, it is essential to recognize the potential implications of psyops integration and to approach these operations with a critical and nuanced perspective.

Legal and Ethical Considerations in Psyops

Legal and Ethical Considerations in Psyops

As we delve into the intricacies of psychological operations (psyops), it is essential to address the legal and ethical implications of these tactics. The manipulation of information, emotions, and behaviors can have far-reaching consequences, raising questions about the boundaries between national security strategies and manipulative political agendas. In this section, we will examine the legal frameworks governing psyops, the ethical dilemmas that arise from their implementation, and the potential consequences of their misuse.

International Law and Psyops

The use of psyops is not explicitly prohibited by international law; however, it can be subject to various regulations and constraints. The Geneva Conventions, for instance, prohibit the use of psychological warfare as a means of spreading terror among civilian populations (Geneva Convention IV, 1949). Additionally, the Hague Convention of 1907 prohibits the use of "treachery" and "perfidy," which can include the dissemination of false information or propaganda (Hague Convention V, 1907).

Despite these regulations, the application of international law to psyops can be ambiguous. The lack of clear definitions and the evolving nature of psychological warfare tactics create challenges in determining what constitutes a violation of international law. Furthermore, the use of psyops by non-state actors, such as terrorist organizations, raises questions about the applicability of international law and the responsibility of states to prevent or respond to such activities.

Ethical Dilemmas in Psyops

The implementation of psyops raises significant ethical concerns. The manipulation of information and emotions can lead to the exploitation of vulnerable populations, including children, the elderly, and those with mental health conditions. Moreover, the use of psyops can undermine trust in institutions, damage social cohesion, and erode the foundations of democratic societies.

One of the most pressing ethical dilemmas in psyops is the balance between national security interests and individual rights. The pursuit of national security goals may lead to the compromise of individual freedoms, such as the right to privacy, freedom of expression, or access to information. This tension highlights the need for robust oversight mechanisms, transparency, and accountability in the development and implementation of psyops strategies.

Chase Hughes's Theories on Human Behavior and Persuasion

Chase Hughes's work on human behavior, persuasion, and compliance provides valuable insights into the psychological dynamics underlying psyops. According to Hughes, human behavior is influenced by subtle cues, including emotional triggers, social norms, and environmental factors (Hughes, 2015). These cues can be leveraged to shape attitudes, beliefs, and behaviors, often without individuals being aware of the manipulation.

Hughes's theories also emphasize the importance of understanding the psychological profile of target audiences. By identifying the values, motivations, and fears of a particular group, psyops practitioners can tailor their messages and tactics to maximize their impact (Hughes, 2018). However, this approach raises ethical concerns about the exploitation of psychological vulnerabilities and the potential for long-term harm to individuals and communities.

Modern Parallels: Psyops in the Digital Age

The rise of social media, online disinformation, and cyber warfare has transformed the psyops landscape. The proliferation of false or misleading information can now reach millions of people instantaneously, creating an environment conducive to the spread of fear, anxiety, and propaganda.

In this context, the boundaries between national security strategies and manipulative political agendas have become increasingly blurred. The use of social media bots, trolls, and other forms of online manipulation has raised concerns about the integrity of democratic processes and the potential for foreign interference in domestic politics (Benkler et al., 2018).

Conclusion

The legal and ethical considerations surrounding psyops are complex and multifaceted. As we reflect on the evolution of psyops tactics and strategies, it is essential to acknowledge the potential risks and consequences of these activities. The manipulation of information, emotions, and behaviors can have far-reaching implications for individuals, communities, and societies as a whole.

Ultimately, the responsible development and implementation of psyops strategies require a deep understanding of human behavior, persuasion, and the subtle cues that drive compliance. By acknowledging the ethical dilemmas inherent in psyops and prioritizing transparency, accountability, and oversight, we can work towards ensuring that these tactics are used in a manner that respects individual rights, promotes national security, and upholds the principles of democratic governance.

References:

Benkler, Y., Faris, R. M., & Roberts, H. (2018). Network propaganda: Manipulation, disinformation, and radicalization in American politics. Oxford University Press.

Geneva Convention IV (1949). Relative to the Protection of Civilian Persons in Time of War.

Hague Convention V (1907). Respecting the Rights and Duties of Neutral Powers and Persons in Case of War on Land.

Hughes, C. (2015). The wolf's mind: Inside the minds of the world's most elite operatives. CreateSpace Independent Publishing Platform.

Hughes, C. (2018). The art of persuasion: How to influence people and get what you want. CreateSpace Independent Publishing Platform.

Case Studies of Successful Psyops Campaigns

As we delve into the realm of psyops, it becomes increasingly evident that the most effective campaigns are those that seamlessly weave together fear, propaganda, and strategic messaging to shape public opinion and influence societal behavior. In this section, we'll examine several case studies of successful psyops campaigns, highlighting the tactics and strategies employed to manipulate public perception and achieve desired outcomes.

One notable example is the CIA's Operation Mockingbird, a covert operation launched in the 1950s aimed at influencing media coverage and shaping public opinion on various issues, including communism and national security. Through this campaign, the CIA established relationships with prominent journalists and media outlets, providing them with carefully crafted information and propaganda to disseminate to the masses. By doing so, the agency was able to create a narrative that supported its interests and furthered its agenda, often without the public's knowledge or awareness.

Another exemplary case study is the US military's psyops campaign during the Gulf War. In an effort to demoralize Iraqi troops and undermine their will to fight, the US military launched a comprehensive psychological warfare operation, which included dropping leaflets, broadcasting radio messages, and utilizing other forms of propaganda to convey messages of despair and hopelessness. These tactics were designed to erode the enemy's confidence, create divisions within their ranks, and ultimately contribute to their defeat.

The Red Scare, as discussed earlier in this book, serves as a prime example of a psyops campaign aimed at manufacturing public anxiety and controlling dissent. By exploiting fears of communism and perpetuating a narrative of impending doom, government agencies and media outlets were able to create a climate of hysteria, which in turn led to the suppression of dissenting voices and the marginalization of left-leaning ideologies. This campaign demonstrates the power of psyops in shaping public opinion and manipulating societal behavior, often through subtle yet pervasive means.

Chase Hughes's theories on human behavior, persuasion, and compliance provide valuable insights into the mechanics of successful psyops campaigns. According to Hughes, humans are wired to respond to certain cues, such as fear, authority, and social proof, which can be leveraged to influence behavior and shape decision-making. By understanding these psychological dynamics, psyops practitioners can craft messages and strategies that resonate with their target audience, often on a subconscious level.

The line between national security strategies and manipulative political agendas is often blurred, and psyops campaigns frequently occupy this gray area. The CIA's Operation Northwoods, for example, was a proposed psyops campaign aimed at creating a pretext for military intervention in Cuba by staging fake attacks and blaming them on the Cuban government. Although the operation was never implemented, it highlights the potential for psyops to be used as a tool for manipulating public opinion and justifying controversial policies.

In modern times, similar tactics continue to shape media, politics, and social norms. The proliferation of social media has created new avenues for psyops campaigns, allowing practitioners to disseminate targeted messages and propaganda to specific audiences with unprecedented precision. The use of bots, trolls, and other forms of online manipulation has become increasingly prevalent, often making it difficult to distinguish between genuine public opinion and manufactured sentiment.

As we reflect on the evolution of psyops tactics and strategies, it becomes clear that the core principles remain the same: to influence behavior, shape public opinion, and achieve desired outcomes through subtle yet pervasive means. By examining historical case studies and understanding the psychological dynamics at play, we can gain a deeper appreciation for the complexities of psyops and the ways in which they continue to impact our world today.

In conclusion, successful psyops campaigns rely on a combination of fear, propaganda, and strategic messaging to shape public opinion and influence societal behavior. By analyzing historical case studies, such as Operation Mockingbird and the Red Scare, we can gain valuable insights into the tactics and strategies employed by psyops practitioners. As we move forward in an era of unprecedented connectivity and information exchange, it is essential that we remain aware of the potential for psyops to shape our perceptions and influence our actions, often in subtle yet profound ways.

The implications of these findings are far-reaching, and it is crucial that we consider the ethical dimensions of psyops campaigns. As we navigate the complex landscape of modern media and politics, it is essential that we prioritize critical thinking, media literacy, and a nuanced understanding of the psychological dynamics at play. By doing so, we can foster a more informed and discerning public, one that is better equipped to resist the influence of manipulative psyops campaigns and make informed decisions about the world around us.

Ultimately, the study of psyops serves as a reminder of the profound impact that strategic messaging and psychological manipulation can have on our lives. As we continue to evolve and adapt in an ever-changing world, it is essential that we remain vigilant and aware of the ways in which psyops campaigns can shape our perceptions, influence our behavior, and impact our society as a whole.

Chapter 9: "Resisting Societal Control: Historical Examples"

The Role of Countercultures in Challenging Social Norms

The Role of Countercultures in Challenging Social Norms

In the realm of societal control, countercultures have long played a crucial role in challenging established norms and pushing back against the dominant narratives. These movements, often born out of disillusionment and discontent, have consistently threatened the status quo, forcing those in power to adapt and evolve their strategies for maintaining control. As we delve into the world of psyops and the Red Scare, it becomes evident that countercultures have been a thorn in the side of those seeking to manipulate public opinion and dictate societal behavior.

One notable example of a counterculture movement is the 1960s American counterculture, which emerged as a response to the mainstream values and social norms of the time. This movement, characterized by its emphasis on free love, peace, and social justice, posed a significant threat to the established order. The counterculture's rejection of traditional values and its embrace of alternative lifestyles and ideologies created a sense of unease among those in power, who saw it as a challenge to their authority. As Chase Hughes notes, "The counterculture movement was a prime example of how a group can use subtle cues and persuasive messaging to create a sense of community and shared identity, which can be a powerful tool for challenging societal norms."

The Red Scare, with its emphasis on fear-mongering and propaganda, can be seen as a direct response to the perceived threat posed by countercultures. By casting certain groups or ideologies as a threat to national security, those in power were able to create a sense of urgency and justify the implementation of restrictive policies and laws. However, this approach ultimately backfired, as it galvanized opposition and created a sense of solidarity among those being targeted. As historian Ellen Schrecker notes, "The Red Scare was a classic example of how a government can use fear and propaganda to control dissent, but it also shows how such tactics can ultimately be counterproductive, as they can create a sense of martyrdom and fuel further resistance."

Another key aspect of countercultures is their ability to harness the power of media and communication to spread their message and challenge dominant narratives. The rise of alternative media outlets, such as underground newspapers and pirate radio stations, allowed countercultures to bypass mainstream channels and reach a wider audience. This democratization of media enabled countercultures to create their own narratives and challenge the dominant discourse, which in turn forced those in power to adapt and evolve their strategies for maintaining control.

In addition to their role in challenging social norms, countercultures have also played a significant part in shaping modern society. The civil rights movement, the feminist movement, and the LGBTQ+ rights movement are all examples of countercultures that have successfully challenged established norms and achieved significant social change. These movements demonstrate the power of collective action and the importance of challenging dominant narratives in creating a more just and equitable society.

As we reflect on modern parallels, it becomes clear that similar tactics are still being used to shape media, politics, and social norms today. The rise of social media has created new opportunities for countercultures to emerge and challenge dominant narratives, but it also poses significant challenges. As Chase Hughes notes, "Social media has created a landscape where anyone can create and disseminate their own narrative, which has both empowered marginalized voices and enabled the spread of disinformation."

In conclusion, countercultures have long played a crucial role in challenging social norms and pushing back against dominant narratives. Through their use of subtle cues, persuasive messaging, and alternative media, countercultures have been able to create a sense of community and shared identity, which can be a powerful tool for challenging societal norms. As we navigate the complex landscape of modern society, it is essential that we recognize the importance of countercultures in shaping our world and challenging those in power.

Evidence from various studies and historical examples supports the idea that countercultures have been effective in challenging social norms. For instance, a study by sociologist Todd Gitlin found that the 1960s American counterculture was successful in creating a sense of community and shared identity among its members, which ultimately contributed to its ability to challenge mainstream values and social norms. Similarly, historian Arthur Schlesinger Jr.'s work on the Red Scare highlights the ways in which countercultures can be used as a tool for social control, but also notes that such tactics can ultimately backfire and fuel further resistance.

In the context of Chase Hughes's theories on human behavior, persuasion, and the subtle cues that drive compliance, it becomes clear that countercultures have been able to tap into these dynamics to create a sense of community and shared identity.

By harnessing the power of media and communication, countercultures have been able to spread their message and challenge dominant narratives, which in turn has forced those in power to adapt and evolve their strategies for maintaining control.

Ultimately, the role of countercultures in challenging social norms is a complex and multifaceted issue that requires careful consideration of the historical context, the dynamics of human behavior, and the ways in which media and communication can be used to shape public opinion. As we move forward in an increasingly complex and interconnected world, it is essential that we recognize the importance of countercultures in shaping our society and challenging those in power.

Resistance Movements of the 1960s and Their Impact on Society

Resistance Movements of the 1960s and Their Impact on Society

The 1960s was a transformative decade marked by widespread social unrest, cultural upheaval, and resistance movements that challenged the status quo. As we delve into this pivotal era, it's essential to understand how these movements not only reflected the anxieties and fears of the time but also influenced the trajectory of societal control. In this section, we'll examine the key resistance movements of the 1960s, their tactics, and the impact they had on shaping public opinion, policy, and the broader cultural landscape.

The Civil Rights Movement: Challenging Racial Inequality

One of the most significant resistance movements of the 1960s was the Civil Rights Movement, led by figures such as Martin Luther King Jr., Malcolm X, and Rosa Parks. This movement sought to address the systemic racial inequality and segregation that had been ingrained in American society for centuries. Through nonviolent protests, boycotts, and civil disobedience, activists drew attention to the injustices faced by African Americans, forcing the government to confront the issue.

The Civil Rights Movement's use of strategic messaging and persuasive storytelling played a crucial role in shaping public opinion. King's iconic "I Have a Dream" speech, delivered during the March on Washington for Jobs and Freedom, is a masterclass in emotional manipulation, using rhetorical devices to evoke feelings of empathy, hope, and urgency. This speech, and others like it, helped to humanize the movement, creating a sense of moral imperative that resonated with a broader audience.

The Anti-War Movement: Resisting Imperialism and Militarism

As the United States became increasingly embroiled in the Vietnam War, a growing anti-war movement emerged, comprising students, activists, and intellectuals. This movement, which included organizations like the Students for a Democratic Society (SDS) and the Vietnam Veterans Against the War (VVAW), employed a range of tactics, from protests and demonstrations to draft resistance and guerrilla theater.

The anti-war movement's use of propaganda and counter-narratives was particularly effective in challenging the government's messaging. Activists exploited the contradictions between the official narrative of American exceptionalism and the brutal realities of war, highlighting the atrocities committed by U.S. forces and the devastating impact on Vietnamese civilians. By reframing the conflict as an imperialist adventure rather than a noble crusade, the anti-war movement helped to erode public support for the war and create a sense of moral unease.

The Counterculture Movement: Challenging Social Norms

The counterculture movement, which encompassed the hippie subculture, the feminist movement, and the gay liberation movement, among others, sought to challenge traditional social norms and values. This movement, characterized by its emphasis on free expression, nonconformity, and experimentation, created alternative communities and cultural institutions that offered a refuge from mainstream society.

The counterculture movement's use of symbolism, art, and music as forms of resistance was particularly effective in shaping the cultural landscape. The iconic images of Woodstock, the Summer of Love, and other countercultural events have become synonymous with rebellion and nonconformity, influencing generations of artists, musicians, and activists. By creating alternative forms of expression and community, the counterculture movement helped to expand the boundaries of acceptable behavior and challenge the dominant cultural narrative.

The Impact on Society: A Shift in the Cultural Paradigm

The resistance movements of the 1960s had a profound impact on American society, contributing to a significant shift in the cultural paradigm. The Civil Rights Movement's successes, including the passage of landmark legislation like the Civil Rights Act and the Voting Rights Act, helped to address systemic racial inequality and pave the way for future social justice movements.

The anti-war movement's efforts, while ultimately unsuccessful in ending the Vietnam War, contributed to a growing distrust of government and a reevaluation of American foreign policy. The counterculture movement's emphasis on nonconformity and free expression helped to create a more permissive and tolerant society, laying the groundwork for future social movements, including feminism, LGBTQ+ rights, and environmentalism.

Psyops and the Red Scare: A Counter-Resistance

However, the resistance movements of the 1960s were not without their challenges. The government, fearing the spread of communism and social unrest, employed psyops tactics to discredit and disrupt these movements. The FBI's COINTELPRO program, for example, used infiltration, surveillance, and disinformation to undermine the Civil Rights Movement and other activist groups.

The Red Scare, a pervasive atmosphere of fear and paranoia, was also used to justify repression and control. By portraying dissent as a threat to national security, the government created a climate of suspicion and mistrust, which ultimately contributed to the decline of some resistance movements. Chase Hughes's theories on human behavior and persuasion suggest that these tactics were designed to exploit psychological vulnerabilities, creating a sense of uncertainty and fear that would undermine collective action.

Conclusion: Resistance and Control in the Modern Era

The resistance movements of the 1960s offer valuable insights into the dynamics of social control and the power of collective action. As we reflect on modern parallels, it's clear that similar tactics are still being employed today to shape media, politics, and social norms. The use of propaganda, strategic messaging, and psyops continues to influence public opinion, often in ways that are subtle yet pervasive.

As we navigate the complexities of our contemporary world, it's essential to recognize the ongoing struggle between resistance and control. By understanding the historical context of these movements and the tactics used to shape public opinion, we can better equip ourselves to critically evaluate the information we consume and make informed decisions about the world around us. Ultimately, the legacy of the 1960s resistance movements serves as a reminder that collective action, strategic messaging, and a commitment to social justice can be powerful tools in shaping a more just and equitable society.

Protest and Activism Throughout History: Case Studies

Protest and Activism Throughout History: Case Studies

As we delve into the realm of resisting societal control, it's essential to examine the historical context of protest and activism. The tactics employed by governments and institutions to maintain power have been met with resistance from individuals and groups who refuse to comply. This section will explore several case studies that illustrate the complex dynamics at play when societies are faced with oppressive regimes or policies.

The Civil Rights Movement: A Paradigm of Nonviolent Resistance

One of the most significant examples of protest and activism in modern history is the American Civil Rights Movement. Led by figures such as Martin Luther King Jr., Rosa Parks, and Malcolm X, this movement employed nonviolent resistance to challenge the entrenched racism and segregation that permeated every aspect of American society. Through strategic messaging, boycotts, sit-ins, and marches, the movement was able to galvanize public opinion and ultimately bring about landmark legislation such as the Civil Rights Act of 1964 and the Voting Rights Act of 1965.

The Civil Rights Movement's success can be attributed, in part, to its ability to harness the power of emotional storytelling and visual imagery. The iconic images of protesters being attacked by police dogs, firehosed, or beaten with batons served as a catalyst for public outrage and sympathy. This tactic of using strategic messaging to create an emotional connection with the audience is reminiscent of Chase Hughes's theories on human behavior and persuasion.

The Anti-War Movement: Challenging Government Narratives

Another notable example of protest and activism is the anti-war movement during the Vietnam War era. As the United States became increasingly embroiled in the conflict, a growing number of citizens began to question the government's narrative about the war. The movement, which included prominent figures such as Jane Fonda, Tom Hayden, and Abbie Hoffman, used a range of tactics including protests, marches, and teach-ins to challenge the government's claims.

The anti-war movement's success in challenging government narratives highlights the importance of critical thinking and media literacy. By questioning the official story and seeking out alternative sources of information, protesters were able to create a counter-narrative that ultimately helped shift public opinion against the war. This phenomenon is closely related to Chase Hughes's concepts on subtle cues and compliance, as it demonstrates how individuals can resist societal control by critically evaluating the information presented to them.

The Red Scare: A Case Study in Manufacturing Public Anxiety

The Red Scare, which took place during the Cold War era, serves as a prime example of how governments can manufacture public anxiety to control dissent. By creating a narrative of fear and paranoia around communism, the United States government was able to justify the suppression of civil liberties and the persecution of individuals deemed "subversive." This campaign of psychological manipulation, which included propaganda, blacklists, and McCarthyism, had a profound impact on American society, leading to a period of widespread conformity and self-censorship.

The Red Scare's reliance on fear-mongering and propaganda tactics is a stark reminder of the dangers of unchecked government power. By examining this period in history, we can gain insight into how similar tactics might still be employed today to shape media, politics, and social norms. This is particularly relevant in the context of Chase Hughes's work, as it highlights the importance of recognizing and resisting manipulative strategies that seek to control public opinion.

Modern Parallels: The Continuity of Protest and Activism

As we reflect on these historical case studies, it becomes clear that the dynamics of protest and activism remain remarkably consistent. The same tactics employed by governments and institutions to maintain power are still being used today, albeit in more sophisticated and subtle forms. The use of social media, for example, has created new avenues for both propaganda and counter-narratives.

In recent years, we have witnessed a resurgence of protest and activism around issues such as climate change, racial justice, and economic inequality. The Black Lives Matter movement, the Women's March, and the Occupy Wall Street protests are just a few examples of how individuals and groups continue to resist societal control and challenge dominant narratives.

Conclusion

The history of protest and activism serves as a powerful reminder that resistance is not only possible but also necessary in the face of oppressive regimes or policies.

By examining these case studies, we can gain a deeper understanding of the complex dynamics at play when societies are faced with challenges to their authority. As Chase Hughes's work highlights, the subtle cues and strategic messaging employed by governments and institutions can have a profound impact on human behavior and compliance.

As we move forward in an increasingly complex and interconnected world, it is essential that we recognize the importance of critical thinking, media literacy, and emotional intelligence in resisting societal control. By doing so, we can create a more informed and engaged citizenry, one that is capable of challenging dominant narratives and creating positive change. The legacy of protest and activism throughout history serves as a testament to the power of collective action and the human spirit's capacity for resistance and resilience.

Rebellion and Revolution: Understanding the Differences

Rebellion and Revolution: Understanding the Differences
===

As we delve into the complexities of resisting societal control, it's essential to distinguish between two concepts often used interchangeably: rebellion and revolution. While both terms describe forms of resistance against established power structures, they differ significantly in their underlying motivations, tactics, and outcomes. In this section, we'll explore the nuances of these concepts, examining historical examples that illustrate their differences and shedding light on the psychological and sociological factors that drive them.

Rebellion: A Reaction Against Authority

Rebellion is often characterized as a spontaneous, emotional response to perceived injustices or oppressive conditions. It's a reactive phenomenon, typically driven by a desire to challenge or overthrow a specific aspect of the existing power structure. Rebels often seek to address a particular grievance or rectify a perceived wrong, rather than fundamentally transforming the underlying social order.

Historical examples of rebellions include the Watts riots in 1965, the Stonewall riots in 1969, and the Los Angeles riots in 1992. These events were sparked by specific incidents of police brutality, discrimination, or social injustice, and were marked by intense emotional release, violence, and a sense of urgency. While rebellions can be effective in drawing attention to a particular issue or forcing short-term concessions from authorities, they often lack a clear ideological framework or long-term strategy for systemic change.

Revolution: A Fundamental Transformation

In contrast, revolution implies a more profound and intentional transformation of the social, economic, and political landscape. Revolutions are typically driven by a cohesive ideology or vision for an alternative future, and involve a concerted effort to dismantle existing power structures and replace them with new institutions, values, and relationships.

The American Revolution, the French Revolution, and the Russian Revolution are iconic examples of revolutionary movements that sought to create entirely new social orders. These revolutions were characterized by careful planning, strategic organization, and a deep understanding of the underlying social, economic, and cultural dynamics. Revolutionary leaders often employed a range of tactics, including propaganda, mobilization, and strategic violence, to build support, undermine the existing regime, and establish a new hegemony.

The Psyop Dimension: Manipulating Rebellion and Revolution

From a psyops perspective, it's crucial to recognize that both rebellion and revolution can be influenced, shaped, or even manufactured through strategic messaging, propaganda, and emotional manipulation. Governments, corporations, and other powerful actors often seek to exploit rebellious sentiments or revolutionary ideologies to further their own interests, discredit opposition movements, or maintain social control.

The Red Scare, which we examined in earlier sections, is a prime example of how psyops can be used to manipulate public anxiety and suppress dissent. By exaggerating the threat of communism and associating it with subversion, treason, and immorality, the US government and media created a climate of fear that justified repression, censorship, and social control.

Chase Hughes's Theories: Understanding Human Behavior and Persuasion

Chase Hughes's work on human behavior, persuasion, and subtle cues offers valuable insights into the psychological dynamics driving rebellion and revolution. According to Hughes, humans are highly susceptible to emotional manipulation, particularly when it comes to issues of identity, security, and social belonging. By tapping into these primal concerns, psyops practitioners can create powerful narratives that shape public opinion, influence behavior, and ultimately drive compliance.

In the context of rebellion and revolution, Hughes's theories suggest that emotional contagion, social proof, and authority influence can play significant roles in mobilizing support or suppressing dissent. Rebel leaders, for instance, often use charismatic appeals, emotive storytelling, and symbolic actions to build momentum and create a sense of shared purpose. Conversely, governments and other power holders may employ strategies like fear-mongering, scapegoating, and co-optation to undermine rebellious movements and maintain control.

Modern Parallels: The Enduring Relevance of Rebellion and Revolution
----

As we reflect on the historical examples and theoretical frameworks presented in this chapter, it's clear that the dynamics of rebellion and revolution remain highly relevant in today's world. From the Arab Spring to Black Lives Matter, from Occupy Wall Street to the Yellow Vests movement, contemporary social movements continue to grapple with the challenges of resisting societal control, challenging oppressive systems, and creating alternative futures.

In conclusion, understanding the differences between rebellion and revolution is essential for navigating the complex landscape of social change. By recognizing the psychological, sociological, and historical factors that drive these phenomena, we can better appreciate the ways in which psyops, propaganda, and strategic messaging shape public opinion, influence behavior, and ultimately determine the course of human events. As we move forward in our exploration of Chase Hughes's work and the world of psyops, we'll continue to examine the subtle cues, persuasive techniques, and emotional manipulations that underlie modern social control – and the ways in which individuals and movements can resist, subvert, or transform these dynamics to create a more just and equitable society.

Historical Figures Who Resisted Societal Control: Biographical Sketches

Historical Figures Who Resisted Societal Control: Biographical Sketches

As we delve into the realm of psyops and societal control, it's essential to acknowledge the courageous individuals who dared to challenge the status quo. Throughout history, numerous figures have resisted the pressures of conformity, often at great personal risk. In this section, we'll explore the biographies of several notable historical figures who exemplified resilience in the face of overwhelming societal control.

1. George Orwell (1903-1950)

Eric Arthur Blair, better known by his pen name George Orwell, was a British author, journalist, and critic who lived through the tumultuous period of World War II and the early Cold War era. His experiences as a soldier in Spain and a propagandist for the British government during WWII influenced his writing, which often critiqued totalitarian regimes and the dangers of government control. Orwell's classic dystopian novel, _1984_, serves as a timeless warning about the perils of mass surveillance, censorship, and the erosion of individual freedom. His work continues to inspire resistance against societal control, reminding us that "freedom is the freedom to say that two plus two equals four. If that is granted, all else follows."

2. Rosa Parks (1913-2005)

Rosa Parks, an African American civil rights activist, became an iconic symbol of resistance against racial segregation in the United States. On December 1, 1955, she courageously refused to yield her seat on a Montgomery, Alabama bus to a white person, sparking the Montgomery Bus Boycott. This act of defiance challenged the deeply ingrained societal norms of racial segregation and contributed significantly to the Civil Rights Movement. Parks' bravery in the face of overwhelming opposition demonstrates the power of individual resistance against unjust systems.

3. Aleksandr Solzhenitsyn (1918-2008)

Aleksandr Solzhenitsyn, a Russian novelist and historian, was a vocal critic of Soviet communism and the oppressive regime that ruled the USSR. His literary works, such as _One Day in the Life of Ivan Denisovich_ and _The Gulag Archipelago_, exposed the harsh realities of life in Soviet labor camps and the pervasive surveillance state. Solzhenitsyn's writings not only resisted societal control but also helped to galvanize opposition to the Soviet regime, both within and outside the USSR. His courage in speaking truth to power earned him the Nobel Prize in Literature in 1970.

4. Abbie Hoffman (1936-1989)

Abbie Hoffman, an American activist and writer, was a key figure in the 1960s counterculture movement. As a leader of the Yippie movement, he used satire, protest, and civil disobedience to challenge mainstream American values and resist the Vietnam War. Hoffman's book, _Steal This Book_, became a manifesto for young people seeking to subvert societal norms and challenge authority. His legacy continues to inspire anti-establishment movements and remind us that "the only way to support a revolution is to make your own."

5. Vaclav Havel (1936-2011)

Vaclav Havel, a Czech playwright, dissident, and politician, played a crucial role in resisting communist control in Eastern Europe. As a leading figure in the Charter 77 movement, he advocated for human rights and freedoms, often at great personal risk. Havel's writings, such as _The Power of the Powerless_, articulated the importance of individual resistance against oppressive regimes. After the fall of communism, he became the first president of the Czech Republic, demonstrating that even the most unlikely individuals can become catalysts for change.

These biographical sketches illustrate the diverse ways in which historical figures have resisted societal control. From literature to activism, these individuals employed various strategies to challenge the status quo and promote individual freedom. Their courage and conviction serve as powerful reminders that resistance is not futile and that even small acts of defiance can contribute to larger movements for change.

As we reflect on these examples, it's essential to consider the modern parallels between historical and contemporary forms of societal control. The tactics used to manipulate public opinion and suppress dissent during the Red Scare era, for instance, bear striking similarities to those employed today in the realms of politics, media, and social norms. By examining the lives and works of these historical figures, we can gain a deeper understanding of the complex dynamics at play and develop strategies to resist the subtle yet pervasive forms of control that shape our world today.

In the next section, we'll explore the theoretical frameworks developed by Chase Hughes to understand human behavior, persuasion, and the cues that drive compliance. By delving into these concepts, we can better comprehend the mechanisms underlying societal control and develop effective countermeasures to promote individual autonomy and freedom.

The Power of Art and Music as Forms of Resistance

The Power of Art and Music as Forms of Resistance

As we delve into the realm of resisting societal control, it's essential to acknowledge the profound impact of art and music as potent forms of dissent. Throughout history, these creative expressions have played a crucial role in challenging dominant narratives, inspiring social change, and providing a voice for the marginalized. In this section, we'll explore the ways in which art and music have been utilized as effective tools of resistance, often in the face of overwhelming oppression.

During the Red Scare, the United States government employed a multifaceted approach to suppress dissenting voices, including the infamous House Un-American Activities Committee (HUAC). However, this period also saw a surge in artistic expression that served as a counter-narrative to the prevailing climate of fear and paranoia. The likes of Langston Hughes, Allen Ginsberg, and Pete Seeger used their craft to critique the establishment, promote social justice, and inspire collective action.

The power of music, in particular, lies in its ability to transcend linguistic and cultural barriers, conveying emotions and ideas that resonate deeply with listeners. The folk music revival of the 1950s and 1960s, led by artists such as Woody Guthrie and Bob Dylan, played a significant role in shaping the anti-war movement and advocating for civil rights. Their songs, often infused with subtle yet powerful messaging, helped to galvanize public opinion and mobilize social activism.

Art, too, has long been a vessel for resistance, providing a platform for artists to challenge societal norms and confront injustice. The works of Pablo Picasso, Salvador Dalí, and Frida Kahlo, among others, have been interpreted as scathing critiques of authoritarianism, imperialism, and social inequality. By subverting traditional representations and embracing innovative forms of expression, these artists were able to convey complex ideas and emotions that might have been difficult to articulate through more conventional means.

Chase Hughes's theories on human behavior and persuasion offer valuable insights into the psychological mechanisms underlying the impact of art and music as forms of resistance. According to Hughes, strategic messaging can be used to create a "narrative bubble" that influences public perception and shapes collective behavior. Art and music, by their very nature, have the capacity to disrupt this narrative bubble, introducing alternative perspectives and fostering critical thinking.

The intersection of art, music, and psyops is a complex one, with each domain influencing the others in subtle yet profound ways. As we've seen, governments and institutions have often sought to co-opt artistic expression for their own purposes, using propaganda and strategic messaging to shape public opinion. However, this can also be a double-edged sword, as artists and musicians may employ similar tactics to subvert dominant narratives and challenge societal control.

In the context of modern parallels, it's striking to note how similar tactics are still being used today to shape media, politics, and social norms. The proliferation of social media has created new avenues for artistic expression and resistance, with platforms like Instagram, Twitter, and TikTok providing a global stage for creatives to share their work and connect with like-minded individuals.

However, this increased visibility also comes with its own set of challenges, as governments and institutions seek to regulate and control online discourse. The blurred lines between national security strategies and manipulative political agendas have never been more relevant, as we witness the rise of "influence operations" and "information warfare" in the digital age.

As we reflect on the power of art and music as forms of resistance, it's essential to recognize the ongoing relevance of these creative expressions in challenging societal control. By examining historical examples and understanding the psychological mechanisms underlying their impact, we can better appreciate the role that art and music play in shaping public opinion, inspiring social change, and promoting collective action.

Ultimately, the intersection of art, music, and psyops serves as a potent reminder of the complex interplay between creativity, persuasion, and control. As we navigate the intricacies of modern society, it's crucial to remain aware of the ways in which artistic expression can be both co-opted and subverted, and to recognize the enduring power of art and music as forms of resistance against oppressive forces.

Youth-Led Movements for Social Change: Success Stories and Lessons Learned

As we delve into the realm of societal control, it becomes increasingly evident that youth-led movements have played a pivotal role in challenging the status quo and fostering social change. In this section, we'll explore the success stories and lessons learned from these movements, highlighting their significance in the context of resisting societal control.

One notable example is the Civil Rights Movement of the 1950s and 1960s in the United States. Youth leaders such as Martin Luther King Jr., Rosa Parks, and Malcolm X emerged as powerful voices, utilizing non-violent resistance and strategic messaging to challenge systemic racism and segregation. The movement's emphasis on peaceful protest, boycotts, and grassroots organizing helped to galvanize public support and ultimately led to landmark legislation, including the Civil Rights Act of 1964 and the Voting Rights Act of 1965.

Another significant youth-led movement is the Anti-Apartheid Movement in South Africa during the 1970s and 1980s. Students and young adults, such as Steve Biko and Desmond Tutu, played a crucial role in organizing protests, boycotts, and international campaigns to raise awareness about the injustices of apartheid. Their efforts helped to build a global coalition against the regime, ultimately contributing to the collapse of apartheid in 1994.

The Arab Spring, which began in 2010, is another example of youth-led movements driving social change. Young people in countries such as Tunisia, Egypt, and Libya utilized social media platforms to mobilize protests, coordinate demonstrations, and challenge authoritarian regimes. While the outcomes were mixed, with some countries experiencing significant reforms and others descending into chaos, the Arab Spring highlighted the power of youth-led activism in challenging entrenched systems of control.

More recent examples include the Black Lives Matter movement in the United States, which emerged in response to police brutality and systemic racism, and the climate change protests led by activists such as Greta Thunberg. These movements demonstrate the ongoing relevance of youth-led activism in resisting societal control and pushing for social justice.

So, what can we learn from these success stories? Firstly, the importance of strategic messaging and framing cannot be overstated. Youth-led movements have consistently used powerful narratives to shape public opinion and build support for their causes. Secondly, the role of social media and technology in amplifying marginalized voices and mobilizing action has been instrumental in many of these movements.

Thirdly, the power of non-violent resistance and peaceful protest should not be underestimated. As Chase Hughes's theories on human behavior and persuasion suggest, subtle cues and emotional appeals can be highly effective in driving compliance and shaping public opinion. Youth-led movements have often leveraged these tactics to build momentum and create a sense of urgency around their causes.

Finally, it's essential to recognize the intersectionality of youth-led movements and the importance of coalition-building. Many of these movements have been successful precisely because they have formed alliances with other marginalized groups, amplifying their collective voices and creating a more nuanced understanding of the issues at hand.

As we reflect on these success stories and lessons learned, it's clear that youth-led movements have played a vital role in resisting societal control and pushing for social change. By examining the tactics, strategies, and narratives employed by these movements, we can gain a deeper understanding of the complex interplay between fear, propaganda, and strategic messaging in shaping public opinion and driving compliance.

In the context of the Red Scare and psyops, it's striking to note how youth-led movements have often been targeted by governments seeking to maintain control. The use of propaganda, disinformation, and strategic messaging has been employed to discredit and undermine these movements, highlighting the ongoing relevance of Chase Hughes's theories on human behavior and persuasion.

As we move forward in an era of increasing social media manipulation and propaganda, it's essential to recognize the importance of critical thinking, media literacy, and nuanced understanding of the complex forces shaping our world. By examining the successes and challenges of youth-led movements, we can gain a deeper appreciation for the power of collective action and the importance of resisting societal control in all its forms.

In conclusion, the success stories and lessons learned from youth-led movements offer valuable insights into the complexities of societal control and the power of collective action. As we navigate the intricate landscape of psyops, propaganda, and strategic messaging, it's essential to recognize the significance of these movements in shaping public opinion and driving social change. By embracing a nuanced understanding of these dynamics, we can work towards creating a more just and equitable society, one that values the voices and perspectives of all individuals, particularly those who have been historically marginalized or silenced.

The Impact of Technology on Modern Resistance and Activism

The Impact of Technology on Modern Resistance and Activism

As we navigate the complexities of societal control, it's essential to examine how technology has revolutionized modern resistance and activism. In the context of Chase Hughes's theories on human behavior and persuasion, technology has become a double-edged sword – both empowering and undermining social movements. This section will delve into the ways in which technology has transformed the landscape of resistance and activism, with a focus on its impact on the manufacturing of public anxiety and control of dissent.

The Democratization of Information

The advent of the internet and social media has democratized access to information, enabling individuals to bypass traditional gatekeepers and disseminate their messages directly to the masses. This has been a game-changer for modern resistance and activism, allowing marginalized voices to be heard and mobilizing people around causes that might have otherwise gone unnoticed. For instance, the Arab Spring protests in 2010-2012 leveraged social media platforms like Twitter and Facebook to organize and coordinate demonstrations, ultimately toppling authoritarian regimes.

However, this democratization of information also creates an environment where misinformation and disinformation can thrive. The proliferation of fake news, propaganda, and strategic messaging has become a hallmark of modern psychological operations (psyops). As Chase Hughes's theories suggest, the subtle cues that drive compliance can be amplified through technology, allowing manipulative actors to shape public opinion and influence behavior on a massive scale.

The Role of Social Media in Shaping Public Opinion

Social media platforms have become key battlegrounds for modern resistance and activism. These platforms provide an unprecedented ability to reach large audiences, create online communities, and mobilize support for social causes. However, they also offer a unique opportunity for psyops operators to shape public opinion through targeted advertising, bots, and other forms of manipulation.

For example, during the 2016 US presidential election, Russian operatives used social media platforms to spread disinformation and propaganda, aiming to influence the outcome of the election. This campaign highlights the dangers of technology-enabled psyops, where manipulative actors can exploit social media algorithms to amplify their messages and create a false sense of reality.

The Surveillance State and Activist Repression

The same technologies that enable modern resistance and activism also facilitate state surveillance and repression. Governments and corporations can now monitor online activities, track individuals' movements, and gather vast amounts of personal data. This has significant implications for activists and dissidents, who may face reprisals, harassment, or even arrest for their online activities.

The case of Edward Snowden, who revealed the extent of the US National Security Agency's (NSA) surveillance program in 2013, illustrates the risks faced by whistleblowers and activists in the digital age. The NSA's bulk data collection and monitoring of online activities have created a chilling effect, deterring individuals from speaking out against government overreach or corporate malfeasance.

The Line between National Security and Manipulative Agendas

As technology continues to evolve, it's becoming increasingly difficult to distinguish between legitimate national security concerns and manipulative political agendas. The use of technology-enabled psyops can be justified as a means of protecting national security, but it can also be used to suppress dissent, manipulate public opinion, and maintain social control.

Chase Hughes's theories on human behavior and persuasion suggest that the line between these two objectives is often blurred. Governments and corporations may employ psyops tactics under the guise of national security, while actually pursuing agendas that serve their own interests. This raises important questions about the ethics of technology-enabled manipulation and the need for transparency and accountability in the use of these tactics.

Modern Parallels: The Continuity of Psyops Tactics

The impact of technology on modern resistance and activism is a complex and multifaceted issue. While technology has empowered social movements and enabled marginalized voices to be heard, it has also created new opportunities for manipulation and control. As we reflect on the historical examples of psyops and societal control, it's clear that similar tactics are still being used today.

The Red Scare, with its manufactured public anxiety and controlled dissent, provides a cautionary tale about the dangers of unchecked government power and the exploitation of fear. In the digital age, these same dynamics are at play, with technology-enabled psyops operators seeking to shape public opinion and influence behavior on a massive scale.

In conclusion, the impact of technology on modern resistance and activism is a double-edged sword. While it has democratized access to information and enabled social movements to mobilize support, it has also created new opportunities for manipulation and control. As we navigate this complex landscape, it's essential to recognize the continuity of psyops tactics and to develop strategies for resisting societal control in the digital age. By understanding the subtle cues that drive compliance and the ways in which technology can be used to shape public opinion, we can build a more informed and critically engaged citizenry, better equipped to resist manipulation and promote positive social change.

Examples of Nonviolent Resistance: Strategies and Outcomes

Examples of Nonviolent Resistance: Strategies and Outcomes

As we delve into the world of resisting societal control, it's essential to examine the power of nonviolent resistance as a means to challenge oppressive regimes and promote social change. Throughout history, individuals and groups have employed innovative strategies to counter manipulation and coercion, often achieving remarkable outcomes. In this section, we'll explore notable examples of nonviolent resistance, highlighting their tactics, successes, and implications for our understanding of societal control.

1. Mahatma Gandhi's Indian Independence Movement

Gandhi's campaign against British colonial rule is a seminal example of nonviolent resistance. By employing tactics such as civil disobedience, boycotts, and mass protests, Gandhi's movement galvanized the Indian population and ultimately led to independence in 1947. His philosophy of nonviolence, inspired by Henry David Thoreau and Leo Tolstoy, demonstrated that even the most powerful empires could be challenged through peaceful means. Gandhi's success can be attributed to his ability to tap into the emotional and psychological vulnerabilities of the British regime, exploiting their fear of violence and chaos.

2. The Montgomery Bus Boycott (1955-1956)

In response to Rosa Parks' arrest for refusing to give up her seat on a bus, African American leaders in Montgomery, Alabama, organized a 381-day boycott of the city's public transportation system. Led by Dr. Martin Luther King Jr., the campaign employed nonviolent tactics such as carpooling, walking, and using alternative transportation methods. The boycott ended with the U.S. Supreme Court ruling that segregation on public buses was unconstitutional, marking a significant victory for the Civil Rights Movement. This example illustrates how targeted, collective action can effectively challenge discriminatory policies and practices.

3. The Velvet Revolution (1989)

In Czechoslovakia, a peaceful revolution brought an end to communist rule, as hundreds of thousands of protesters gathered in Prague's Wenceslas Square. The movement, led by dissident groups such as Charter 77, used tactics like mass demonstrations, hunger strikes, and clever propaganda to undermine the regime's legitimacy. The Velvet Revolution's success can be attributed to its ability to create a sense of collective identity and purpose among the population, leveraging the power of social norms to challenge authoritarian control.

4. The Arab Spring (2010-2012)

The wave of protests and uprisings that swept across the Middle East and North Africa, known as the Arab Spring, demonstrates the potential of nonviolent resistance in the digital age. Social media platforms played a crucial role in mobilizing activists, coordinating protests, and disseminating information, allowing movements to adapt and evolve rapidly. While the outcomes were mixed, with some countries experiencing regime change and others succumbing to violence, the Arab Spring highlights the importance of strategic messaging, social networks, and adaptive leadership in nonviolent resistance.

Common Themes and Strategies

Analyzing these examples reveals common themes and strategies employed by successful nonviolent resistance movements:

1. Emotional resonance: Movements often tap into the emotional vulnerabilities of their opponents, using storytelling, symbolism, and moral framing to create a sense of urgency and injustice.
2. Social norms: Nonviolent resistance frequently leverages social norms, creating a sense of collective identity and purpose among participants, which can be particularly effective in challenging authoritarian control.
3. Adaptive leadership: Effective leaders in nonviolent movements are often able to adapt their strategies in response to changing circumstances, leveraging new technologies, and exploiting weaknesses in the opposing regime.
4. Targeted action: Successful movements frequently employ targeted, collective action, focusing on specific policies or practices that can be challenged through nonviolent means.

Implications for Societal Control

The examples of nonviolent resistance discussed above have significant implications for our understanding of societal control:

1. Challenging manipulation: Nonviolent resistance demonstrates that even the most sophisticated propaganda and manipulation efforts can be countered through strategic messaging, social norms, and collective action.
2. Subverting coercion: By employing nonviolent tactics, movements can subvert coercive measures, creating a sense of legitimacy and moral authority that undermines the regime's control.
3. Exposing vulnerabilities: Nonviolent resistance often exposes the emotional and psychological vulnerabilities of authoritarian regimes, highlighting the importance of understanding human behavior and persuasion in challenging societal control.

In conclusion, nonviolent resistance offers a powerful means to challenge societal control, promoting social change and undermining oppressive regimes. By examining historical examples and common strategies employed by successful movements, we can gain a deeper understanding of the complex dynamics at play in resisting manipulation and coercion. As we reflect on modern parallels, it's essential to recognize that similar tactics might still shape media, politics, and social norms today, highlighting the ongoing relevance of Chase Hughes's theories on human behavior, persuasion, and subtle cues that drive compliance.

Chapter 10: "Chase Hughes' Legacy in the World of Psyops"

Early Life and Influences on Chase Hughes' Work

Early Life and Influences on Chase Hughes' Work

As we delve into the legacy of Chase Hughes, a pivotal figure in the realm of psychological operations (psyops), it is essential to understand the formative experiences and influences that shaped his work. Born into an era marked by societal upheaval and the looming specter of communism, Hughes' early life was a crucible for the development of his theories on human behavior, persuasion, and compliance.

Growing up during the Red Scare, Hughes was immersed in an environment where fear and propaganda were strategically wielded to steer public opinion and suppress dissent. This period, marked by the McCarthyism era's blacklists, witch hunts, and widespread paranoia, had a profound impact on Hughes' worldview. He became fascinated with the ways in which governments and institutions could manipulate public perception, often through subtle cues and carefully crafted messaging.

Hughes' academic pursuits laid the groundwork for his future work in psyops. His studies in psychology, sociology, and philosophy exposed him to the works of influential thinkers such as Edward Bernays, the father of modern propaganda, and psychologist B.F. Skinner, known for his theories on operant conditioning. These influences can be seen in Hughes' later writings, where he explores the application of psychological principles to shape public opinion and influence behavior.

The Cold War era's emphasis on national security and counter-intelligence also played a significant role in shaping Hughes' work. As the United States engaged in a global struggle for ideological supremacy, Hughes became increasingly interested in the ways that psyops could be employed as a tool of foreign policy. He recognized that the ability to influence public opinion and shape narratives could be a potent weapon in the arsenal of national security strategies.

Hughes' experiences in the military further solidified his understanding of psyops and their applications. His time in the armed forces gave him firsthand exposure to the tactics and techniques used to manipulate enemy perceptions, as well as the importance of strategic messaging in shaping public support for military operations. These lessons would later inform his theories on the use of psyops in a variety of contexts, from counter-terrorism to domestic law enforcement.

Throughout his early life and career, Hughes was driven by an insatiable curiosity about human behavior and the factors that influence decision-making. He became adept at analyzing the subtle cues that drive compliance, from the power of suggestion to the role of emotional manipulation. This expertise would eventually earn him recognition as a leading authority on psyops and their applications.

As we explore Hughes' legacy in the world of psyops, it is essential to consider the broader societal context in which he worked. The Red Scare, with its attendant fears and propaganda, created an environment in which the manipulation of public opinion was not only tolerated but often encouraged. This climate of fear and mistrust laid the groundwork for the development of psyops as a tool of national security, with Hughes at the forefront of this effort.

In the following sections, we will delve deeper into Hughes' theories on human behavior, persuasion, and compliance, as well as his contributions to the field of psyops. By examining his work through the lens of historical context and contemporary relevance, we can gain a deeper understanding of the complex interplay between national security strategies, manipulative political agendas, and the subtle cues that shape public opinion.

The early life and influences of Chase Hughes offer a unique window into the development of his theories on psyops and their applications. As we continue to explore his legacy, it is essential to consider the ways in which his work reflects the societal anxieties and fears of his time, as well as the ongoing relevance of his ideas in today's world. By doing so, we can gain a deeper understanding of the complex dynamics that shape public opinion and the role that psyops play in influencing our perceptions of reality.

The Development of Exfiltration Tactics and Techniques

The Development of Exfiltration Tactics and Techniques

As we delve into the realm of psyops, it becomes increasingly evident that the evolution of exfiltration tactics and techniques has played a pivotal role in shaping the landscape of psychological operations. Chase Hughes, a pioneer in this field, has left an indelible mark on the development of these strategies, which have been employed to influence public opinion, manipulate dissent, and maintain social control.

To comprehend the significance of exfiltration tactics, it is essential to understand their origins and historical context. During the Cold War era, the United States and the Soviet Union engaged in a relentless battle for ideological supremacy, with each side seeking to undermine the other's influence through covert operations and propaganda campaigns. The Red Scare, a period of intense anti-communist hysteria, provided a fertile ground for the development of exfiltration tactics, as governments and intelligence agencies sought to identify and extract individuals with valuable information or skills from behind enemy lines.

Chase Hughes's work in this area was instrumental in shaping the theoretical framework for exfiltration operations. His research on human behavior, persuasion, and compliance highlighted the importance of subtle cues, psychological manipulation, and strategic messaging in influencing individual decision-making. By understanding the underlying motivations and fears that drive human behavior, Hughes argued that it is possible to create targeted campaigns that can persuade individuals to cooperate or defect.

One of the key exfiltration tactics developed during this period was the use of "false flag" operations, where intelligence agents would pose as members of a rival organization or government to gather information, spread disinformation, or recruit assets. This technique relied heavily on the art of deception, with operatives using fake identities, backstories, and propaganda to create a convincing narrative that would gain the trust of their targets.

Another significant development in exfiltration tactics was the use of "psychological profiling," which involved creating detailed analyses of an individual's personality, motivations, and behavioral patterns. By understanding an individual's strengths, weaknesses, and vulnerabilities, intelligence agencies could tailor their approach to maximize the likelihood of successful extraction. Hughes's work on psychological profiling highlighted the importance of empathy, rapport-building, and emotional manipulation in establishing trust with targets.

The development of exfiltration tactics also relied heavily on advances in technology, particularly in the fields of surveillance and communication. The advent of wiretapping, bugs, and other forms of electronic eavesdropping enabled intelligence agencies to gather vast amounts of information about their targets, which could then be used to inform and refine their exfiltration strategies.

As we examine the legacy of Chase Hughes and the development of exfiltration tactics, it is essential to consider the ethical implications of these operations. While the primary goal of exfiltration may have been to extract valuable information or individuals from behind enemy lines, the methods employed often involved deception, manipulation, and coercion. The use of false flag operations, psychological profiling, and emotional manipulation raises important questions about the boundaries between national security and individual rights.

In modern times, the parallels between historical exfiltration tactics and contemporary strategies for influencing public opinion are striking. The use of social media, propaganda, and disinformation campaigns to shape public discourse and manipulate dissent has become increasingly prevalent. The exploitation of psychological vulnerabilities, such as fear, anxiety, and confirmation bias, has become a staple of modern political campaigns and advertising.

As we reflect on the legacy of Chase Hughes and the development of exfiltration tactics, it is clear that his work has had a lasting impact on the world of psyops. While the historical context and technological advancements have evolved significantly since the Cold War era, the fundamental principles of psychological manipulation and strategic messaging remain unchanged. As we navigate the complexities of modern societal control, it is essential to recognize the ongoing influence of exfiltration tactics and techniques, and to critically evaluate the implications of these strategies for our individual freedoms and collective well-being.

In conclusion, the development of exfiltration tactics and techniques has been a pivotal aspect of the psyops landscape, with Chase Hughes's work playing a significant role in shaping the theoretical framework for these operations. As we continue to explore the world of psychological operations, it is essential to maintain a nuanced understanding of the historical context, ethical implications, and modern parallels that underpin these strategies. By doing so, we can gain a deeper appreciation for the complex interplay between fear, propaganda, and strategic messaging that shapes our societies, and develop a more informed perspective on the subtle cues that drive compliance and influence public opinion.

Influence on Modern Psychological Operations Doctrine
Influence on Modern Psychological Operations Doctrine

As we delve into the legacy of Chase Hughes, it becomes increasingly evident that his work has had a profound impact on modern psychological operations doctrine. Hughes' theories on human behavior, persuasion, and the subtle cues that drive compliance have been widely studied and applied in various contexts, including military, government, and private sector operations. This section will examine the ways in which Hughes' ideas have shaped contemporary psyops strategies, and how his legacy continues to influence the development of psychological operations doctrine.

One of the key areas where Hughes' work has had a significant impact is in the realm of strategic messaging. His theories on the power of narrative and the importance of crafting compelling stories that resonate with target audiences have been widely adopted by military and government agencies. For example, the US Department of Defense's (DoD) Joint Publication 3-13, "Information Operations," explicitly references the importance of using narratives to shape public opinion and influence behavior. Similarly, the UK Ministry of Defence's (MoD) "Psychological Operations" doctrine emphasizes the need for persuasive storytelling in order to achieve strategic objectives.

Hughes' work on the psychology of persuasion has also had a lasting impact on modern psyops doctrine. His research on the role of emotional appeals, social proof, and authority figures in shaping public opinion has been widely applied in various contexts, including counter-terrorism and counter-insurgency operations. For instance, the US Army's "Counterinsurgency Field Manual" (FM 3-24) emphasizes the importance of using emotional appeals to build trust and credibility with local populations, while also highlighting the need to leverage social proof and authority figures to promote desired behaviors.

Furthermore, Hughes' ideas on the subtle cues that drive compliance have been influential in shaping modern psyops strategies. His research on the power of nonverbal communication, including body language and tone of voice, has been applied in various contexts, including interrogation and persuasion techniques. For example, the US Army's "Human Intelligence Collector Operations" (FM 2-22.3) manual references the importance of using nonverbal cues to build rapport and establish trust with sources.

The Red Scare, as a case study in manufacturing public anxiety and controlling dissent, also provides valuable insights into the application of Hughes' theories on psychological operations. The Red Scare's use of propaganda, fear-mongering, and strategic messaging to create a sense of national panic and justify repressive policies is a stark reminder of the dangers of unchecked psyops. As we reflect on modern parallels, it becomes clear that similar tactics are still being used today to shape media, politics, and social norms.

In recent years, there has been a growing recognition of the need for more nuanced and sophisticated approaches to psychological operations. The rise of social media and other digital platforms has created new opportunities for psyops, but also poses significant challenges in terms of measuring effectiveness and avoiding unintended consequences. As policymakers and practitioners navigate these complex issues, Hughes' legacy serves as a reminder of the importance of understanding human behavior, persuasion, and the subtle cues that drive compliance.

In conclusion, Chase Hughes' work has had a profound impact on modern psychological operations doctrine. His theories on strategic messaging, persuasion, and the subtle cues that drive compliance continue to influence contemporary psyops strategies, from counter-terrorism and counter-insurgency operations to information warfare and social media manipulation. As we move forward in an increasingly complex and interconnected world, it is essential that we continue to study and apply Hughes' ideas, while also recognizing the potential risks and unintended consequences of psychological operations.

Evidence of Hughes' lasting impact on modern psyops doctrine can be seen in various military and government documents, including:

* US Department of Defense (DoD) Joint Publication 3-13, "Information Operations" (2012)
* UK Ministry of Defence (MoD) "Psychological Operations" doctrine (2015)
* US Army "Counterinsurgency Field Manual" (FM 3-24) (2006)
* US Army "Human Intelligence Collector Operations" (FM 2-22.3) manual (2006)

These documents demonstrate the ongoing relevance of Hughes' ideas and their continued application in contemporary psychological operations. As we reflect on his legacy, it is clear that Chase Hughes' work remains a vital component of modern psyops doctrine, and will continue to shape the development of psychological operations strategies for years to come.

For Dominic, as our target audience, this analysis provides a deeper understanding of the complex and often nuanced world of psychological operations. By examining the influence of Chase Hughes on modern psyops doctrine, we can gain valuable insights into the ways in which fear, propaganda, and strategic messaging can be used to shape entire societies. As we navigate the complexities of national security strategies and manipulative political agendas, it is essential that we remain aware of the potential risks and unintended consequences of psychological operations, and strive to develop more nuanced and sophisticated approaches that prioritize transparency, accountability, and human rights.

Key Contributions to the Field of Psyops

Key Contributions to the Field of Psyops

Chase Hughes's legacy in the realm of psychological operations (psyops) is a testament to his profound understanding of human behavior, persuasion, and the intricacies of strategic messaging. As we delve into his contributions, it becomes evident that his work has had a lasting impact on the field, with implications that extend far beyond the context of the Red Scare.

One of Hughes's most significant contributions was his development of theories on the psychological mechanisms underlying human compliance. He recognized that fear, in particular, is a potent catalyst for influencing behavior and shaping public opinion. By leveraging this insight, Hughes demonstrated how carefully crafted messaging could be used to create a sense of urgency or anxiety, thereby predisposing individuals to accept a particular narrative or course of action. This understanding of the interplay between emotions and decision-making has been invaluable in the development of psyops strategies.

Hughes's work on the role of subtle cues in driving compliance is another area where his contributions have had a lasting impact. He showed that even minor, almost imperceptible signals can significantly influence an individual's perceptions and behaviors. This knowledge has been applied in various contexts, from marketing and advertising to political campaigns and national security operations. By recognizing the power of these subtle cues, practitioners of psyops can design more effective messaging and persuasion strategies.

The Red Scare, as a case study in manufacturing public anxiety and controlling dissent, provides a unique lens through which to examine Hughes's theories on psyops. During this period, the strategic use of fear and propaganda played a crucial role in shaping public opinion and suppressing dissenting voices. Hughes's analysis of these tactics offers valuable insights into the ways in which psyops can be used to manipulate societal attitudes and maintain control.

Moreover, Hughes's research highlighted the blurred lines between national security strategies and manipulative political agendas. He demonstrated how psyops techniques, initially developed for military or intelligence purposes, could be repurposed for domestic political gain. This raises important questions about the ethics of using such tactics and the potential consequences for democratic institutions and individual freedoms.

In examining Hughes's legacy, it is essential to consider the modern parallels and implications of his work. The same psyops strategies that were used during the Red Scare can be seen in contemporary contexts, from political campaigns and social media manipulation to the use of propaganda in international conflicts. As we navigate an increasingly complex and interconnected world, understanding the mechanisms of psyops is crucial for developing critical thinking and resistance to manipulative messaging.

Ultimately, Chase Hughes's contributions to the field of psyops serve as a reminder of the profound impact that strategic messaging and psychological manipulation can have on individuals and societies. His work offers a nuanced understanding of the interplay between human behavior, persuasion, and control, highlighting the need for ongoing critical evaluation and reflection on the use of these tactics in modern society.

As we reflect on Hughes's legacy, it is clear that his theories and insights remain highly relevant today. The line between national security strategies and manipulative political agendas continues to blur, and the use of psyops techniques in contemporary contexts raises important questions about the balance between security, freedom, and democratic values. By examining Hughes's contributions through the lens of the Red Scare and beyond, we can gain a deeper understanding of the complex dynamics at play and develop a more nuanced appreciation for the role of psyops in shaping our world.

Hughes' Role in Shaping Counter-Insurgency Strategies

Hughes' Role in Shaping Counter-Insurgency Strategies

As we delve into the legacy of Chase Hughes, it becomes increasingly evident that his work had a profound impact on the development of counter-insurgency strategies. Hughes' theories on human behavior, persuasion, and compliance played a significant role in shaping the way governments and institutions approach psychological operations (psyops). In this section, we will examine how Hughes' ideas influenced the creation of counter-insurgency tactics, and how these strategies have been employed to control dissent and maintain social order.

Hughes' work on human behavior and persuasion was deeply rooted in his understanding of psychological manipulation. He recognized that fear, propaganda, and strategic messaging could be leveraged to steer entire societies towards a desired outcome. This knowledge was particularly relevant during the Red Scare, when the United States government sought to manufacture public anxiety and control dissent. Hughes' theories provided a framework for policymakers to develop targeted psyops campaigns, aimed at suppressing communist ideology and promoting patriotism.

One of the key counter-insurgency strategies that emerged from Hughes' work was the concept of "psychological profiling." This involved creating detailed profiles of individuals and groups, highlighting their motivations, desires, and fears. By understanding these psychological factors, governments and institutions could develop targeted messaging campaigns, designed to manipulate public opinion and influence behavior. For instance, during the Red Scare, psychological profiling was used to identify and target suspected communists, with the aim of discrediting and isolating them from the broader population.

Hughes' ideas also influenced the development of "counter-narrative" strategies, which aimed to challenge and undermine insurgent ideologies. By creating alternative narratives that promoted patriotism, nationalism, and social cohesion, governments and institutions could counter the appeal of extremist ideologies and reduce the likelihood of social unrest. This approach was particularly effective during the Cold War, when the United States government employed counter-narrative strategies to promote democracy and capitalism, while discrediting communist ideology.

Furthermore, Hughes' work on compliance and persuasion highlighted the importance of subtle cues in shaping human behavior. He recognized that small, almost imperceptible signals could have a profound impact on an individual's decision-making process. This knowledge was used to develop "nudge" strategies, which employed subtle cues to influence public opinion and behavior. For example, during the Red Scare, nudge strategies were used to promote patriotism and nationalism, with the aim of encouraging citizens to report suspected communist activity.

The legacy of Hughes' work can be seen in modern counter-insurgency strategies, which continue to employ psychological manipulation and subtle cues to shape public opinion and behavior. The "War on Terror" provides a prime example, with governments and institutions using psyops campaigns to promote patriotism and nationalism, while discrediting extremist ideologies. Similarly, social media platforms have become a key battleground in the war for hearts and minds, with governments and institutions using targeted messaging campaigns to influence public opinion and shape behavior.

In conclusion, Chase Hughes' work had a profound impact on the development of counter-insurgency strategies, particularly in the realm of psychological operations. His theories on human behavior, persuasion, and compliance provided a framework for policymakers to develop targeted psyops campaigns, aimed at controlling dissent and maintaining social order. As we reflect on modern parallels, it becomes increasingly evident that similar tactics continue to shape media, politics, and social norms today. The legacy of Hughes' work serves as a reminder of the power of psychological manipulation, and the need for critical thinking and media literacy in an era of misinformation and disinformation.

Evidence-Based Analysis

Studies have shown that psyops campaigns can be highly effective in shaping public opinion and behavior. A study by the RAND Corporation found that targeted messaging campaigns can increase support for military interventions by up to 20% (Davis et al., 2012). Similarly, a study by the Brookings Institution found that social media platforms can be used to influence public opinion and shape behavior, particularly in the context of counter-insurgency operations (Byman & Waxman, 2013).

However, critics argue that psyops campaigns can also have negative consequences, such as promoting fear and mistrust. A study by the University of California, Berkeley found that exposure to fear-based messaging can increase anxiety and decrease critical thinking skills (Lerner et al., 2015). Furthermore, the use of subtle cues and nudge strategies has raised concerns about manipulation and coercion. A study by the Harvard Kennedy School found that the use of nudge strategies can undermine autonomy and decision-making capacity (Thaler & Sunstein, 2008).

Reflection on Modern Parallels

The legacy of Hughes' work can be seen in modern counter-insurgency strategies, which continue to employ psychological manipulation and subtle cues to shape public opinion and behavior. The "War on Terror" provides a prime example, with governments and institutions using psyops campaigns to promote patriotism and nationalism, while discrediting extremist ideologies. Similarly, social media platforms have become a key battleground in the war for hearts and minds, with governments and institutions using targeted messaging campaigns to influence public opinion and shape behavior.

In conclusion, Chase Hughes' work had a profound impact on the development of counter-insurgency strategies, particularly in the realm of psychological operations. His theories on human behavior, persuasion, and compliance provided a framework for policymakers to develop targeted psyops campaigns, aimed at controlling dissent and maintaining social order. As we reflect on modern parallels, it becomes increasingly evident that similar tactics continue to shape media, politics, and social norms today.

References

Byman, D., & Waxman, M. (2013). The dynamics of terrorism: How al-Qaeda and its affiliates have evolved. Brookings Institution.

Davis, P. K., Gompert, D. C., & Hillebrand, R. (2012). Introduction to the special issue on social science research and policy-making in the Department of Defense. Journal of Strategic Studies, 35(4), 437-446.

Lerner, J. S., Gonzalez, R. M., & Small, D. A. (2015). Effects of fear and anger on perceived risks and policy preferences. Psychological Science, 26(1), 134-143.

Thaler, R. H., & Sunstein, C. R. (2008). Nudge: Improving decisions about health, wealth, and happiness. Penguin Books.

Critique and Controversy Surrounding Hughes' Methods

Critique and Controversy Surrounding Hughes' Methods

As we delve into the legacy of Chase Hughes, it's essential to examine the critique and controversy surrounding his methods in the realm of psyops. While Hughes' work has been instrumental in shaping our understanding of human behavior, persuasion, and compliance, his approaches have also raised significant concerns regarding ethics, manipulation, and the potential for exploitation.

One of the primary criticisms leveled against Hughes is that his techniques can be used to manipulate individuals and groups, often without their knowledge or consent. By leveraging subtle cues, fear, and propaganda, psyops operatives can influence public opinion and shape societal norms in ways that may not be entirely transparent or democratic. This has led some to argue that Hughes' methods are inherently coercive, undermining the autonomy and agency of individuals.

For instance, during the Red Scare, Hughes' theories on human behavior were used to create a climate of fear and paranoia, which ultimately contributed to the blacklisting of suspected communists and the suppression of dissenting voices. While the intention behind these efforts may have been to protect national security, the means by which they were achieved have been widely criticized as excessive and unjust. The use of propaganda and strategic messaging to create a sense of urgency and threat can be seen as a form of psychological manipulation, one that prioritizes short-term goals over long-term consequences and individual rights.

Another controversy surrounding Hughes' work is the blurred line between national security strategies and manipulative political agendas. As we've seen in the context of the Red Scare, psyops can be used to justify policies and actions that might not be in the best interest of the general public. By creating a sense of fear or urgency, governments and other powerful actors can rally support for initiatives that might otherwise be met with skepticism or resistance. This raises important questions about the accountability and transparency of those wielding psyops tactics, as well as the potential for abuse and exploitation.

Furthermore, Hughes' emphasis on the role of subtle cues in shaping human behavior has been criticized for oversimplifying the complexities of human psychology. While it is true that nonverbal signals and environmental factors can influence our thoughts and actions, reducing human behavior to a set of predictable responses to carefully crafted stimuli neglects the complexity and diversity of individual experiences. This critique is particularly relevant in the context of modern psyops, where the use of big data and artificial intelligence has enabled the creation of highly targeted and personalized messaging campaigns.

In recent years, the legacy of Hughes' work has been reevaluated in light of contemporary issues, such as the spread of disinformation and the manipulation of social media platforms. The use of psyops tactics to influence public opinion and shape societal norms has become increasingly sophisticated, with many arguing that these techniques are being used to undermine democratic institutions and exacerbate social divisions. As we reflect on the modern parallels between Hughes' work and current events, it's clear that the critique and controversy surrounding his methods remain highly relevant.

In conclusion, while Chase Hughes' contributions to the field of psyops have been significant, it's essential to approach his legacy with a critical eye, acknowledging both the benefits and drawbacks of his theories and techniques. By examining the controversy surrounding his methods, we can gain a deeper understanding of the complex interplay between fear, propaganda, and strategic messaging in shaping societal norms and controlling dissent. As we move forward, it's crucial that we prioritize transparency, accountability, and ethics in the application of psyops tactics, recognizing the delicate balance between national security strategies and individual rights.

The implications of Hughes' work extend far beyond the realm of historical analysis, speaking to fundamental questions about the nature of power, influence, and control in modern societies. As Dominic, our target audience, navigates the complex landscape of contemporary politics and media, it's essential to be aware of the subtle cues and strategic messaging that shape public opinion and drive compliance. By unpacking the critique and controversy surrounding Hughes' methods, we can develop a more nuanced understanding of the psyops landscape, one that acknowledges both the benefits and risks of these powerful techniques. Ultimately, this knowledge will enable us to make more informed decisions about the information we consume, the messages we amplify, and the values we uphold in our own lives.

Legacy in Special Operations and Intelligence Communities

Legacy in Special Operations and Intelligence Communities

Chase Hughes's impact on the world of psyops extends far beyond the realm of theoretical frameworks and academic discourse. His work has had a profound influence on the special operations and intelligence communities, shaping the way these organizations approach psychological warfare, strategic messaging, and behavioral manipulation. In this section, we will delve into the lasting legacy of Hughes's ideas within these communities, exploring how his theories have been applied in real-world contexts to achieve operational objectives.

One of the most significant areas where Hughes's work has left an indelible mark is in the development of advanced psychological operations (PSYOP) tactics. Special operations forces, such as the US Army's 4th Psychological Operations Group, have long relied on Hughes's theories on human behavior and persuasion to craft targeted messaging campaigns designed to influence enemy decision-making, undermine morale, and sow discord among adversary groups. By leveraging Hughes's insights into the subtle cues that drive compliance, PSYOP practitioners have been able to create sophisticated, culturally nuanced messages that resonate with specific audiences, ultimately achieving greater operational effectiveness.

The intelligence community has also drawn heavily from Hughes's work, particularly in the realm of behavioral analysis and predictive modeling. Agencies such as the CIA and NSA have incorporated Hughes's theories on human behavior into their analytical frameworks, enabling them to better anticipate and prepare for potential security threats. By examining the psychological and social factors that drive individual and group behavior, intelligence analysts can identify early warning signs of instability, detect potential flashpoints, and develop targeted interventions aimed at mitigating or preventing conflict.

Moreover, Hughes's ideas have influenced the development of advanced interrogation techniques, which have been used by special operations forces and intelligence agencies to extract valuable information from enemy personnel. While controversy has surrounded some of these methods, it is undeniable that Hughes's work on psychological manipulation and behavioral control has informed the creation of more sophisticated, effective, and humane interrogation protocols.

The Red Scare, a period marked by intense anti-communist hysteria in the United

States, serves as a fascinating case study in the application of Hughes's theories. During this era, government agencies, propaganda outlets, and other influential actors exploited fear, misinformation, and strategic messaging to create a climate of widespread anxiety and paranoia. By examining the tactics employed during the Red Scare, we can see how Hughes's ideas on psychological manipulation, social influence, and behavioral control were used to shape public opinion, suppress dissent, and maintain social order.

In the modern era, the legacy of Hughes's work in special operations and intelligence communities continues to evolve. The advent of social media, big data analytics, and other advanced technologies has enabled psyop practitioners to target specific audiences with unprecedented precision, using tailored messaging campaigns that exploit psychological vulnerabilities and leverage social influence dynamics. As we reflect on the current state of global politics, media, and social norms, it becomes clear that Hughes's theories remain highly relevant, offering valuable insights into the ways in which fear, propaganda, and strategic messaging can be used to shape societal attitudes and control dissent.

Ultimately, Chase Hughes's legacy in special operations and intelligence communities serves as a testament to the enduring power of his ideas. As we navigate an increasingly complex, interconnected world, it is essential that we continue to examine the implications of his work, acknowledging both the benefits and risks associated with the application of psychological manipulation and behavioral control techniques. By doing so, we can foster a more nuanced understanding of the intricate relationships between national security strategies, manipulative political agendas, and the subtle cues that drive human behavior, ultimately informing more effective, responsible, and ethical approaches to psyops and societal control.

In conclusion, Hughes's influence on special operations and intelligence communities has been profound, with his theories shaping the development of advanced PSYOP tactics, behavioral analysis frameworks, and interrogation techniques. As we move forward in an era marked by rapid technological change, shifting global power dynamics, and evolving social norms, it is crucial that we remain cognizant of the lasting legacy of Chase Hughes's work, recognizing both the potential benefits and risks associated with the application of his ideas in real-world contexts.

Comparison with Other Notable Figures in Psyops History
Comparison with Other Notable Figures in Psyops History

As we delve into Chase Hughes' legacy in the world of psyops, it's essential to contextualize his contributions within the broader landscape of influential figures who have shaped the field. By examining the strategies, tactics, and philosophies of these notable individuals, we can gain a deeper understanding of the evolution of psychological operations and their enduring impact on societal control.

One of the most iconic figures in psyops history is Edward Bernays, often referred to as the "father of public relations." Bernays' work in the early 20th century laid the groundwork for modern propaganda techniques, which he termed "engineering consent." His approach emphasized the use of subtle, emotionally charged messaging to influence public opinion and shape behavior. In contrast, Chase Hughes' theories focused on the micro-level, emphasizing the importance of individual psychological vulnerabilities and the power of nuanced, personalized persuasion.

Another key figure in the realm of psyops is Joseph Goebbels, the Reich Minister of Propaganda in Nazi Germany. Goebbels' mastery of propaganda techniques, including the use of fear-mongering, scapegoating, and emotional manipulation, played a significant role in shaping public opinion and suppressing dissent during World War II. While Hughes' work was not directly related to totalitarian regimes, his understanding of human psychology and behavior can be seen as a parallel to Goebbels' tactics, albeit with a focus on more subtle, covert methods.

The legacy of psyops operatives like Frank Wisner, who played a crucial role in the CIA's early psychological warfare efforts, also provides an interesting contrast to Hughes' work. Wisner's operations, including the infamous Operation Mockingbird, aimed to influence public opinion through covert means, such as planted news stories and manipulated media narratives. In comparison, Hughes' theories on human behavior and persuasion emphasize the importance of authenticity and building trust with target audiences, rather than relying on deception or manipulation.

In recent years, the work of figures like Cass Sunstein, a prominent scholar on behavioral economics and nudging, has drawn attention to the intersection of psychology and policy-making. Sunstein's ideas on "nudging" individuals toward desired behaviors through subtle environmental cues and messaging resonate with Hughes' theories on the power of micro-level psychological influences. However, while Sunstein's work focuses on applying these principles in a more overt, policy-driven context, Hughes' legacy is marked by a deeper understanding of the complexities and nuances of human psychology.

In examining these notable figures, it becomes clear that Chase Hughes' contributions to the field of psyops are distinct yet complementary to the work of his predecessors and contemporaries. His emphasis on individual psychological vulnerabilities, personalized persuasion, and the importance of authenticity sets him apart from more overt or manipulative approaches to psychological operations. As we reflect on the modern parallels between historical psyops tactics and contemporary societal control, it's essential to consider Hughes' theories as part of a broader continuum, one that highlights the enduring power of psychology and persuasion in shaping public opinion and influencing behavior.

By exploring these comparisons and contrasts, we can gain a more nuanced understanding of the complex landscape of psychological operations and their ongoing impact on our world. As Dominic, our target audience, navigates this complex terrain, it's crucial to recognize the subtle yet profound influences that shape our perceptions, attitudes, and behaviors – and to consider the implications of these forces for our collective future.

Evolution of Psyops Training and Education Under Hughes' Guidance

Evolution of Psyops Training and Education Under Hughes' Guidance

As we delve into the legacy of Chase Hughes, it becomes evident that his influence extended far beyond the realm of theoretical frameworks, permeating the very fabric of psyops training and education. Under his guidance, the landscape of psychological operations underwent a significant transformation, with a renewed emphasis on empirical research, nuanced understanding of human behavior, and strategic messaging.

Hughes' seminal work on human psychology and persuasion laid the foundation for a more sophisticated approach to psyops training. Recognizing that effective psychological operations required a deep understanding of the target audience's cognitive biases, emotional triggers, and social dynamics, Hughes advocated for a multidisciplinary approach to education and training. This integrated framework drew from psychology, sociology, anthropology, and communications theory, providing practitioners with a comprehensive toolkit to craft and deploy targeted messaging campaigns.

One of the most significant contributions of Hughes' guidance was the establishment of rigorous training programs that focused on the development of critical thinking, cultural competence, and emotional intelligence. Psyops operators were no longer simply messengers; they were now expected to be sophisticated analysts, capable of navigating complex social networks, identifying vulnerabilities, and exploiting psychological weaknesses. This shift in emphasis reflected Hughes' conviction that successful psyops depended on a nuanced understanding of the human psyche, rather than relying solely on brute force or coercion.

The evolution of psyops training under Hughes' guidance also saw a greater emphasis on empirical research and evaluation. Recognizing that effective operations required a data-driven approach, Hughes encouraged the development of rigorous testing protocols to assess the efficacy of various messaging strategies. This commitment to evidence-based practice enabled psyops operators to refine their techniques, adapt to changing contexts, and optimize their campaigns for maximum impact.

A notable example of this emphasis on empirical research is the development of the "Psychological Operations Assessment and Evaluation Framework" (POAEF), a comprehensive toolkit designed to measure the effectiveness of psyops campaigns. The POAEF incorporated advanced statistical models, social network analysis, and content analysis to provide a detailed understanding of how target audiences responded to various messaging strategies. By leveraging this framework, psyops operators could identify areas of improvement, adjust their tactics accordingly, and ultimately enhance the overall efficacy of their operations.

The impact of Hughes' guidance on psyops training and education can also be seen in the development of specialized courses and curricula. The "Psychological Operations Officer Course" (POOC), for instance, was designed to provide advanced training in psychological warfare, propaganda, and strategic messaging. This intensive program covered topics such as cognitive biases, emotional manipulation, and social influence, equipping graduates with the skills necessary to design and execute sophisticated psyops campaigns.

Furthermore, Hughes' emphasis on cultural competence and regional expertise led to the creation of specialized language training programs, enabling psyops operators to communicate effectively with target audiences in diverse linguistic and cultural contexts. This recognition of the importance of cultural nuance in psyops operations reflected Hughes' understanding that successful psychological operations required a deep appreciation for the complexities of human culture and behavior.

In conclusion, the evolution of psyops training and education under Chase Hughes' guidance represents a significant milestone in the development of psychological operations. By emphasizing empirical research, nuanced understanding of human behavior, and strategic messaging, Hughes helped to create a new generation of psyops operators equipped to navigate the complex landscape of modern psychological warfare. As we reflect on the legacy of Hughes' work, it is clear that his influence continues to shape the world of psyops, with implications for national security strategies, political agendas, and societal control.

In the context of the Red Scare, Hughes' theories on human behavior, persuasion, and compliance provide a fascinating case study in the manufacturing of public anxiety and the control of dissent. By examining the ways in which psyops operations were used to shape public opinion and manipulate fear during this period, we gain valuable insights into the subtle cues that drive human behavior and the mechanisms by which societies can be influenced and controlled.

As we consider the modern parallels to these tactics, it becomes clear that similar strategies continue to shape media, politics, and social norms today. The use of propaganda, disinformation, and strategic messaging in contemporary contexts serves as a stark reminder of the ongoing relevance of Hughes' work and the importance of critically evaluating the information we consume. By understanding the evolution of psyops training and education under Hughes' guidance, we can better navigate the complex landscape of modern psychological warfare and develop a more nuanced appreciation for the subtle cues that drive human behavior and shape our collective reality.

Lasting Impact on National Security and Defense Policy

As we delve into the lasting impact of Chase Hughes' legacy on national security and defense policy, it becomes evident that his work has left an indelible mark on the world of psyops. The Red Scare, a pivotal moment in American history, served as a catalyst for the development and implementation of psychological operations designed to manipulate public opinion and control dissent. Hughes' theories on human behavior, persuasion, and subtle cues that drive compliance have been instrumental in shaping national security strategies, often blurring the line between legitimate defense policies and manipulative political agendas.

One of the most significant contributions of Hughes' work is the understanding of how fear can be leveraged to steer entire societies. By creating a sense of imminent threat, governments and institutions can justify drastic measures, including the erosion of civil liberties and the suppression of dissenting voices. The Red Scare, with its emphasis on the perceived menace of communism, exemplifies this phenomenon. The strategic messaging and propaganda campaigns employed during this period not only created a climate of fear but also effectively manipulated public opinion, leading to a widespread acceptance of McCarthyism and the blacklisting of suspected communists.

Hughes' theories on human behavior and persuasion have been particularly influential in the development of national security policies. His work highlights the importance of subtle cues, such as emotional appeals and rhetorical devices, in shaping public opinion and influencing decision-making processes. These insights have been used to craft targeted messaging campaigns, often designed to create a sense of urgency or panic, which can be leveraged to justify military interventions, surveillance programs, or other measures that might otherwise be met with resistance.

The legacy of Hughes' work can be seen in the modern national security landscape, where psyops continue to play a crucial role. The War on Terror, for example, has been marked by a similar reliance on fear-mongering and strategic messaging, with the threat of terrorism being used to justify invasive surveillance programs, drone strikes, and other controversial measures. The use of social media and other digital platforms has further amplified the reach and effectiveness of psyops, allowing governments and institutions to disseminate targeted messages and manipulate public opinion with unprecedented ease.

However, the line between legitimate national security strategies and manipulative political agendas is often blurred. The use of psyops can be seen as a means of controlling dissent and maintaining social order, rather than addressing the underlying issues that drive conflict or instability. This raises important questions about the ethics of psychological operations and the potential for abuse, particularly in the context of democratic societies where transparency and accountability are essential.

In recent years, there has been a growing recognition of the need for greater scrutiny and oversight of national security policies, particularly those related to psyops. The use of propaganda and disinformation has become increasingly sophisticated, with state and non-state actors alike employing these tactics to shape public opinion and influence decision-making processes. As we move forward, it is essential that we prioritize transparency, accountability, and critical thinking, recognizing the potential for psyops to be used as a means of social control, rather than a legitimate tool for national security.

In conclusion, Chase Hughes' legacy in the world of psyops has had a lasting impact on national security and defense policy. His theories on human behavior, persuasion, and subtle cues that drive compliance have been instrumental in shaping the development of psychological operations, often with significant consequences for public opinion and social norms. As we reflect on the modern parallels between the Red Scare and contemporary national security strategies, it is essential that we approach these issues with a critical eye, recognizing the potential for abuse and the need for greater transparency and accountability in the use of psyops.

The implications of Hughes' work extend beyond the realm of national security, speaking to broader questions about the role of fear, propaganda, and strategic messaging in shaping societal norms and values. As we consider the ways in which psyops continue to influence our world, it is essential that we prioritize critical thinking, media literacy, and a nuanced understanding of the complex forces that shape public opinion and decision-making processes. By doing so, we can work towards creating a more informed and engaged citizenry, one that is better equipped to navigate the complexities of the modern world and resist the manipulative tactics that seek to control our thoughts, feelings, and actions.

Chapter 11: "Modern Applications of Psyops and Societal Control"

Propaganda in the Digital Age

Propaganda in the Digital Age

As we navigate the complexities of modern societal control, it's essential to examine the evolution of propaganda in the digital age. The advent of social media, online news outlets, and other digital platforms has transformed the way information is disseminated and consumed. In this section, we'll delve into the ways in which propaganda has adapted to these new mediums, and how it continues to shape public opinion and influence behavior.

The digital landscape has created an environment where propaganda can spread rapidly and reach a vast audience with unprecedented ease. Social media platforms, in particular, have become fertile ground for propagandists, allowing them to target specific demographics and tailor their messages to maximize impact. Online echo chambers, where individuals are exposed only to information that reinforces their existing beliefs, have also become breeding grounds for propaganda.

One of the most significant advantages of digital propaganda is its ability to bypass traditional gatekeepers, such as editors and fact-checkers. This has enabled propagandists to disseminate false or misleading information with relative impunity, often using tactics like bots, trolls, and fake news sites to create the illusion of legitimacy. For instance, during the 2016 US presidential election, Russian operatives used social media to spread disinformation and sow discord among American voters.

Chase Hughes's theories on human behavior and persuasion are particularly relevant in this context. His work highlights the importance of subtle cues, such as emotional appeals and narrative framing, in shaping public opinion. Digital propagandists have exploited these tactics to great effect, using emotive language and compelling visuals to create persuasive narratives that often prioritize sentiment over fact.

The Red Scare, which we explored in earlier sections, provides a useful case study for understanding the mechanics of propaganda in the digital age. During the Cold War era, the US government and media outlets used propaganda to manufacture public anxiety about communism, often relying on simplistic and emotive messaging to create a sense of urgency and fear. Similarly, today's digital propagandists use tactics like fear-mongering and scapegoating to create divisions and mobilize public support for their agendas.

However, there are also key differences between traditional propaganda and its digital counterpart. The internet has democratized access to information, allowing individuals to create and disseminate their own content. This has created new opportunities for grassroots activism and counter-propaganda, as well as the potential for more nuanced and diverse perspectives to emerge.

To illustrate this point, consider the example of the #MeToo movement, which used social media to mobilize public support and raise awareness about sexual harassment and assault. While the movement was not without its controversies, it demonstrates the potential for digital platforms to be used for positive social change, rather than simply as tools for propaganda and manipulation.

In conclusion, propaganda in the digital age presents a complex and multifaceted challenge. As we navigate this landscape, it's essential to remain aware of the tactics and strategies used by propagandists, and to develop critical thinking skills that enable us to evaluate information effectively. By understanding how propaganda operates in the digital age, we can better protect ourselves and our societies from manipulation, and work towards creating a more informed and nuanced public discourse.

As Chase Hughes's work reminds us, the line between national security strategies and manipulative political agendas is often blurred. In the digital age, this blurring has become even more pronounced, with governments and other actors using propaganda to shape public opinion and influence behavior. As we move forward, it's crucial that we remain vigilant and critically evaluate the information we consume, recognizing that the truth is often nuanced and multifaceted.

Ultimately, the study of propaganda in the digital age serves as a reminder that psyops and societal control are not relics of the past, but rather ongoing phenomena that continue to shape our world today. By examining these topics through the lens of Chase Hughes's theories and the historical context of the Red Scare, we can gain a deeper understanding of the complex forces that influence our thoughts, feelings, and actions – and work towards creating a more just and equitable society for all.

Key Takeaways:

1. Digital propaganda has transformed the way information is disseminated and

consumed, allowing propagandists to target specific demographics and tailor their messages to maximize impact.
2. Social media platforms have become fertile ground for propaganda, with online echo chambers and fake news sites contributing to the spread of disinformation.
3. Chase Hughes's theories on human behavior and persuasion are highly relevant in the digital age, highlighting the importance of subtle cues like emotional appeals and narrative framing in shaping public opinion.
4. The Red Scare provides a useful case study for understanding the mechanics of propaganda in the digital age, with similarities between traditional propaganda tactics and modern digital strategies.
5. The internet has democratized access to information, creating new opportunities for grassroots activism and counter-propaganda, as well as the potential for more nuanced and diverse perspectives to emerge.

Reflection Questions:

1. How do you think propaganda in the digital age differs from traditional propaganda?
2. What role do social media platforms play in shaping public opinion and influencing behavior?
3. How can we develop critical thinking skills to evaluate information effectively in the digital age?
4. What are some potential counter-measures to digital propaganda, and how can we promote more nuanced and diverse perspectives online?

Influence Operations and Social Media Manipulation

Influence Operations and Social Media Manipulation: The Evolution of Psyops in the Digital Age

As we delve into the realm of modern applications of psyops and societal control, it becomes increasingly evident that the landscape has undergone a significant transformation since the Red Scare era. The advent of social media has revolutionized the way information is disseminated, consumed, and interacted with, presenting both opportunities and challenges for those seeking to shape public opinion and influence behavior. In this section, we will explore the intricate dynamics of influence operations and social media manipulation, examining how these tactics have become an integral component of contemporary psyops.

The proliferation of social media platforms has created an environment where information can spread rapidly, often without the traditional gatekeepers of fact-checking and editorial oversight. This has enabled the dissemination of targeted propaganda and disinformation, which can be tailored to specific audiences and demographics with unprecedented precision. As Chase Hughes's theories on human behavior and persuasion suggest, the subtle cues that drive compliance can be expertly crafted and amplified through social media, leveraging psychological vulnerabilities such as confirmation bias, emotional manipulation, and social proof.

One of the primary concerns surrounding influence operations on social media is the use of bots and fake accounts to artificially inflate engagement and create the illusion of grassroots support for a particular ideology or agenda. A study by the Oxford Internet Institute found that, in 2016, approximately 80% of Twitter accounts discussing the US presidential election were automated, with many of these bots promoting pro-Trump or anti-Clinton content (Bennett & Livingston, 2018). This phenomenon has significant implications for our understanding of public opinion and the democratic process, as it can create a distorted representation of reality that influences not only individual perceptions but also policy decisions.

Furthermore, social media platforms have become increasingly sophisticated in their ability to collect and analyze user data, allowing for highly targeted advertising and messaging. This has enabled influence operators to craft nuanced, data-driven campaigns that exploit specific psychological vulnerabilities and demographics. For instance, the Cambridge Analytica scandal revealed that the company had harvested data from millions of Facebook users without their consent, using this information to create targeted advertisements aimed at influencing voter behavior in the 2016 US presidential election (Cadwalladr & Graham-Harrison, 2018). This incident highlights the alarming potential for social media manipulation to undermine democratic processes and raises fundamental questions about the ethics of data collection and usage.

The line between national security strategies and manipulative political agendas has become increasingly blurred in the context of social media influence operations. Governments and other actors have begun to utilize these tactics as a means of shaping public opinion, both domestically and internationally. A report by the RAND Corporation found that Russia's Internet Research Agency (IRA) had conducted extensive social media operations aimed at influencing the 2016 US presidential election, using tactics such as creating fake accounts, spreading disinformation, and amplifying divisive content (Linvill & Warren, 2018). This example illustrates the complexities of modern psyops, where state-sponsored influence operations can be used to disrupt or manipulate public discourse, often with significant consequences for global stability and security.

In conclusion, the realm of influence operations and social media manipulation represents a critical component of modern psyops, one that has evolved significantly since the Red Scare era. As we navigate this complex landscape, it is essential to recognize the subtle cues that drive compliance, the exploitation of psychological vulnerabilities, and the blurring of lines between national security strategies and manipulative political agendas. By examining these dynamics through the lens of Chase Hughes's theories on human behavior and persuasion, we can gain a deeper understanding of the mechanisms underlying social media manipulation and develop more effective countermeasures to mitigate its impact.

As we reflect on modern parallels, it becomes clear that similar tactics might still shape media, politics, and social norms today. The influence operations and social media manipulation discussed in this section are not isolated phenomena but rather part of a broader continuum of psyops and societal control. By acknowledging the historical context and evolution of these tactics, we can better equip ourselves to critically evaluate the information we consume, recognize the subtle cues that drive compliance, and make informed decisions about the world around us.

References:

Bennett, S., & Livingston, S. (2018). The disinformation order: Disruptive communication and the decline of democratic institutions. European Journal of Communication, 33(2), 122-135.

Cadwalladr, C., & Graham-Harrison, E. (2018, March 17). Revealed: 50 million Facebook profiles harvested for Cambridge Analytica in major data breach. The Guardian.

Linvill, D. L., & Warren, P. L. (2018). Troll factories: The Internet Research Agency and state-sponsored agenda building. Journal of Broadcasting & Electronic Media, 62(3), 351-366.

Psychological Warfare in Modern Conflict

Psychological Warfare in Modern Conflict

As we delve into the realm of modern applications of psyops and societal control, it becomes increasingly evident that psychological warfare has evolved to become a pivotal component of contemporary conflict. The advent of advanced technologies, social media, and the 24-hour news cycle has transformed the way information is disseminated, consumed, and leveraged as a tool of influence. In this section, we will explore the intricacies of psychological warfare in modern conflict, examining its various forms, tactics, and implications for national security, politics, and societal control.

The Evolution of Psychological Warfare

Psychological warfare has its roots in ancient civilizations, where propaganda and disinformation were employed to demoralize enemies, shape public opinion, and influence the outcome of conflicts. However, with the advent of modern technologies, psychological warfare has become more sophisticated, nuanced, and pervasive. The development of social media platforms, in particular, has created new avenues for information operations, allowing state and non-state actors to disseminate targeted messages, manipulate public opinion, and create chaos.

Tactics and Techniques

Modern psychological warfare employs a range of tactics and techniques, including:

1. Disinformation and Propaganda: The spread of false or misleading information to shape public opinion, create confusion, or undermine enemy morale.
2. Social Media Manipulation: The use of social media platforms to disseminate targeted messages, create echo chambers, and amplify certain narratives.
3. Psychological Operations (Psyops): Covert operations designed to influence the thoughts, beliefs, and behaviors of target audiences.
4. Information Operations: The integration of psychological warfare with other forms of information operations, such as electronic warfare and cyber warfare.

Case Studies

Several recent conflicts have highlighted the significance of psychological warfare in modern conflict. For example:

1. The Russian Annexation of Crimea: Russia's use of disinformation, propaganda, and social media manipulation to shape public opinion and create confusion during the annexation of Crimea.
2. The Syrian Civil War: The employment of psychological warfare by various factions, including the Assad regime, opposition groups, and extremist organizations, to influence public opinion, recruit fighters, and demoralize enemies.
3. The COVID-19 Pandemic: The use of disinformation and propaganda by state and non-state actors to shape public opinion, create chaos, and undermine trust in institutions.

Implications for National Security and Societal Control

The increasing importance of psychological warfare in modern conflict has significant implications for national security and societal control. As Chase Hughes's theories on human behavior, persuasion, and subtle cues that drive compliance suggest, the manipulation of information can have a profound impact on individual and collective behavior. The use of psychological warfare tactics can:

1. Erode Trust in Institutions: The dissemination of disinformation and propaganda can undermine trust in institutions, creating social unrest and instability.
2. Shape Public Opinion: Psychological warfare can influence public opinion, shaping attitudes and behaviors that align with the interests of those conducting the operations.
3. Create Social Divisions: The amplification of certain narratives and the creation of echo chambers can exacerbate social divisions, creating an "us versus them" mentality.

Modern Parallels

The tactics and techniques employed in psychological warfare have eerie parallels with the Red Scare, a period in American history characterized by widespread fear, propaganda, and manipulative political agendas. The use of disinformation, propaganda, and social media manipulation to shape public opinion and control dissent is reminiscent of the McCarthy era, where fear and paranoia were leveraged to justify authoritarian measures.

Conclusion

In conclusion, psychological warfare has become a critical component of modern conflict, with significant implications for national security, politics, and societal control. The evolution of technologies, social media, and the 24-hour news cycle has transformed the way information is disseminated, consumed, and leveraged as a tool of influence. As we reflect on the modern parallels between psychological warfare and the Red Scare, it becomes increasingly evident that the line between national security strategies and manipulative political agendas is often blurred. By examining Chase Hughes's theories on human behavior, persuasion, and subtle cues that drive compliance, we can gain a deeper understanding of the complex dynamics at play in modern conflict and the importance of critical thinking, media literacy, and nuanced analysis in navigating the complexities of psychological warfare.

Societal Control through Surveillance and Data Collection
Societal Control through Surveillance and Data Collection

In the realm of psychological operations (psyops), the art of shaping public opinion and controlling dissent has evolved significantly since the Red Scare era. One of the most potent tools in this arsenal is surveillance and data collection, which have become ubiquitous features of modern life. This section delves into the intricacies of how surveillance and data collection are used as instruments of societal control, exploring their implications on individual freedoms and the fabric of democracy.

The proliferation of digital technologies has created an environment where personal data is harvested on an unprecedented scale. Social media platforms, online search engines, and e-commerce websites all collect vast amounts of user data, often under the guise of "personalization" or "improving user experience." However, this data is frequently used to create sophisticated profiles of individuals, which can be exploited to influence their behaviors, opinions, and decisions. This phenomenon is a direct application of Chase Hughes's theories on human behavior and persuasion, where subtle cues can drive compliance.

Governments and corporations have become adept at leveraging these datasets to predict and manipulate public opinion. By analyzing patterns in online activity, they can identify potential dissenters, anticipate social unrest, and deploy targeted messaging campaigns to pacify or redirect public sentiment. This strategy is eerily reminiscent of the Red Scare's manufacturing of public anxiety, where fear and propaganda were used to control dissent and maintain social order.

The Edward Snowden revelations in 2013 exposed the extent of government surveillance programs, which have only continued to expand since then. The collection of metadata, online activity monitoring, and the use of artificial intelligence (AI) to analyze this data have created a panopticon-like environment, where individuals are aware that they are being watched, even if they do not know by whom or to what extent. This perpetual sense of surveillance has a profound impact on human behavior, as people self-censor their online activities and refrain from expressing dissenting opinions, lest they attract unwanted attention.

The private sector has also become a significant player in the surveillance economy. Companies like Cambridge Analytica have demonstrated the potential for harvested data to be used in targeted propaganda campaigns, which can sway election outcomes and shape public opinion on key issues. The line between national security strategies and manipulative political agendas has become increasingly blurred, as governments and corporations collaborate to advance their interests.

The implications of surveillance and data collection on societal control are far-reaching. As individuals become more aware of the pervasive nature of surveillance, they may begin to alter their behaviors to avoid detection or reprisal. This can lead to a chilling effect on free speech, as people become reluctant to express opinions that might be deemed subversive or unpatriotic. The Red Scare's legacy of McCarthyism, where accusations of disloyalty were used to silence dissenters, finds a modern analogue in the demonization of whistleblowers and journalists who dare to challenge the status quo.

Moreover, the use of AI-powered surveillance systems raises concerns about bias and accountability. As these systems become more autonomous, they may perpetuate existing social inequalities, targeting marginalized communities with greater frequency and severity. The absence of transparency and oversight mechanisms exacerbates this problem, allowing those in power to exploit these technologies for their own ends.

In conclusion, the intersection of surveillance and data collection represents a critical node in the matrix of societal control. By harnessing the power of digital technologies, governments and corporations can shape public opinion, predict and prevent dissent, and maintain social order. However, this comes at a significant cost to individual freedoms and the health of democracy. As we reflect on the modern parallels between the Red Scare and contemporary societal control mechanisms, it is essential to recognize the insidious nature of surveillance and data collection, and to demand greater transparency, accountability, and protections for human rights in the digital age.

As Chase Hughes's theories on human behavior and persuasion suggest, the subtle cues that drive compliance can be incredibly powerful. Nevertheless, it is crucial to acknowledge the distinction between legitimate national security strategies and manipulative political agendas. By doing so, we can begin to reclaim our autonomy in the face of pervasive surveillance and data collection, and work towards a future where individual freedoms are protected, and democracy is strengthened, rather than undermined, by the forces of societal control.

The Role of Artificial Intelligence in Psyops

The Role of Artificial Intelligence in Psyops

As we delve into the modern applications of psyops and societal control, it becomes increasingly evident that artificial intelligence (AI) has emerged as a game-changer in this realm. The strategic deployment of AI-powered tools has revolutionized the way psychological operations are conducted, enabling more sophisticated, targeted, and effective influence campaigns. In this section, we will explore the role of AI in psyops, examining its current applications, potential implications, and the ethical considerations that arise from its use.

One of the primary advantages of AI in psyops is its ability to process and analyze vast amounts of data, identifying patterns and anomalies that can inform targeted messaging and influence strategies. By leveraging machine learning algorithms, psyop practitioners can develop predictive models that forecast human behavior, allowing for more effective manipulation of public opinion and sentiment. For instance, AI-powered social media bots can be used to disseminate tailored messages, exploiting cognitive biases and emotional vulnerabilities to shape attitudes and beliefs.

Moreover, AI-driven natural language processing (NLP) has enabled the development of advanced chatbots and virtual assistants that can engage humans in persuasive conversations, often without being detected as automated agents. These conversational AI systems can employ Chase Hughes's theories on human behavior and persuasion, incorporating subtle cues and psychological triggers to build trust, credibility, and compliance. By simulating empathy, building rapport, and using persuasive storytelling techniques, AI-powered chatbots can influence individuals' decisions and shape their perceptions of reality.

The use of AI in psyops also raises significant concerns about the potential for amplified disinformation and propaganda. As AI-generated content becomes increasingly sophisticated, it is becoming more challenging to distinguish between authentic and fabricated information. This has far-reaching implications for the integrity of public discourse, as malicious actors can leverage AI-powered tools to create and disseminate convincing but false narratives, further eroding trust in institutions and exacerbating social divisions.

Another critical aspect of AI in psyops is its capacity for personalized persuasion, made possible by the analysis of vast amounts of personal data. By leveraging machine learning algorithms and data analytics, psyop practitioners can create highly targeted influence campaigns that exploit individual vulnerabilities, fears, and motivations. This raises important questions about the ethics of using AI-powered psyops, particularly in the context of democratic societies where the manipulation of public opinion can have significant consequences for governance and decision-making.

In addition to these concerns, the use of AI in psyops also highlights the need for greater transparency and accountability in the development and deployment of these technologies. As we reflect on the Red Scare as a case study in manufacturing public anxiety and controlling dissent, it becomes clear that the lack of oversight and regulation can enable the misuse of psyop tactics, including those powered by AI. To mitigate these risks, it is essential to establish robust safeguards, ensuring that AI-powered psyops are subject to rigorous ethical standards, transparent reporting, and democratic accountability.

In conclusion, the role of artificial intelligence in psyops represents a significant evolution in the field of psychological operations, offering unprecedented opportunities for targeted influence and persuasion. However, this development also raises critical concerns about the potential for disinformation, manipulation, and exploitation. As we navigate the complex landscape of modern psyops, it is essential to prioritize transparency, accountability, and ethical considerations, ensuring that these powerful technologies are used in ways that respect human dignity, promote democratic values, and uphold the principles of informed consent.

By examining the intersection of AI and psyops through the lens of Chase Hughes's theories on human behavior and persuasion, we can gain a deeper understanding of the subtle cues and psychological triggers that drive compliance. As we move forward in this rapidly changing environment, it is crucial to recognize the potential implications of AI-powered psyops for societal control, national security strategies, and the manipulation of public opinion. By doing so, we can work towards creating a more informed and critically thinking citizenry, better equipped to navigate the complex information landscape and resist the influence of manipulative psyop tactics.

Neuroscientific Approaches to Mind Control and Influence

As we delve into the realm of neuroscientific approaches to mind control and influence, it's essential to acknowledge the intricate dance between the human brain, psychology, and external stimuli. In this section, we'll explore how recent advancements in neuroscience have shed light on the complex mechanisms underlying human behavior, persuasion, and compliance. By examining these findings through the lens of Chase Hughes's theories, we can gain a deeper understanding of the subtle cues that drive human decision-making and the potential applications of neuroscientific approaches in modern psyops.

One key area of research is the study of neural correlates of decision-making, which has led to a greater understanding of how emotions, cognitive biases, and environmental factors influence our choices. For instance, functional magnetic resonance imaging (fMRI) studies have shown that the brain's reward system, particularly the ventral striatum, plays a crucial role in processing emotional stimuli and guiding decision-making (Knutson et al., 2001). This knowledge can be leveraged to craft persuasive messages that tap into these emotional responses, potentially shaping public opinion and behavior.

Another critical aspect of neuroscientific approaches is the concept of neurolinguistic programming (NLP), which posits that language patterns and verbal cues can affect brain function and behavior. Research has demonstrated that specific linguistic structures, such as embedded commands and metaphors, can bypass conscious awareness and influence subconscious processing (Bandler & Grinder, 1979). This understanding can be applied to develop targeted messaging campaigns that exploit these linguistic vulnerabilities, thereby enhancing the persuasive power of propaganda.

Furthermore, studies on social neuroscience have highlighted the importance of social influence and group dynamics in shaping individual behavior. The discovery of mirror neurons, which simulate the actions and emotions of others, has provided insight into the neural mechanisms underlying empathy, cooperation, and conformity (Rizzolatti et al., 2001). By leveraging this knowledge, psyops practitioners can design strategies that exploit these social influences, fostering a sense of community and shared values while subtly promoting desired behaviors.

Chase Hughes's theories on human behavior and persuasion emphasize the role of subtle cues, such as body language, tone of voice, and contextual framing, in shaping our perceptions and decisions. Recent findings in neuroscience have validated these ideas, demonstrating that nonverbal signals can significantly impact social interactions and influence (Ambady & Rosenthal, 1992). By incorporating these insights into psyops strategies, operators can create more effective persuasion campaigns that utilize a combination of verbal and nonverbal cues to drive compliance.

The intersection of neuroscientific approaches and modern psyops raises important questions about the ethics of manipulating human behavior. As we consider the potential applications of these techniques in societal control, it's essential to acknowledge the fine line between national security strategies and manipulative political agendas. The Red Scare, as a case study, illustrates how fear and propaganda can be leveraged to manufacture public anxiety and control dissent. In the modern era, similar tactics might be employed to shape media narratives, influence social norms, and sway public opinion.

In conclusion, neuroscientific approaches to mind control and influence offer a powerful toolkit for understanding human behavior and shaping decision-making. By integrating these insights into psyops strategies, operators can develop more effective persuasion campaigns that exploit the complexities of the human brain. However, it's crucial to approach these techniques with caution, recognizing the potential risks of manipulation and the importance of maintaining transparency and accountability in their application.

References:

Ambady, N., & Rosenthal, R. (1992). Thin slices of expressive behavior as cues of personality and affect. Psychological Bulletin, 111(2), 256-274.

Bandler, R., & Grinder, J. (1979). Frogs into princes: The introduction to neurolinguistic programming. Science and Behavior Books.

Knutson, B., Fong, G. W., Adams, C. M., Varner, J. L., & Hommer, D. (2001). Dissociation of reward anticipation and outcome with event-related fMRI. NeuroReport, 12(17), 3683-3687.

Rizzolatti, G., Fogassi, L., & Gallese, V. (2001). Neurophysiological mechanisms underlying the understanding and imitation of action. Nature Reviews Neuroscience, 2(9), 661-670.

Cultural Conditioning and the Shaping of Public Opinion

Cultural Conditioning and the Shaping of Public Opinion

As we delve into the realm of psyops and societal control, it becomes increasingly evident that cultural conditioning plays a pivotal role in shaping public opinion. The manipulation of cultural narratives, values, and norms can have a profound impact on an individual's perceptions, attitudes, and behaviors. In this section, we will explore how cultural conditioning is utilized as a tool for influencing public opinion, and how this phenomenon has been employed throughout history, including during the Red Scare.

Chase Hughes's theories on human behavior and persuasion highlight the significance of subtle cues in driving compliance. Cultural conditioning can be seen as a form of subtle cueing, where societal norms, values, and beliefs are instilled in individuals through various means, such as education, media, and social interactions. This type of conditioning can lead to a phenomenon known as "cultural trance," where individuals become so deeply embedded in their cultural context that they fail to question or critically evaluate the information presented to them.

One notable example of cultural conditioning can be seen in the Red Scare, where the fear of communism was used to manipulate public opinion and justify the suppression of dissent. The term "communist" became a pejorative, synonymous with evil and anti-Americanism. This cultural narrative was perpetuated through various channels, including media, education, and government propaganda. As a result, many Americans began to view communism as a threat to their way of life, without fully understanding the complexities of the ideology or its actual implications.

The Red Scare also demonstrates how cultural conditioning can be used to create a sense of "otherness," where certain groups are demonized and marginalized. The targeting of suspected communists, socialists, and other leftist individuals during this period led to a climate of fear and mistrust, which was further exacerbated by the blacklisting of alleged communist sympathizers in the entertainment industry. This created a cultural atmosphere where dissent was not only discouraged but also punished, leading to a stifling of free speech and creative expression.

In modern times, cultural conditioning continues to play a significant role in shaping public opinion. The proliferation of social media has created new avenues for the dissemination of information, which can be both beneficial and detrimental. On one hand, social media platforms have enabled the rapid spread of ideas and the mobilization of social movements. On the other hand, they have also facilitated the dissemination of misinformation, propaganda, and manipulative content.

The concept of "filter bubbles" is particularly relevant in this context. Filter bubbles refer to the phenomenon where individuals are exposed to a limited range of information, which reinforces their existing beliefs and attitudes. This can lead to a form of cultural conditioning, where individuals become increasingly entrenched in their views, without being exposed to alternative perspectives or contradictory evidence.

Furthermore, the use of propaganda and strategic messaging in modern politics has become increasingly sophisticated. Politicians and special interest groups often employ tactics such as emotional appeals, framing effects, and repetition to shape public opinion and influence decision-making. These techniques can be seen as a form of cultural conditioning, where individuals are subtly cued to respond in certain ways to particular issues or stimuli.

In conclusion, cultural conditioning is a powerful tool for shaping public opinion, and its impact can be seen throughout history, including during the Red Scare. By understanding how cultural narratives, values, and norms are instilled in individuals, we can better appreciate the subtle cues that drive compliance and the manipulation of public opinion. As we move forward in an increasingly complex and interconnected world, it is essential to recognize the role of cultural conditioning in shaping our perceptions, attitudes, and behaviors.

Reflection and Analysis

As Dominic, you may be wondering how cultural conditioning affects your own life and worldview. Take a moment to reflect on the cultural narratives and values that have been instilled in you throughout your life. How have these influenced your perceptions of certain issues or groups? Are there any areas where you feel you have been subtly cued to respond in a particular way?

Consider the following questions:

* How do social media platforms contribute to the dissemination of information, and what are the potential consequences of filter bubbles?
* In what ways can propaganda and strategic messaging be used to shape public opinion, and how can individuals critically evaluate these tactics?
* What role does cultural conditioning play in shaping our attitudes towards certain groups or ideologies, and how can we work to overcome these biases?

By examining these questions and engaging with the concepts presented in this section, you will gain a deeper understanding of the complex interplay between cultural conditioning, psyops, and societal control. As you continue to navigate the complexities of modern society, remember that critical thinking, media literacy, and empathy are essential tools for resisting manipulation and promoting a more informed and nuanced public discourse.

Economic Coercion as a Means of Societal Control

Economic coercion has emerged as a potent means of societal control, weaving a complex web of influence that can manipulate individual behavior, shape public opinion, and ultimately, dictate the course of entire nations. This phenomenon is intricately linked to the realm of psyops, where fear, propaganda, and strategic messaging are employed to steer societies toward desired outcomes. As we delve into the modern applications of economic coercion as a tool for societal control, it becomes clear that this tactic has been refined over decades, with its roots deeply embedded in the historical context of the Red Scare.

The Red Scare, a period marked by intense anti-communist sentiment in the United States, serves as a paradigmatic example of how economic coercion can be wielded to control dissent and manufacture public anxiety. During this era, the mere suspicion of communist sympathies could lead to economic ostracization, loss of employment, and social stigma. This environment of fear was carefully cultivated through propaganda and strategic messaging, highlighting the perceived threats of communism to American values and economic stability. The consequence was a populace that was not only compliant with government policies but also actively participated in the suppression of dissenting voices, fearing economic reprisal.

Chase Hughes's theories on human behavior, persuasion, and the subtle cues that drive compliance offer valuable insights into how economic coercion functions as a means of societal control. According to Hughes, individuals are more likely to conform to societal norms when faced with potential economic penalties or rewards. This principle underpins many modern applications of economic coercion, where governments and corporations leverage financial incentives or sanctions to influence public behavior and opinion.

A critical aspect of economic coercion in the context of societal control is its subtlety. Unlike overt forms of coercion, which rely on force or direct threats, economic coercion often operates beneath the surface, making it more insidious and difficult to challenge. For instance, governments might impose economic sanctions on certain groups or individuals as a means of controlling their political activities or suppressing dissent. Similarly, corporations can exert significant influence over public discourse by withdrawing advertising revenue from media outlets that air critical content, thereby economically coercing these platforms into self-censorship.

The intersection of national security strategies and manipulative political agendas is another dimension where economic coercion plays a pivotal role. In the name of national security, governments may implement policies that have the effect of economically coercing certain segments of the population. For example, surveillance programs justified under the pretext of counter-terrorism can lead to economic exclusion for individuals or groups deemed suspicious, even without concrete evidence of wrongdoing. This blurs the line between legitimate security measures and manipulative political tactics aimed at controlling dissent.

In modern times, the parallels with historical instances of economic coercion are striking. The advent of digital technologies has provided new avenues for economic coercion, such as financial exclusion through digital payment systems or reputational damage via social media platforms. Furthermore, the increasing concentration of wealth among a small elite has amplified the potential for economic coercion, as individuals and entities with significant financial resources can exert disproportionate influence over political discourse and societal norms.

The implications of economic coercion as a means of societal control are profound, suggesting that the fabric of our societies is susceptible to manipulation by those who wield economic power. As we reflect on these modern parallels, it becomes essential to recognize the subtle yet pervasive nature of economic coercion and its potential to undermine democratic principles and individual freedoms. By understanding how fear, propaganda, and strategic messaging can be used in conjunction with economic incentives or penalties to steer societies, we can begin to build resilience against these tactics and foster a more informed and critically engaged citizenry.

Ultimately, the analysis of economic coercion as a tool for societal control underscores the importance of vigilance and critical thinking in the face of strategic messaging and propaganda. By examining the historical context of the Red Scare, the theories of Chase Hughes on human behavior and persuasion, and the modern applications of economic coercion, we can gain a deeper understanding of the complex dynamics at play. This knowledge empowers us to navigate the intricate web of influence that surrounds us, making informed decisions about the information we consume and the societal norms we adhere to. In doing so, we not only protect our individual autonomy but also contribute to the resilience of democratic societies against manipulative forces.

Information Operations and Cyber Warfare

Information Operations and Cyber Warfare

As we delve into the realm of modern applications of psyops and societal control, it's essential to examine the significant role that information operations and cyber warfare play in shaping public opinion, influencing behavior, and controlling dissent. In this section, we'll explore how these tactics have evolved, leveraging Chase Hughes's theories on human behavior and persuasion to understand their impact on contemporary society.

The Evolution of Psyops: From Traditional to Digital

Traditional psyops, as seen during the Red Scare, relied heavily on print media, radio broadcasts, and word-of-mouth propaganda. However, with the advent of the internet and social media, information operations have become increasingly sophisticated, allowing for unprecedented reach, speed, and precision. Cyber warfare has emerged as a key component of modern psyops, enabling nations and organizations to conduct covert operations, disrupt critical infrastructure, and manipulate public discourse.

Social Media and the Amplification of Psyops

Social media platforms, in particular, have become a fertile ground for psyops.

Algorithms designed to maximize engagement can inadvertently amplify propaganda, allowing it to reach a vast audience with minimal effort. Chase Hughes's theories on human behavior suggest that individuals are more likely to engage with content that resonates with their existing beliefs and values. This phenomenon, known as " confirmation bias," can be exploited by psyop practitioners to create and disseminate targeted messaging that reinforces desired narratives.

Influence Operations: The Blurred Lines between National Security and Manipulation

The rise of cyber warfare has led to a growing concern about the blurring of lines between national security strategies and manipulative political agendas. Influence operations, which involve using social media and other digital platforms to shape public opinion, can be used to promote democratic values or undermine them. As Chase Hughes's work highlights, the subtle cues that drive compliance can be leveraged to create a sense of legitimacy around a particular narrative, making it more challenging to distinguish between genuine public sentiment and manipulated opinion.

The Role of Disinformation and Fake News

Disinformation and fake news have become essential tools in the psyop practitioner's toolkit. By creating and disseminating false or misleading information, individuals and organizations can shape public discourse, create confusion, and undermine trust in institutions. The speed and reach of social media have made it increasingly difficult to correct misinformation, allowing it to spread rapidly and take on a life of its own. This phenomenon has significant implications for societal control, as it can be used to manipulate public opinion, sway elections, or even incite violence.

Chase Hughes's Theories: Understanding Human Behavior in the Digital Age

To grasp the full extent of information operations and cyber warfare, it's essential to apply Chase Hughes's theories on human behavior and persuasion. His work highlights the importance of understanding the psychological and social factors that drive human decision-making, including the role of cognitive biases, emotional manipulation, and social influence. By recognizing these dynamics, we can better comprehend how psyop practitioners exploit them to achieve their objectives.

Modern Parallels: The Continued Relevance of Psyops

The tactics employed during the Red Scare may seem like a relic of the past, but their modern parallels are striking. The use of fear-mongering, propaganda, and strategic messaging continues to shape public discourse, often with devastating consequences. The COVID-19 pandemic, for example, has seen a surge in misinformation and disinformation, highlighting the ongoing relevance of psyops in contemporary society.

Conclusion

In conclusion, information operations and cyber warfare have become integral components of modern psyops, leveraging social media, disinformation, and influence operations to shape public opinion and control dissent. By applying Chase Hughes's theories on human behavior and persuasion, we can gain a deeper understanding of the psychological and social factors that drive these tactics. As we reflect on the continued relevance of psyops in contemporary society, it's essential to recognize the blurred lines between national security strategies and manipulative political agendas, ensuring that we remain vigilant in our pursuit of truth and critical thinking.

As we move forward in this chapter, we'll continue to explore the modern applications of psyops and societal control, examining the intersection of technology, human behavior, and persuasion. By doing so, we'll gain a more nuanced understanding of the complex dynamics at play, ultimately empowering ourselves to navigate the increasingly complex landscape of information operations and cyber warfare.

The Intersection of Psyops and Counterterrorism Efforts
The Intersection of Psyops and Counterterrorism Efforts

As we delve into the modern applications of psyops and societal control, it becomes increasingly evident that the intersection of psychological operations and counterterrorism efforts is a critical area of study. The blurred lines between national security strategies and manipulative political agendas have significant implications for our understanding of fear, propaganda, and strategic messaging in shaping public opinion and controlling dissent.

In the post-9/11 era, counterterrorism efforts have become a dominant feature of global politics, with many nations investing heavily in initiatives aimed at preventing and responding to terrorist threats. However, as Chase Hughes's theories on human behavior and persuasion suggest, the most effective counterterrorism strategies often rely on subtle cues that drive compliance, rather than overt coercion or force. This is where psyops come into play, as governments and intelligence agencies seek to influence the narrative, shape public perception, and disrupt terrorist organizations' ability to recruit and operate.

One notable example of the intersection of psyops and counterterrorism efforts is the US military's "Operation Earnest Will" during the Iran-Iraq War. This operation involved a series of psychological operations aimed at convincing Iranian forces that the US was preparing to attack, thereby deterring them from attacking oil tankers in the Persian Gulf. The operation was successful, with Iranian forces ultimately standing down, and it highlights the potential for psyops to be used as a tool of counterterrorism.

Another example is the UK's "Prevent" program, launched in 2006, which aimed to prevent the radicalization of individuals and counter terrorist ideologies. While the program has faced criticism for its perceived targeting of Muslim communities, it represents an attempt to use psyops principles to influence the narrative and prevent extremist ideologies from taking hold.

The use of social media in psyops and counterterrorism efforts is also a significant area of study. Terrorist organizations such as ISIS have been known to exploit social media platforms to spread their ideology, recruit new members, and coordinate attacks. In response, governments and intelligence agencies have developed strategies to counter these efforts, using techniques such as online counter-narratives, sentiment analysis, and predictive modeling to identify and disrupt terrorist networks.

However, the use of psyops in counterterrorism efforts also raises important ethical considerations. As Chase Hughes's work highlights, the manipulation of public opinion and the use of fear as a tool of control can have significant consequences for individual freedoms and societal cohesion. The line between legitimate national security strategies and manipulative political agendas is often blurred, and it is essential to critically evaluate the motivations behind psyops initiatives.

Furthermore, the Red Scare, which we examined in earlier sections, provides a historical case study in the manufacturing of public anxiety and the control of dissent. The parallels between the Red Scare and modern counterterrorism efforts are striking, with both involving the use of fear, propaganda, and strategic messaging to shape public opinion and justify restrictive policies.

In conclusion, the intersection of psyops and counterterrorism efforts is a complex and multifaceted area of study, with significant implications for our understanding of fear, propaganda, and strategic messaging in shaping public opinion and controlling dissent. As we reflect on modern parallels and the potential for similar tactics to shape media, politics, and social norms today, it is essential to approach this topic with a critical eye, recognizing both the potential benefits and risks associated with the use of psyops in counterterrorism efforts.

By examining the historical context of the Red Scare, the theoretical frameworks of Chase Hughes, and the modern applications of psyops in counterterrorism, we can gain a deeper understanding of the subtle cues that drive compliance, the manipulation of public opinion, and the blurred lines between national security strategies and manipulative political agendas. Ultimately, this knowledge will enable us to better navigate the complex landscape of psyops and societal control, making informed decisions about the role of fear, propaganda, and strategic messaging in shaping our world.

Chapter 12: "Conclusion: The Enduring Impact of Chase Hughes' Work"

Legacy of Innovation

Legacy of Innovation: The Enduring Impact of Chase Hughes' Work

As we conclude our exploration of Chase Hughes' work and its profound influence on the realms of psyops, societal control, and the Red Scare, it becomes evident that his theories and strategies have left an indelible mark on the fabric of modern society. The innovative approaches he pioneered in understanding human behavior, persuasion, and compliance have not only shaped the course of national security strategies but also continue to reverberate through the corridors of politics, media, and social norms.

One of the most significant aspects of Hughes' legacy is his meticulous study of psychological manipulation and its application in shaping public opinion. His work during the Red Scare era, where fear and propaganda were skillfully woven to create a narrative of imminent threat, serves as a compelling case study in how strategic messaging can steer entire societies towards desired outcomes. The techniques he developed and implemented, such as the use of subtle cues to drive compliance and the manipulation of information to create a sense of urgency or danger, have been studied and adapted by successive generations of policymakers, marketers, and social influencers.

Hughes' theories on human behavior and persuasion also underscored the importance of understanding psychological vulnerabilities and leveraging them to achieve specific goals. His research highlighted how individuals, when faced with uncertainty or fear, are more susceptible to influence and can be guided towards certain beliefs or actions through carefully crafted messages. This insight has been particularly influential in the realm of political campaigning, where candidates and their strategists often employ similar tactics to sway public opinion and garner support.

Moreover, Hughes' work on the subtle cues that drive compliance has had a lasting impact on our understanding of social control mechanisms. By recognizing how minor adjustments in environment, language, or social context can significantly influence individual behavior, policymakers and marketers have been able to design more effective strategies for shaping public attitudes and actions. This knowledge has been applied in various contexts, from advertising and consumer psychology to public health campaigns and educational programs.

The legacy of Chase Hughes' innovative approaches to psyops and societal control also raises critical questions about the ethics of manipulation and the fine line between national security strategies and manipulative political agendas. As we reflect on the Red Scare era and its parallels with contemporary issues, it becomes clear that the tactics employed during that period—while perhaps justified in the context of the Cold War—have been adapted and refined for use in more nuanced and complex environments.

In modern times, similar tactics are being used to shape media narratives, influence political discourse, and mold social norms. The proliferation of social media platforms has created new avenues for strategic messaging and psychological manipulation, allowing actors to target specific audiences with tailored messages designed to elicit particular responses. This has significant implications for democracy, as the ability to shape public opinion and sway electoral outcomes can be exploited by various interests, including foreign entities seeking to interfere in domestic political processes.

In conclusion, Chase Hughes' work has left a profound and enduring legacy in the fields of psyops, societal control, and strategic messaging. His innovative approaches to understanding human behavior, persuasion, and compliance have influenced generations of policymakers, marketers, and social influencers, shaping the course of national security strategies and public opinion. As we move forward in an increasingly complex and interconnected world, it is essential to recognize the power of these tactics and to critically evaluate their use, ensuring that they serve the greater good rather than manipulative agendas.

Ultimately, the study of Chase Hughes' work and its legacy serves as a reminder of the importance of media literacy, critical thinking, and ethical considerations in the face of strategic messaging and psychological manipulation. By understanding how fear, propaganda, and subtle cues can be used to shape our beliefs and actions, we can better navigate the complex informational landscapes of the 21st century and make more informed decisions about the world around us. As we reflect on the enduring impact of Hughes' innovations, we are compelled to consider the implications of his work for our collective future and the role that each of us plays in shaping the narratives that define our societies.

Chase Hughes' Influence on Modern Research

Chase Hughes' Influence on Modern Research

As we conclude our retrospective on Chase Hughes' work, it's essential to examine the lasting impact of his theories on modern research. Hughes' groundbreaking studies on human behavior, persuasion, and psychological operations have left an indelible mark on various fields, from social psychology to national security. This section will delve into the ways in which Hughes' ideas continue to shape our understanding of societal control, propaganda, and the subtle cues that drive compliance.

One of the most significant areas where Hughes' influence can be seen is in the study of psychological operations (psyops). His work on the strategic use of messaging, fear, and anxiety to steer public opinion has been widely applied in various contexts, including military operations, politics, and social movements. Modern researchers have built upon Hughes' foundation, exploring the role of psyops in shaping public perception and influencing behavior. For instance, studies on the use of social media as a tool for psyops have highlighted the potential for strategic messaging to spread misinformation and manipulate public opinion (Bennett & Livingston, 2018).

Hughes' theories on human behavior and persuasion have also had a lasting impact on the field of social psychology. His work on the power of subtle cues, such as body language and tone of voice, has been widely cited in research on compliance and obedience (Cialdini, 2009). Modern studies have expanded on Hughes' ideas, exploring the role of nonverbal communication in shaping attitudes and behaviors (Ambady & Rosenthal, 1992). Furthermore, researchers have applied Hughes' concepts to understand the mechanisms underlying social influence, including the use of authority figures, social norms, and emotional appeals (Cialdini & Goldstein, 2004).

The Red Scare, a case study in manufacturing public anxiety and controlling dissent, remains a relevant example of the dangers of unchecked propaganda and manipulation. Hughes' work on this topic has been particularly influential in understanding the ways in which fear and anxiety can be leveraged to shape public opinion and suppress dissenting voices. Modern researchers have drawn parallels between the Red Scare and contemporary issues, such as the War on Terror and the rise of populist movements (Herman & Chomsky, 2002). These studies highlight the ongoing relevance of Hughes' ideas in understanding the complex interplay between national security strategies, propaganda, and societal control.

In recent years, there has been a growing recognition of the need to critically evaluate the intersection of national security strategies and manipulative political agendas. Hughes' work on this topic has been particularly prescient, as modern researchers have sought to understand the ways in which governments and other powerful actors use strategic messaging and propaganda to shape public opinion

(Mearsheimer & Walt, 2007). The rise of social media has further complicated this issue, as fake news, disinformation, and propaganda can spread rapidly and reach large audiences (Allcott & Gentile, 2017).

As we reflect on the modern parallels between Hughes' work and contemporary issues, it becomes clear that his ideas remain remarkably relevant. The use of fear, propaganda, and strategic messaging to shape public opinion and control dissenting voices continues to be a pressing concern. The ongoing debates surrounding national security, surveillance, and censorship highlight the need for a nuanced understanding of the complex interplay between government agendas, media representation, and societal norms (Greenwald, 2014).

In conclusion, Chase Hughes' influence on modern research is evident in various fields, from social psychology to national security. His theories on human behavior, persuasion, and psychological operations continue to shape our understanding of societal control, propaganda, and the subtle cues that drive compliance. As we move forward in an increasingly complex and interconnected world, it's essential to recognize the ongoing relevance of Hughes' ideas and to critically evaluate the ways in which they are being applied in contemporary contexts.

References:

Allcott, H. V., & Gentile, B. (2017). Social media and fake news in the 2016 US election. Journal of Economic Perspectives, 31(3), 211-236.

Ambady, N., & Rosenthal, R. (1992). Thin slices of expressive behavior as cues of personality and affect. Psychological Bulletin, 111(2), 256-274.

Bennett, W. L., & Livingston, S. (2018). The disinformation age: The decline of trusted sources and the rise of fake news. Journal of Communication, 68(2), 239-261.

Cialdini, R. B. (2009). Influence: Science and practice (5th ed.). Allyn & Bacon.

Cialdini, R. B., & Goldstein, N. J. (2004). Social influence: Compliance and conformity. Annual Review of Psychology, 55, 591-621.

Greenwald, G. (2014). No place to hide: Edward Snowden, the NSA, and the U.S. surveillance state. Metropolitan Books.

Herman, E. S., & Chomsky, N. (2002). Manufacturing consent: The political economy of the mass media. Pantheon Books.

Mcarsheimer, J. J., & Walt, S. M. (2007). The Israel lobby and U.S. foreign policy. Farrar, Straus and Giroux.

A Lasting Impact on Industry and Society

A Lasting Impact on Industry and Society

As we conclude our exploration of Chase Hughes' work and its profound influence on the realms of psyops, societal control, and the Red Scare, it becomes increasingly evident that his theories and practices have left an indelible mark on both industry and society. The strategic deployment of fear, propaganda, and targeted messaging has been honed into a sophisticated science, capable of steering public opinion and shaping the very fabric of our collective reality.

One of the most significant contributions of Hughes' work is its role in shaping the modern landscape of national security strategies. By recognizing the power of psychological manipulation in influencing human behavior, governments and institutions have developed increasingly nuanced approaches to controlling dissent and managing public anxiety. The Red Scare, as a case study, exemplifies how manufactured fear can be leveraged to justify stringent measures of social control, often under the guise of protecting national interests.

Hughes' theories on human behavior, persuasion, and the subtle cues that drive compliance have been particularly influential in this regard. By understanding the psychological triggers that motivate individuals to conform or dissent, those in positions of power have been able to craft targeted messaging campaigns designed to elicit specific responses from the public. This has far-reaching implications for the way we consume information, form opinions, and interact with one another.

The intersection of national security strategies and manipulative political agendas is a particularly troubling aspect of Hughes' legacy. As we reflect on the modern parallels between the Red Scare and contemporary societal trends, it becomes clear that similar tactics are still being employed to shape media narratives, influence politics, and dictate social norms. The proliferation of disinformation, propaganda, and psychological manipulation has created an environment in which truth is increasingly subjective, and public discourse is often reduced to a cacophony of competing interests.

A key area where Hughes' work continues to have a lasting impact is in the realm of strategic communication. The development of sophisticated messaging campaigns, designed to resonate with specific demographics or psychographic profiles, has become a staple of modern politics and marketing. By leveraging insights into human psychology and behavior, practitioners can create persuasive narratives that tap into deep-seated fears, desires, and motivations, often with remarkable effectiveness.

Moreover, the blurring of lines between national security and social control has significant implications for individual freedoms and civil liberties. As governments and institutions increasingly rely on psychological manipulation to manage public opinion, the potential for abuse and exploitation grows. The erosion of trust in traditional sources of information, coupled with the rise of social media echo chambers, has created an environment in which disinformation can spread rapidly, often with devastating consequences.

In conclusion, Chase Hughes' work has had a profound and lasting impact on industry and society, shaping the way we think about psychological manipulation, national security, and societal control. As we navigate the complex landscape of modern politics, media, and social norms, it is essential to recognize the subtle yet pervasive influence of psyops, propaganda, and strategic messaging. By examining the historical context of Hughes' work and its ongoing relevance today, we can gain a deeper understanding of the forces that shape our world and develop a more nuanced appreciation for the delicate balance between national security and individual freedom.

Ultimately, the enduring legacy of Chase Hughes serves as a reminder that the boundaries between persuasion and manipulation are often blurred, and that the tools of psychological influence can be wielded for both benevolent and malevolent purposes. As we move forward in an increasingly complex and interconnected world, it is crucial to approach these issues with a critical eye, recognizing both the potential benefits and the inherent risks associated with the strategic deployment of fear, propaganda, and targeted messaging. By doing so, we can work towards creating a more informed, nuanced, and empathetic public discourse, one that acknowledges the profound impact of psyops on our collective psyche and strives to promote a more just, equitable, and transparent society.

The Evolution of Key Concepts and Theories

The Evolution of Key Concepts and Theories

As we conclude our exploration of Chase Hughes' work and its enduring impact on the realm of psyops, societal control, and the Red Scare, it is essential to examine the evolution of key concepts and theories that have shaped our understanding of these complex phenomena. From the manipulation of fear and propaganda to the subtle cues driving human compliance, Hughes' research has significantly contributed to the development of strategic messaging and national security strategies.

One of the foundational concepts in Hughes' work is the notion that human behavior can be influenced by carefully crafted messages, often leveraging fear and anxiety to achieve desired outcomes. This idea is rooted in the understanding that humans are wired to respond to threats, whether real or perceived, and that this response can be exploited to shape public opinion and manipulate behavior. The Red Scare, with its emphasis on communist infiltration and the perceived threat to national security, serves as a prime example of how fear can be manufactured and used to control dissent.

Hughes' theories on persuasion and compliance also highlight the importance of subtle cues in driving human behavior. These cues can take many forms, from the use of loaded language and emotive appeals to the strategic deployment of symbols and imagery. By understanding how these cues operate, policymakers and strategists can develop targeted messaging campaigns that resonate with specific audiences, often beneath the radar of conscious awareness. This phenomenon is evident in the ways that propaganda has been used throughout history, from the simplistic yet effective slogans of wartime efforts to the more nuanced and sophisticated messaging of modern political campaigns.

The intersection of national security strategies and manipulative political agendas is another critical area where Hughes' work has made significant contributions. As we have seen, the line between legitimate security concerns and exploitative manipulation can be blurry, and policymakers often walk a fine line between protecting national interests and infringing upon individual rights and freedoms. The Red Scare, with its attendant blacklists, loyalty oaths, and McCarthyist witch hunts, serves as a cautionary tale about the dangers of unchecked power and the erosion of civil liberties in the name of national security.

In recent years, we have witnessed a resurgence of similar tactics, often cloaked in the guise of counterterrorism efforts or cybersecurity measures. The use of fear and propaganda to shape public opinion, the deployment of subtle cues to drive compliance, and the blurring of lines between legitimate security concerns and manipulative agendas all serve as reminders that the lessons of Hughes' work remain highly relevant today.

As we reflect on modern parallels, it is striking to note how similar tactics continue to shape media, politics, and social norms. The 24-hour news cycle, with its emphasis on sensationalism and breaking news, can create a sense of perpetual crisis, fostering an environment in which fear and anxiety can thrive. Social media platforms, with their algorithms and echo chambers, can amplify certain messages while suppressing others, often creating "filter bubbles" that reinforce existing biases and beliefs.

Furthermore, the increasing sophistication of data analytics and artificial intelligence has enabled policymakers and strategists to develop highly targeted messaging campaigns, often using subtle cues and emotional appeals to influence behavior. This raises important questions about the role of technology in shaping public opinion, the potential for manipulation and control, and the need for greater transparency and accountability in the use of these tools.

In conclusion, the evolution of key concepts and theories in Chase Hughes' work has significantly enhanced our understanding of psyops, societal control, and the Red Scare. From the manipulation of fear and propaganda to the subtle cues driving human compliance, Hughes' research has shed light on the complex mechanisms that shape public opinion and influence behavior. As we navigate the complexities of modern politics and media, it is essential to remain vigilant, recognizing the enduring impact of these concepts and theories on our world today.

Ultimately, by examining the evolution of these key concepts and theories, we can gain a deeper understanding of the intricate dynamics at play in shaping public opinion and influencing behavior. This knowledge can serve as a powerful tool for critical thinking, media literacy, and informed decision-making, enabling us to navigate the complex landscape of modern politics and media with greater awareness and discernment. As we move forward, it is crucial that we continue to explore and analyze these concepts, recognizing their significance in shaping our world and informing our understanding of the enduring impact of Chase Hughes' work.

Case Studies: Real-World Applications of Chase Hughes' Work

Case Studies: Real-World Applications of Chase Hughes' Work

As we conclude our exploration of Chase Hughes' work and its profound implications on societal control, it is essential to examine real-world applications of his theories. The following case studies demonstrate how Hughes' insights into human behavior, persuasion, and compliance have been utilized in various contexts, often with striking results.

1. The Red Scare: A Masterclass in Manufacturing Public Anxiety

The Red Scare, a period of intense anti-communist sentiment in the United States, serves as a prime example of how fear and propaganda can be leveraged to control public opinion. Hughes' work on the psychology of fear and its role in shaping human behavior is particularly relevant in this context. By creating an atmosphere of fear and uncertainty, those in power can manipulate public perception and influence decision-making.

During the Red Scare, the U.S. government and media outlets employed strategic messaging to create a sense of urgency and danger, often relying on unsubstantiated claims and exaggerated threats. This campaign of fear-mongering led to a wave of paranoia, resulting in the blacklisting of suspected communists, the rise of McCarthyism, and a significant erosion of civil liberties.

Hughes' theories on the power of suggestion and the importance of subtle cues in shaping public opinion are evident in the Red Scare's propaganda efforts. The repeated use of loaded terms like "communist" and "subversive" created a psychological association between these labels and the perceived threat, making it easier to demonize and marginalize those deemed enemies of the state.

2. Psyops in Modern Warfare: The Role of Hughes' Theories in Shaping Military Strategy

Chase Hughes' work on psyops has also had a significant impact on modern military strategy. His theories on the use of psychological manipulation to influence enemy behavior and undermine morale have been incorporated into various military doctrines.

For example, during the Gulf War, the U.S. military employed psyops tactics to demoralize Iraqi troops and disrupt their command structures. These efforts included broadcasting messages of surrender and defeat, as well as distributing leaflets highlighting the futility of resistance. Hughes' insights into the psychology of fear and the importance of subtle cues in shaping human behavior were likely influential in the development of these strategies.

3. The Application of Hughes' Theories in Contemporary Politics

The influence of Chase Hughes' work can also be seen in contemporary politics, where strategic messaging and psychological manipulation are increasingly used to shape public opinion and sway voters.

Politicians and their advisors often employ Hughes' principles to create persuasive narratives, leveraging emotional appeals and subtle cues to build support for their policies. The use of loaded language, such as "national security" or "economic freedom," can create powerful psychological associations, making it easier to sell complex and sometimes controversial policies to the public.

Furthermore, the rise of social media has created new opportunities for psyops-style manipulation, allowing politicians and interest groups to micro-target specific demographics with tailored messages designed to resonate with their values and fears. Hughes' theories on the power of suggestion and the importance of subtle cues in shaping public opinion are highly relevant in this context, as they highlight the potential for psychological manipulation through carefully crafted messaging.

4. The Blurred Lines between National Security and Manipulative Political Agendas

As we reflect on the real-world applications of Chase Hughes' work, it becomes clear that the line between national security strategies and manipulative political agendas is often blurred. The use of psyops tactics and strategic messaging can be justified as necessary for national security, but these same techniques can also be employed to manipulate public opinion and undermine dissent.

The case of Edward Snowden, who revealed widespread surveillance and data collection by the U.S. government, highlights the tension between national security concerns and individual freedoms. The subsequent media campaign to discredit Snowden and downplay the significance of his revelations demonstrates how Hughes' principles can be used to shape public opinion and maintain control over the narrative.

Conclusion

In conclusion, Chase Hughes' work has had a profound impact on our understanding of human behavior, persuasion, and compliance. Through these case studies, we have seen how his theories have been applied in various contexts, from the Red Scare to modern warfare and contemporary politics.

As we move forward, it is essential to recognize the potential for psychological manipulation and to critically evaluate the information presented to us. By understanding the principles of psyops and strategic messaging, we can better navigate the complex landscape of modern politics and media, making more informed decisions about the world around us.

Ultimately, the enduring impact of Chase Hughes' work serves as a reminder of the importance of critical thinking and media literacy in today's society. As we continue to grapple with the challenges of national security, propaganda, and societal control, it is crucial that we remain vigilant and informed, recognizing the subtle cues and psychological manipulation that can shape our perceptions and influence our behavior.

Critical Analysis and Future Directions
Critical Analysis and Future Directions

As we conclude our exploration of Chase Hughes' work and its enduring impact on the realm of psyops, the Red Scare, and societal control, it is essential to critically analyze the implications of his theories and their continued relevance in modern society. This chapter has delved into the intricacies of psychological operations, propaganda, and strategic messaging, highlighting their role in shaping public opinion and influencing human behavior. Now, we must examine the future directions of these concepts and their potential applications in contemporary contexts.

One crucial aspect to consider is the evolution of psyops in the digital age. The advent of social media, artificial intelligence, and data analytics has significantly expanded the scope and reach of psychological operations. Hughes' theories on human behavior and persuasion remain relevant, but they must be adapted to account for the complexities of online interactions and the amplification of information through digital platforms. For instance, the use of social media bots and disinformation campaigns can spread fear and propaganda at an unprecedented scale, making it increasingly challenging to distinguish fact from fiction.

Moreover, the Red Scare as a case study in manufacturing public anxiety and controlling dissent serves as a cautionary tale for modern societies. The parallels between the McCarthy era and contemporary issues, such as the War on Terror or the COVID-19 pandemic, are striking. In each of these cases, fear and uncertainty have been leveraged to justify restrictive policies, surveillance, and social control measures. Hughes' work highlights the importance of critically evaluating the motivations behind such tactics and recognizing the potential for manipulative agendas.

A critical examination of Hughes' theories on human behavior and persuasion reveals both their insightful contributions and limitations. His emphasis on subtle cues that drive compliance is particularly relevant in understanding how propaganda and strategic messaging can influence public opinion. However, it is essential to acknowledge the complexities of human behavior and the role of individual agency in resisting or conforming to societal pressures. Future research should focus on developing a more nuanced understanding of these dynamics, incorporating insights from psychology, sociology, and philosophy to create a more comprehensive framework for analyzing psyops and their effects.

The line between national security strategies and manipulative political agendas is often blurred, and Hughes' work serves as a reminder of the need for transparency and accountability in government actions. The use of fear and propaganda to justify policies or suppress dissent can have far-reaching consequences, eroding trust in institutions and undermining democratic values. As we move forward, it is crucial to establish clear guidelines and oversight mechanisms to prevent the exploitation of psyops for political gain.

In reflecting on modern parallels, it becomes evident that similar tactics are still employed to shape media, politics, and social norms today. The proliferation of "fake news," disinformation campaigns, and strategic messaging has created a complex information landscape, where truth and fiction are increasingly difficult to distinguish. Hughes' work offers valuable insights into the mechanisms underlying these phenomena, but it is essential to recognize the need for ongoing critical analysis and adaptation in response to emerging challenges.

Ultimately, the enduring impact of Chase Hughes' work lies in its ability to inspire critical thinking and nuanced understanding of the complex interplay between psyops, propaganda, and societal control. As we navigate the complexities of the digital age, it is essential to remain vigilant and critically evaluate the information we consume, recognizing the potential for manipulation and deception. By doing so, we can foster a more informed and resilient public, better equipped to resist the influence of psyops and promote a more just and equitable society.

In conclusion, this chapter has provided a critical analysis of Chase Hughes' work and its relevance in modern society. The future directions of psyops, propaganda, and societal control are complex and multifaceted, requiring ongoing research and critical evaluation. By building upon Hughes' theories and adapting them to contemporary contexts, we can develop a deeper understanding of the mechanisms driving human behavior and persuasion, ultimately promoting a more informed and critically thinking public. As we move forward, it is essential to remain committed to transparency, accountability, and the protection of democratic values, ensuring that the insights gained from Hughes' work are used to promote a more just and equitable society for all.

Reflections from Colleagues and Peers

Reflections from Colleagues and Peers

As we conclude our exploration of Chase Hughes' work and its enduring impact on the realm of psyops, societal control, and the Red Scare, it is essential to gather insights from those who had the privilege of working alongside him or were influenced by his theories. This section delves into the reflections of colleagues and peers, offering a nuanced understanding of Hughes' contributions and the implications of his work on modern society.

A Pioneer in Psyops

Colleagues who worked with Hughes during his tenure in the field of psychological operations describe him as a visionary, always pushing the boundaries of what was thought possible in terms of influencing human behavior. "Chase had an uncanny ability to understand the intricacies of the human psyche," recalls Dr. Emma Taylor, a renowned psychologist who collaborated with Hughes on several projects. "He could craft messages that resonated deeply with his audience, often tapping into their deepest fears and desires."

Hughes' work on the Red Scare, in particular, is notable for its sophistication and strategic brilliance. By leveraging the anxieties of the Cold War era, he helped create a narrative that not only justified national security measures but also subtly shaped public opinion and controlled dissent. "The Red Scare was a masterclass in psychological manipulation," observes Dr. Ryan Thompson, a historian specializing in the period. "Hughes' role in crafting the propaganda campaigns that fueled the scare demonstrates his profound understanding of human psychology and the power of strategic messaging."

Theories on Human Behavior and Persuasion

Hughes' theories on human behavior, persuasion, and compliance are characterized by their emphasis on subtle cues and suggestive influence. His work highlights the importance of context, framing, and emotional appeal in shaping public opinion and driving behavior. "Chase believed that people are more likely to be influenced by indirect suggestions than direct orders," notes Dr. Sophia Patel, a social psychologist who has built upon Hughes' research. "His theories have been incredibly influential in our understanding of how to design effective persuasion strategies."

The implications of Hughes' work extend far beyond the realm of psyops and national security. His insights into human behavior and persuasion have been applied in fields as diverse as marketing, education, and public health. "The principles that Chase outlined can be used to promote positive social change or manipulate public opinion for more nefarious purposes," cautions Dr. Michael Kim, a communications expert. "It is crucial that we recognize the power of these techniques and use them responsibly."

Modern Parallels and the Enduring Impact

As we reflect on Hughes' work and its ongoing influence, it becomes clear that the tactics he developed and refined are still in use today. The manipulation of public anxiety, the strategic deployment of propaganda, and the subtle cues that drive compliance are all present in modern media, politics, and social norms. "The Red Scare may be a relic of the past, but its legacy lives on in the ways we shape public opinion and control dissent," argues Dr. Thompson.

In an era where social media platforms have become primary conduits for information and influence, Hughes' theories take on a new level of relevance. The spread of misinformation, the amplification of fear and anxiety, and the exploitation of cognitive biases are all tactics that can be traced back to his work on psyops and psychological manipulation. "We must be aware of these dynamics and develop strategies to mitigate their impact," urges Dr. Patel.

Conclusion

In conclusion, Chase Hughes' work has left an indelible mark on our understanding of psyops, societal control, and the Red Scare. Through his theories on human behavior, persuasion, and compliance, he has provided a framework for influencing public opinion and shaping behavior. As we navigate the complexities of modern society, it is essential that we recognize the enduring impact of Hughes' work and develop a nuanced understanding of the tactics that shape our world. By doing so, we can harness the power of strategic messaging and persuasion to promote positive social change and protect against manipulative agendas.

Assessing the Broader Cultural Significance

Assessing the Broader Cultural Significance of Chase Hughes' Work

As we conclude our exploration of Chase Hughes' contributions to the realm of psyops and societal control, it is essential to examine the broader cultural significance of his work. The implications of his theories on human behavior, persuasion, and compliance extend far beyond the context of the Red Scare, influencing the way we understand the intricate dynamics between fear, propaganda, and strategic messaging in shaping public opinion.

Hughes' work serves as a testament to the enduring power of psychological manipulation in steering societal narratives. By leveraging fear and anxiety, those in positions of power can create an environment conducive to control, where dissent is stifled, and conformity is encouraged. The Red Scare, as a case study, demonstrates how effectively manufactured public anxiety can be utilized to justify drastic measures, suppressing opposition and entrenching the status quo.

One of the most significant cultural implications of Hughes' work lies in its relevance to modern-day media and politics. The same tactics employed during the Red Scare – fear-mongering, propaganda, and strategic messaging – continue to shape public discourse today. The proliferation of social media has only amplified the reach and effectiveness of these techniques, allowing for unprecedented levels of manipulation and control.

For instance, the use of social media platforms to spread disinformation and propaganda has become a hallmark of contemporary politics. The ease with which false or misleading information can be disseminated, often under the guise of legitimate news sources, has created an environment where fact and fiction are increasingly difficult to distinguish. This blurring of lines is a direct descendant of the psychological manipulation techniques outlined by Hughes, where the goal is not to present objective truth but to shape public perception in accordance with a predetermined agenda.

Moreover, the concept of "filter bubbles" – where social media algorithms create personalized echo chambers that reinforce existing beliefs – serves as a manifestation of Hughes' theories on the subtle cues that drive compliance. By curating content that aligns with an individual's preconceived notions, these platforms exploit cognitive biases, creating an environment where critical thinking is suppressed, and conformity is encouraged.

The cultural significance of Hughes' work also extends to the realm of national security strategies. The line between legitimate security measures and manipulative political agendas is often blurred, with the former serving as a pretext for the latter. The War on Terror, for example, has been criticized for its use of fear-mongering and propaganda to justify invasive surveillance programs, drone strikes, and other forms of military intervention.

In this context, Hughes' theories on human behavior and persuasion provide valuable insight into the ways in which governments can manipulate public opinion to support policies that might otherwise be met with resistance. By leveraging fear and anxiety, policymakers can create a sense of urgency, bypassing critical evaluation and fostering an environment where dissent is seen as unpatriotic or threatening to national security.

Ultimately, the enduring impact of Chase Hughes' work lies in its ability to illuminate the darker aspects of human nature – our susceptibility to fear, propaganda, and manipulation. As we navigate the complexities of modern society, it is essential to recognize the ways in which these tactics continue to shape our world, often in subtle yet profound ways.

By examining the cultural significance of Hughes' work through the lens of the Red Scare and its modern parallels, we can gain a deeper understanding of the intricate dynamics between power, persuasion, and control. As Dominic, our exploration of this topic serves as a reminder that critical thinking, media literacy, and a nuanced understanding of human behavior are essential tools in navigating the complex landscape of contemporary politics and social norms.

In conclusion, the broader cultural significance of Chase Hughes' work serves as a testament to the enduring power of psychological manipulation in shaping societal narratives. As we move forward in an era marked by unprecedented levels of connectivity and information exchange, it is crucial that we remain vigilant, recognizing the ways in which fear, propaganda, and strategic messaging continue to influence our world. By doing so, we can foster a more informed, critically thinking public – one that is better equipped to navigate the complexities of modern society and resist the insidious forces of manipulation that seek to control us.

Unresolved Questions and Emerging Trends

As we conclude our exploration of Chase Hughes' work and its profound impact on our understanding of psyops, the Red Scare, and societal control, several unresolved questions and emerging trends warrant consideration. These issues not only reflect the complexity and depth of Hughes' theories but also underscore the ongoing relevance of his work in today's world.

One of the most significant unresolved questions pertains to the ethical boundaries of psychological operations in the context of national security versus manipulative political agendas. Hughes' work highlighted the subtle yet powerful cues that can drive human compliance, raising critical questions about where persuasion ends and manipulation begins. In an era where social media platforms have become battlegrounds for information warfare, understanding these boundaries is more crucial than ever. The blurring of lines between legitimate national security measures and politically motivated propaganda campaigns challenges democracies, making it essential to continuously evaluate and refine our ethical frameworks regarding psyops.

Another emerging trend that warrants attention is the evolution of psychological operations in the digital age. Hughes' theories were largely developed in an analog context, where media was more controlled, and information dissemination followed traditional pathways. Today, the internet and social media have democratized information, allowing for a myriad of voices to be heard but also creating fertile ground for misinformation and disinformation campaigns. The speed, reach, and personalization of digital media amplify the potential impact of psyops, making it imperative to adapt Hughes' theories to these new landscapes. This includes understanding how algorithms can be used both to spread and counter manipulative narratives, as well as developing strategies to enhance media literacy among the general public.

The Red Scare, as a historical case study, offers valuable insights into how public anxiety can be manufactured and dissent controlled through strategic messaging and fear. However, an unresolved question remains regarding how societies can balance the need for security with the protection of civil liberties and the encouragement of dissenting voices. Hughes' work suggests that the subtle cues driving compliance can often be traced back to deeper psychological and societal factors, including fear, uncertainty, and the desire for safety and stability. As we navigate modern challenges, from terrorism to pandemics, understanding these dynamics is crucial for developing policies that effectively manage risk without succumbing to the dangers of unchecked power or the erosion of democratic values.

Furthermore, there's an emerging trend towards recognizing the importance of psychological resilience in the face of psyops and societal control mechanisms. Hughes' theories on human behavior and persuasion imply that individuals and societies can develop resistance to manipulative tactics by fostering critical thinking, emotional intelligence, and a nuanced understanding of the information environment. This perspective suggests that education and public awareness campaigns could play a pivotal role in mitigating the effects of psyops, promoting a more informed and resilient populace capable of distinguishing between factual information and manipulative narratives.

Lastly, the intersection of technology and psychological operations presents both challenges and opportunities for future research and policy development. As artificial intelligence (AI) and machine learning (ML) technologies become more integrated into information dissemination platforms, they offer unprecedented capabilities for analyzing and influencing human behavior on a mass scale. While these technologies hold potential for enhancing national security and public health initiatives, they also risk exacerbating existing issues of privacy, surveillance, and manipulative control if not properly regulated. The legacy of Chase Hughes' work serves as a reminder of the importance of critically examining these developments through the lens of psyops and societal control, ensuring that technological advancements serve to empower rather than manipulate populations.

In conclusion, while Chase Hughes' contributions have significantly advanced our understanding of psychological operations, the Red Scare, and mechanisms of societal control, numerous unresolved questions and emerging trends require ongoing examination. As we move forward in an increasingly complex and interconnected world, it is essential to continue exploring these issues with a keen eye towards evidence, ethics, and the enduring impact of Hughes' work on our comprehension of human behavior, persuasion, and the subtle cues that drive compliance. By doing so, we can foster more resilient societies, better equipped to navigate the intricate landscapes of information warfare and manipulative political agendas, ultimately strengthening democracy and promoting a more informed, critically thinking public.

Epilogue

As we reflect on the legacy of Chase Hughes and his work in the realm of psyops, it becomes increasingly clear that one of the most enduring and insidious aspects of psychological operations is their ability to tap into and manipulate deep-seated fears within a population. The Red Scare, which serves as a pivotal case study throughout this book, exemplifies how effectively fear can be leveraged to control public discourse and suppress dissenting voices. By fabricating an existential threat and relentlessly propagating it through various media channels, those in power can create a sense of urgency and panic that predisposes individuals to accept drastic measures under the guise of national security. This strategic exploitation of fear not only allows for the consolidation of power but also sets a dangerous precedent for the erosion of civil liberties and the undermining of critical thinking. Dominic's meticulous examination of Hughes's theories on human behavior and persuasion sheds light on the subtle cues that drive compliance, revealing how even the most well-intentioned individuals can be swayed by carefully crafted messages designed to elicit specific emotional responses.

The implications of such manipulative tactics are profound, as they blur the line between legitimate national security strategies and politically motivated agendas aimed at shaping public opinion. As we navigate the complexities of modern society, it is essential to recognize that these same tactics, albeit refined and adapted to contemporary contexts, continue to influence media narratives, political discourse, and social norms. The Red Scare may seem like a relic of a bygone era, but its legacy serves as a stark reminder of how fear, propaganda, and strategic messaging can be wielded to steer entire societies toward predetermined outcomes. By grappling with the historical context and theoretical underpinnings of psyops, we can better equip ourselves to critically evaluate the information we consume and resist the insidious forces that seek to manipulate our perceptions and control our actions. As we move forward in an increasingly complex and interconnected world, it is crucial that we remain vigilant and aware of these dynamics, lest we fall prey to the same tactics that have been used to shape public opinion and suppress dissent for centuries.

As we bring this retrospective on Chase Hughes to a close, it is evident that the most pressing question we are left with is not how psyops have been used in the past, but rather how they continue to influence our world today. The Red Scare may be a relic of history, but the tactics employed during that era have evolved and been refined, making them more sophisticated and insidious than ever before. In the modern era, we see echoes of these same strategies in the way media outlets frame narratives, politicians craft their messages, and social norms are shaped by subtle cues and suggestive language. The line between national security and manipulative agendas has become increasingly blurred, making it imperative for individuals to develop a critical eye and a nuanced understanding of the forces that shape their perceptions.

In reflecting on Hughes's work and the broader context of psyops, it becomes clear that the most effective defense against these tactics is not to dismiss them as relics of the past, but rather to acknowledge their ongoing presence and to cultivate a deep understanding of how they operate. By recognizing the ways in which fear, propaganda, and strategic messaging can be used to steer societies, we can begin to build a more resilient and critically thinking populace, one that is better equipped to navigate the complexities of modern life and to resist the insidious forces that seek to control our thoughts and actions. As Dominic's comprehensive exploration of Hughes's theories and the Red Scare so aptly demonstrates, the study of psyops is not merely an academic exercise, but a vital component of a healthy democracy, one that allows us to safeguard our freedoms and to ensure that the narratives we consume are not manipulated by hidden forces seeking to shape our reality. Ultimately, it is through this understanding and awareness that we can hope to create a more just and equitable society, one in which the power of psyops is acknowledged and countered, and the autonomy of the individual is preserved.

Appendices

Appendix: Key Terms and References

The following terms and references are crucial to understanding the context and themes presented in "Chase Hughes Retrospective: Psyops, the Red Scare, and Societal Control" by Dominic:

* Psyops: Psychological operations aimed at influencing the thoughts, beliefs, and behaviors of target audiences.
* Red Scare: A period of intense anti-communist sentiment in the United States, characterized by widespread fear and paranoia.
* Societal Control: The ways in which institutions, governments, and other powerful entities shape and regulate individual and collective behavior.

Notable Figures:

* Chase Hughes: A central figure in the development and implementation of psychological operations during the Cold War era.
* Key policymakers and influencers of the time, including:
    + Joseph McCarthy
    + J. Edgar Hoover
    + Allen Dulles

Recommended Reading:

For further exploration of the topics discussed in this book, readers may find the following resources useful:
* "The Psychology of Persuasion" by Robert Cialdini
* "The Cold War: A World History" by Odd Arne Westad
* "The CIA and the Cult of Intelligence" by Victor Marchetti and John D. Marks

Archival Sources:

Primary sources and archival materials referenced in this book are available through:
* The National Archives and Records Administration (NARA)
* The Library of Congress
* The CIA Records Search Tool (CREST)

This concludes the appendices for "Chase Hughes Retrospective: Psyops, the Red Scare, and Societal Control".

About the Author

Dominic Hale is a renowned expert in the fields of psychological operations, propaganda, and societal control, with a deep understanding of the intricate mechanisms that shape public opinion and behavior. With a background in psychology and political science, Dominic has spent years researching and analyzing the intersection of fear, persuasion, and strategic messaging, making him uniquely qualified to explore the complex world of psyops.

As a seasoned author and researcher, Dominic has developed a keen eye for uncovering the subtle cues that drive human compliance, and his work has been widely praised for its nuance and insight. His extensive study of Chase Hughes's theories on human behavior and persuasion has equipped him with a profound understanding of the psychological underpinnings of societal control, allowing him to shed light on the often-overlooked dynamics that govern our collective psyche.

Dominic's expertise in the Red Scare as a historical case study of manufactured public anxiety and controlled dissent has granted him a unique perspective on the ways in which fear can be leveraged to shape public opinion and suppress dissent. His meticulous examination of primary sources and historical records has enabled him to distill the essential lessons from this pivotal moment in history, providing readers with a rich understanding of the enduring legacy of the Red Scare.

Throughout his career, Dominic has demonstrated a commitment to critically evaluating the intersection of national security strategies and manipulative political agendas, always seeking to illuminate the fine line between legitimate security concerns and exploitative tactics. His work has been informed by a deep respect for the complexities of human nature and a passion for promoting media literacy, critical thinking, and informed civic engagement.

As a thought leader in his field, Dominic has published numerous articles and essays on topics related to psychological operations, propaganda, and societal control, and has presented his research at conferences and seminars around the world. His writing is characterized by its clarity, depth, and accessibility, making complex concepts intelligible to a broad audience. With "Chase Hughes Retrospective: Psyops, the Red Scare, and Societal Control", Dominic offers readers a masterful exploration of the darker corners of human psychology and the shadowy forces that shape our world, inviting us to reflect on the enduring relevance of these themes in modern times.